Praise for *A History of Luther Seminary*

"This is an institutional history about challenges. Mark Granquist clearly and accessibly sorts through the theological challenges—regarding the Augsburg Confession, predestination, low and high church worship practice—and shifting institutional relationships that shaped the origin and early development of Luther Seminary. He then moves on to the social and financial challenges that have impacted it since the 1960s. Avoiding nostalgia and boosterism, he presents a picture of midwestern Lutheran diversity that many will find surprising, and some, uncomfortable. Written at a time when seminary education generally and Luther Seminary specifically are facing perhaps their greatest challenges ever due to declining enrollments, this book will be of great value to not only alumni interested in the history of Lutheranism but also anyone concerned with the question of how mainline Protestant seminary education will survive in the upcoming decades."

– **Jeanne Halgren Kilde**, director of religious studies program, University of Minnesota

"The history of Luther Seminary is not only long, it is also the story of multiple institutions each with its own characters, setting, and distinctive concerns. Granquist conducts his readers through the twists and turns of these intertwining stories with clarity. He highlights each school's relationship with its larger ecclesiastical (and often ethnic) community. At the same time, he points to the similarities of purpose and practice that allowed these schools to undertake the challenging process of combining their work. This complex story also illumines the ways in which the churches associated with these schools adapted to their ever-changing cultural context."

– **L. DeAne Lagerquist**, Harold H. Ditmanson Professor of Religion, St. Olaf College

"This book does an admirable job of consistently integrating the history of Luther Seminary into the larger story of developments in the Lutheran community. Though these interactions are often complex, Granquist's account is readable, clear, and interesting. Readers come to see the remarkable changes experienced by the seminary during the last century and a half."
– **Darrell Jodock**, professor emeritus, Gustavus Adolphus College

"*A History of Luther Seminary: 1869–2019* is much more than the history of particular theological seminary. In this telling of Luther Seminary's story, Mark Granquist offers a primer on Lutheran theological education in America from the time of the first Lutheran immigrants to the New World, and he ushers readers into a centuries-long conversation concerning what ministers of the gospel need from their academic and pastoral formation. Anyone interested in how today's church prepares its leaders will be engaged by this story and inspired to continue that conversation."
– **Mary Hinkle Shore**, rector and dean, Lutheran Theological Southern Seminary, Lenoir-Rhyne University

"Luther Seminary traces its roots back to the mid-nineteenth century and Norwegian immigrants who sought a new life in the fertile soil of the Midwest. Lutheranism, whether churchly or pietist, is above all a theological movement in the church that demands an educated clergy with seminary training. In this regard, theological conflict is inevitable, part and parcel of Lutheran identity, with seminaries serving as the chief battleground. Predestination verses conversion, legalism verses antinomianism, congregationalism verses clericalism, liturgical formalism verses free expression in worship, and, most important of all, the evangelical impulse verses cultural accommodation—these are the battles. Luther Seminary has seen them all, its faculty often at the center of the fray. With sympathy, fairness, and candor, Mark Granquist tells the story of Luther Seminary as it has played itself out. His book is admirable and trustworthy."
– **Walter C. Sundberg Jr.**, professor emeritus, Luther Seminary

"Mark Granquist's history of Luther Seminary places the story of this vital school in the midst of the challenges of the world. Faculty and alums developed the capacity to turn in new directions as times and the church required. Granquist helps us see in a compelling way the intimate and dynamic relationship between a seminary and the congregations it serves as they together seek to be relevant for the dramatic challenges facing the churches today."
– **Maria E. Erling**, United Lutheran Seminary

"In the hands of distinguished historian Mark Granquist, this history of the ELCA's largest seminary is much more than the story of one institution. Luther Seminary is a microcosm of American Lutheranism's remarkable odyssey from ethnic insularity to mainline establishment. It wasn't always a smooth journey. Granquist tells it straight, recounting bygone battles (when Norwegian-speaking professors fought over the fine points of predestination) and recent ones (when sexuality, ecumenism, and budgets were the flash points). Through it all emerges a picture of a seminary that remains adaptable and strong—an enduring witness to Christian truth in a secular age."
– **Peter J. Thuesen**, Indiana University-Purdue University Indianapolis

A History of Luther Seminary

A History of Luther Seminary

1869–2019

Mark Granquist

Fortress Press

Minneapolis

A HISTORY OF LUTHER SEMINARY
1869–2019

Print ISBN: 978-1-5064-5662-1
eBook ISBN: 978-1-5064-5663-8

Copyright © 2019 Fortress Press. All rights reserved. Except for brief quotations in critical articles or reviews, no part of this book may be reproduced in any manner without prior written permission from the publisher. Email copyright@fortresspress.com or write to Permissions, Fortress Press, PO Box 1209, Minneapolis, MN 55440-1209.

Scripture quotations are from the New Revised Standard Version Bible © 1989 Division of Christian Education of the National Council of the Churches of Christ in the United States of America. Used by permission.

Cover design: Laurie Ingram
Cover images: Top row, left to right: Dedication of United Church Seminary (1902), building named Bockman Hall in the 1950s (photo by Server P. Eggan, courtesy of the Luther Seminary Archives); "Crucifixion" by Paul Granlund (1967), Chapel of the Cross (photo by Beth Ann Gaede, 2018); Bockman and Gullixson Halls (courtesy of the Luther Seminary Archives). Bottom row, left to right: Celtic cross in front of Bockman Hall (courtesy of Luther Seminary); Seminary group in front of vacant hotel (Robbinsdale, Minnesota) where Luther Seminary was located 1895–1899 (courtesy of the Luther Seminary Archives); cross atop Olson Campus Center (courtesy of Luther Seminary).

This book is dedicated to Lloyd and Annelotte Svendsbye and their family for their support of the study of the history of Christianity at Luther Seminary. It is further dedicated to those numerous men and women who have sacrificially given of themselves to further the work of Luther Seminary and its mission of educating leaders for Christian communities.

Contents

	Introduction	1
1.	The Lutheran Tradition in Theological Education	5
2.	The Beginnings of Norwegian American Theological Education	37
3.	The Center of Norwegian American Lutheranism	67
4.	Luther Theological Seminary, 1917–1963	97
	Gallery	127
5.	Augsburg Seminary, 1890–1963	143
6.	Northwestern Lutheran Theological Seminary, 1920–1982	173
7.	Moving into the Mainstream: Luther Seminary, 1960–1988	205
8.	Expansion and Change: Luther Seminary, 1988–2019	235
	Epilogue	267
	Appendix: Professors and Numbers of Graduates to 1936	273
	Bibliography	277
	Index	285

Introduction

On the surface, the need for this book is fairly obvious. Luther Seminary has been around now, in one iteration or another, for 150 years, and as a major Lutheran and Protestant seminary in the United States, it is worth an updated history at this point. The fact that a narrative history of the seminary has not yet been written is itself another impetus for proceeding, as is the point that its history is an interesting story in and of itself and should be told. But these are rather pedestrian reasons to write a book such as this. Rather, the history of Luther Seminary is an integral part of the broader story of American Lutheranism and an important part of American religious history, especially the development of Protestant theological education within this larger narrative. So this book will not only tell the story of Luther Seminary and its people but also place its history within the context of these larger movements.

This work will trace the story of Luther Seminary from its beginnings in 1869 to its 150th year in 2019. The current title of the institution, Luther Seminary, will at times be used anachronistically, because the seminary is, in fact, an amalgamation of a number of predecessor institutions that have been merged at various points and times, mainly (but not exclusively) out of the broader world of Norwegian American Lutheranism; in its present form the seminary dates from its last merger in 1982. But even the beginning date of the seminary, 1869, is rather arbitrary. One could trace this history back to 1855 with the first, short-lived attempt of the Eielsen Synod to establish a seminary, or to the founding of a Norwegian-language professorate at Concordia Seminary in 1859, or to the Augustana Seminary of the Scandinavian Augustana Synod in 1860. The year 1869 marks the withdrawal of the Norwegian professor August Weenaas and his Norwegian American students from Augustana Seminary to found Augsburg Seminary and has been generally noted as the beginning of Luther Seminary, at least in continuity with the present institution.

This history is roughly chronological, beginning with a brief overview of the Lutheran traditions in theological education, especially in North America, as a means of situating the narrative of Luther Seminary within this context. Chapters 2 and 3 attempt to give some definition to the sometimes bewildering early history of Norwegian American Lutheranism and its initial attempts at theological education. The second chapter examines the two ideological bookends of this tradition, the low-church Eielsen Synod and the Haugean tradition, and its opposite, the Norwegian Synod, representing the formal, confessional group much in harmony with the Church of Norway. Chapter 3 returns to pick up the story of the Norwegian American Lutheran "center," with the beginnings of Augsburg Seminary in 1869 and the formations of the United Norwegian Lutheran Church in 1890 and the United Church Seminary to 1917. Chapter 4 continues the history of Luther Seminary from the Norwegian American Lutheran merger of 1917 through to 1963. The fifth chapter resumes the history of Augsburg Seminary from its breakaway in 1893, through the formation of the Lutheran Free Church in 1897, to its end in the merger in 1963 that formed the American Lutheran Church. Chapter 6 then begins with the story of the founding of the Northwestern Lutheran Theological Seminary in 1922, the only part of the current institution that does not have its roots in Norwegian American Lutheranism, and takes this narrative to 1982. The seventh chapter resumes the history of Luther Seminary in 1963 at the time when Augsburg Seminary joined it, continues through its merger with Northwestern in 1982, and concludes with the merger that created the Evangelical Lutheran Church in America in 1988. The final chapter completes the history of Luther Seminary to its 150th year in 2019.

As can be seen from the preceding description, the history of Luther Seminary has been full of mergers and other institutional rearrangements. Set in the larger context of American Lutheranism, and especially the labyrinthine history of nineteenth-century Norwegian American Lutheranism, this narrative could easily be overwhelmed by the institutional details of seminary and denominational mergers, schisms, and new formations. This history will endeavor to keep such details of institutional formation and rearrangements to a minimum, to provide the necessary outlines of this history without overwhelming the reader with too much detail. The bibliography at the end of this work can direct the reader to more details about these events, should they be desired. Hopefully this rather complicated history will be clear enough in the pages of this work.

Trying to condense the 150-year history of Luther Seminary into a single book of this size is a challenge, and there were many good stories that simply could not be told within the confines of this present work. This is obviously the history of an institution, Luther Seminary, but it hopes not to be an institutional history. Rather, the intended focus is on the history of the people who themselves have constituted these institutions—the faculty, staff, and students who comprised the seminary communities themselves and their supporters in the Lutheran denominations who made such institutions possible. This book, too, is a work of history, of the history of Christianity in this time and place. Some might object that there is not enough of the history of Christian theology in this work, and that perhaps is a fair complaint. But though the history of theology does have an important role in this story, it is not the key element of the narrative. Rather, this is primarily a history of Lutheran theological education in North America, through the lens of a single institution, and especially through the people who made this institution possible.

There are many themes that recur through this narrative, but overall it seems that the most prominent are the twin themes of challenge and response. The establishment of this institution of theological education by nineteenth-century immigrants and its continuation by their descendants has been a constant struggle, not only on the financial and logistical end, but also because of ongoing questions of mission and identity. The story is not just how these experiments in theological education have been established and continued but, perhaps more importantly, why they did what they did. The transition from Europe to the United States in the nineteenth century, the shifts in language and acculturation to the mainstream of American society in the twentieth century, and the shifting contours of American religion in the twenty-first century have all been an immense challenge to the community of Luther Seminary. The pages of this history show how the people of the Luther Seminary community met these ongoing challenges and their attempts to innovate and develop a sustainable and meaningful form of theological education in light of the challenges and opportunities they encountered.

The writing of this history has been made possible by many different individuals and groups. Support for this work has been provided in part by Luther Seminary, especially through the auspices of President Robin Steinke and Vice President of Seminary Relations Heidi Droegemueller. The archivist at Luther Seminary, Paul Daniels, and the staff of the seminary library have been extremely helpful in the research for this volume, as have been those whose previous research and historical writing undergird this work. The people at Fortress Press, including Will Bergkamp, Scott Tunseth, and especially editor Beth Gaede, have been of immense assistance in bringing this project to conclusion. Faculty colleagues and friends of the author have read chapters and made invaluable suggestions and corrections. Many in the community of Luther Seminary have given great encouragement toward the completion of this work, encouragement that is often priceless during the long periods of solitary drafting, writing, and revision. Of course, great thanks is due to the author's family, who put up with long periods of writing and research; their dear support is best of all. Many people contributed to the making of this book, although the author alone assumes responsibility for the materials contained therein.

Mark Granquist
Luther Seminary
July 2019

1

The Lutheran Tradition in Theological Education

The history of one particular theological institution, such as Luther Seminary, is not an isolated narrative. This history comes in a context, a trajectory of theological education that stretches back to the beginnings of the Christian movement. It is important to understand the rise and development of Christian theological education in general, specifically in Western Europe, and more specifically among the Lutheran Protestants. It is equally important to understand the development of theological education in the North American context, and even more the context of American Lutheranism, to see where Luther Seminary fits in the larger narrative. The patterns of piety and education that can be seen in the history of Luther Seminary do owe a great deal to these historical traditions of theological education.

THE DEVELOPMENT OF THEOLOGICAL EDUCATION IN EUROPE

From its beginnings, the Christian movement relied on recognized leaders both to spread the new teachings about Christ to new audiences and to lead established communities of faith. Jesus Christ himself spent a great deal of his ministry on earth teaching and preaching to his disciples and the crowds that followed him about God and the coming kingdom of God. Jesus also commissioned disciples and apostles as an extension of this teaching and preaching, and sent out the seventy to proclaim the good news (Matt 10:1–16; Luke 10:1–11). The Gospel accounts record Jesus's explicit instructions to these evangelists as to how they should carry out their tasks. In Acts, the apostolic teaching is spread from Jerusalem by those who had been selected by the Holy Spirit, and the teaching and preaching of the gospel was carried to the wider world through the efforts of evangelists, apostles, and prophets. While Acts follows primarily the ministry of Paul and his companions, many other such leaders and their efforts are also mentioned. A detailed record of Paul's ministry is seen in the letters he wrote to communities he had founded. The letters show his theological leadership and his work in teaching and preaching to these new Christians.[1]

While Paul, like the disciples and the seventy, was commissioned directly by Christ, the New Testament also records that the early Christians raised up and recognized leaders within the communities both to spread the gospel and to minister to the needs of the local churches. These leaders were called by various titles, including *elder*, *presbyter*, *bishop*, *deacon*, and *pastor*, and descriptions of their qualifications can be seen in 1 Timothy 3:1–13 and Titus 1:7–9. Gradually, the terms *bishop* and *deacon* were applied to local church leaders, elected from within the community on the basis of their spiritual qualifications and leadership skills—the bishops leading and teaching, while the deacons assisted with service to the community.[2] Gradually, these local leaders begin to take on more prominence in the wider Christian community in place of the spiritual offices such as prophets and evangelists. This trend is accelerated in the second and third centuries because of tensions with spiritual prophets such as the Montanists, who claimed that their direct experience of the Holy Spirit gave them precedence in leadership, even over the Scriptures. In response, the Christian community increasingly emphasized structural elements to define leadership, including the training and qualifications for leaders to lead the local community. This dispute, which

William Placher refers to as the tension between "spirit and structure," has been a perennial issue when it comes to defining and recognizing Christian leaders.[3]

In some of the larger cities, such as Alexandria and Rome, Christians developed educational schools for teachers and leaders, although most early Christian leaders were still educated within the local Christian communities. These famous catechetical schools were generally intended to provide higher education for Christian intellectuals so they would be able to propound on theological topics and defend the Christian movement against pagan intellectual attacks. In general, Christian leaders were expected to be literate, having received formal education in the classical schools.

Much of the theological education in the early church was a general education of new Christians in the catechumenate, a process by which they were prepared to receive baptism and to enter the Christian community as a full member, including admission to the Lord's Supper. In some areas of the Christian world, this process of general theological education could be quite lengthy, lasting many months or even several years. This education was required of all, but those who were destined to become recognized leaders in the community did no further formal education, although they might continue to study the specific responsibilities of their new positions. With the dramatic expansion of Christianity in the Roman Empire after Constantine's official recognition of it, the flood of new Christians overwhelmed the catechetical system, and the length of the catechumenate and its educational requirements were drastically reduced. Infant baptism grew in popularity, and the process of adult catechumenate leading to baptism fell out of favor.

AFTER CONSTANTINE

As Christianity developed, especially after the fourth century, many of the local Christian communities, especially in the cities, became too large for the personal pastoral leadership of a single bishop. Rather, multiple worshipping communities (eventually called parishes) were developed within a single location, all in an administrative unit known as the diocese, headed by the bishop. The bishops relied on local presbyters or elders to carry out the ministry within the parishes, and gradually these local leaders were named *priests* because of their sacramental role, especially in presiding at the Lord's Supper. The bishops were responsible for the selection of these priests (in consultation with the community) and for their education and formation. The example of Augustine and his community in North Africa shows this pattern as it develops in the Latin West—essentially an "apprenticeship" model. It was expected that bishops and the leading clergy had a good education from the classical Roman schools, but their theological education was largely tutorial, as was the case with Ambrose, Augustine, and many other Christian leaders and theologians.

The decline of learning and education in the West, especially with the collapse of centralized Roman authority, made theological education difficult. Some teaching and learning continued in the monasteries and around the cathedral or episcopal schools, such as the one established by Alcuin and Charlemagne in the ninth century, but these schools could educate only a limited number of students, and most priests were still trained locally. Standards of educational literacy were generally low, books were not readily available, and many local priests were essentially illiterate. Candidates for the priesthood were taught the Creeds, the Lord's Prayer, some selected psalms, and the canon of the Mass by rote memorization, usually while apprenticing to a local priest or perhaps the household of the bishop. More formal literary education was maintained in the monasteries, but mainly for the monks themselves. From the seventh to the eleventh centuries, the monasteries in Ireland were particularly known for their education and scholarship, which eventually was spread to other areas of Western Europe.

With the rise of Western universities in the twelfth and thirteenth centuries, a new avenue for formal theological education developed among the theology faculties of these institutions. These faculties were generally independent of the direct control of bishops or religious orders. Some who wished to become priests came to the universities to study theology, and many of them lived in student dormitories established in proximity to the universities by various religious groups and orders, who supervised the students. The new mendicant orders, such as the Dominicans and Franciscans, were primarily involved in university education, training candidates for tasks of preaching and apologetics. The theological training in the universities was generally academic in nature, and pastoral formation was handled outside the classroom. The priests and religious who received such training were generally destined for positions in the upper ranks of the Western church. The large majority of priests during this time still had no formal education whatsoever. Many of the local priests did carry out their ministries with care and devotion, to be sure, but with only the rudiments of training and often living in grinding poverty, their ability to be effective was severely limited. The emphasis was on the local priest's sacramental duties—to see that the Mass was celebrated and the other sacraments were performed. Illiteracy and a lack of Bibles were common.

REFORMATION-ERA IMPROVEMENTS

The sixteenth-century Protestant Reformation in Europe brought major improvements in theological education for pastors and other local church leaders. Martin Luther was educated and trained for the ministry in both his monastery and at the university in Wittenberg, and his model of theological education included elements of these two traditions. Luther's movement for the evangelical reform of the church was based on the proclamation of the word of God, which required educated preachers who were trained to preach the word effectively. The ministry of theologically trained and educated preachers also needed to be supplemented by educated laypeople, who could read the Bible themselves and teach children and others the basics of the Christian faith. In the 1520s, Luther and other leaders visited the local parishes and were appalled by the illiteracy and theological ignorance of not only the laypeople but also the pastors.[4] The goal of the Lutheran leaders was to have all pastoral candidates be literate and theologically educated, preferably by the new evangelical theology faculties in universities. The reality was that because the world of the early Reformation was often chaotic, this was not always possible. In Wittenberg itself from 1537 to 1560 there were ordinations of 772 university-trained pastors but also of 868 pastors with much less formal education.[5] Because of the need for new evangelical pastors, the goal of university education was often not possible, though this situation in Lutheran parts of Germany did improve as the sixteenth-century progressed.

The development of theological education necessitated an improvement in education from the bottom up. Parents and heads of households were enjoined to teach their families the elements of the Christian faith through the *Small Catechism* (1529). Luther developed his *Large Catechism* (1529) to enable these family leaders to carry out this charge. Local Lutheran parishes were charged with establishing local parochial schools that taught the elements of literacy and of the evangelical faith to children, so that they too could read the Bible and devotional literature. Those chosen for leadership in the church and society were sent for further schooling, especially at local Latin schools (later, gymnasiums) that provided education in classical languages and curriculum, preparatory to admission to the universities. Universities prepared individuals to become pastors and teachers for local parishes and schools, as well as those needing advanced degrees to join the theological faculties.

One of the key individuals to shape Protestant education, and particularly theological education, was Luther's younger colleague Philipp Melanchthon, who became known as the *Preaceptor Germaniae* (Teacher of Germany). Melanchthon influenced all levels of education, from the common schools to the universities, and he developed a comprehensive outline for education that lasted for several centuries. He also wrote a number of the textbooks used in university-level theological education and assisted in the formation of a number of new Protestant universities in Europe in the sixteenth century.

Thus, the Protestant universities in Germany and Scandinavia, and especially their theological faculties, became the loci for pastoral and theological education.[6] Not only did they prepare candidates for the ministry, in many places they were the ones to examine these candidates for ordination and approve them, along with other church leaders. After the death of Luther in 1546, the theological faculties also began to serve as a type of theological "magisterium," deliberating on contested theological issues and passing their judgments on the questions. Students from all over Europe flocked to Lutheran universities, such as the one in Wittenberg, and took their new theological education back to their home areas.

The growth and maturation of theological education in the Lutheran areas was also spurred by external developments in Europe and the need to define and defend the Lutheran theological tradition against the attacks of Roman Catholics and other Protestants. The Roman church was slow to respond to the Protestants in theological education, but after the Council of Trent (1545–1563), the Roman Catholics (especially the Jesuit order) aggressively established new, high-quality schools throughout Europe that sought to counter the Protestants. As theological polemics, to define the faith for their communities and to counter the definitions of the faith provided by others, became an increasingly important aspect of the task of pastors and professors, theological education was sharpened.

By the beginning of the seventeenth century, most Lutheran pastors had received a solid classical education and at least some training in the universities, although not all of them completed a degree. Having received a theological education, their practical ministerial training was generally completed under the supervision of a senior clergyperson or, later, at a practical training school set up by the churches. Church officials and the theological faculty examined the candidates for ordination and ruled on their suitability for the ordained ministry. Others sought the somewhat less prestigious position of schoolteacher, which was still a largely academic position. Often, ministerial candidates had a difficult time finding a permanent pastoral position, and many served for a time as either teachers or private chaplains to institutions or wealthy families.

The theological education at this time was heavily weighted toward formal dogmatic and polemical theology, classical languages, and exegetical and biblical knowledge. Instruction was in Latin, and the chosen intellectual foundation was the philosophy of Aristotle. Luther himself had strongly dismissed Aristotelianism, but since it was the general basis of learning and scholarship for Europe, this philosophy was judged to be the proper basis for intellectual and theological learning. This was the age of creating massive volumes of theological dogmatics for the purpose of supporting academic disputation and "correct doctrine." Later critics dismissed this as a "sterile" Age of Orthodoxy. This charge is not completely correct, for this was also a period when deeply moving hymns and devotional works were written, often by the same dogmatic theology professors. However, theological education was still focused mainly on correct doctrine and the defense of the faith.

This system of theological education and ministerial formation was deeply stressed by the Thirty Years' War (1618–1648), especially in Lutheran Germany. This period of confessional warfare between Protestant and Roman Catholic forces was deeply destructive of the social fabric of many areas in Germany; institutions were disrupted or destroyed, and the warfare and its attendant hunger and disease reduced the population in some places by half or more. Many universities and schools were partially or completely destroyed, and the existing system of theological education was compromised, as was the moral fabric of many areas. Decades of work were necessary to rebuild the systems of theological education and ministerial formation in Germany after the Peace of Westphalia in 1648.

PIETISM, RATIONALISM, AND OTHER CHALLENGES

Toward the end of the seventeenth century, the traditional system of Lutheran theological education was challenged again, this time from within the church by the movement known as Pietism, generally dated to begin with the publication of Philipp Jakob Spener's work, *Pia Desideria* (1675). Spener and other reformers thought that the Lutheranism of their day, with its stress on correct doctrine, had led to a rigid (even dead) orthodoxy, an overemphasis on the ordained clergy, and a moral decline among the laypeople. The pietists sought to reemphasize Luther's idea of the "priesthood of all believers," the necessity of conversion or a subjective religious experience, and a deep biblical faith for all, both clergy and laity. These reformers sought to push theological education away from dogmatics and formal apologetics and toward the devotional study of the Bible and practical ministerial training. They were also as much concerned with the spiritual formation of Christian leaders as they were with their education, an emphasis that ironically they shared with contemporary Roman Catholic ministerial education. The center of Pietism was in the city of Halle, Germany, where pietist leaders such as August Hermann Francke established the University of Halle (1694) as a training school along Pietist lines not only for clergy but also for missionaries and other church leaders. Pietism was deeply controversial among the Lutherans, but it made an impact on subsequent theological and ministerial education.

In the aftermath of the Thirty Years' War and with the influence of Pietism, the training of Lutheran candidates for ordination shifted toward a more practical course of study. Candidates still had to study at the universities, where they were examined by the faculty for their academic learning—a universal requirement by the beginning of the eighteenth century. But church leaders also implemented a second, practical examination that usually measured preaching, teaching, pastoral care, and elements of worship and apologetics. Both exams were required in order to successfully achieve ordination. While Lutheran officials sought to upgrade these academic and practical requirements, reports indicate that at times these high standards were not always achievable and were sometimes relaxed to meet individual needs and circumstances.

With the rise of the Enlightenment and rationalism during the eighteenth century, there were changes in the universities with implications for theological and ministerial education. The universities, including the theological faculties, generally moved away from specifically confessional positions and proposed instead to study and teach theology from a rationalistic or "scientific" position. Universities developed general Protestant or Roman Catholic faculties (sometimes both), with much less emphasis on dogmatic and confessional theology; the heavy, classical education faculties, in favor of philosophy, linguistics, and other rationalistic subjects. Some university faculties attempted to maintain their traditional confessional positions, but the trend was generally toward rationalism. Much of the confessional and practical education of pastors was shifted to practical seminaries (*Predigarseminar*), established by local Lutheran churches, where theological students continued their education after the university. The rationalism of the universities was increasingly influential among the Lutheran clergy and was noticeable in the sermons and other religious writings of the age.

In the nineteenth century, a number of alternatives were developed by those dissatisfied with religious rationalism, naturalism, and deism. The romantic movements, in reaction to traditional classicalism, found their religious proponents in certain theologians, most notably the German theologian Friedrich Schleiermacher, who developed a theological system on the basis of universal human feelings or intuitions, a subjective approach. More immediately influential for Lutheran theological education, however, were forms of neoconfessional theology that attempted to counter rationalism. Sparked by the action of German pastor Claus Harms, who in 1817 issued a series of ninety-five theses against religious rationalism, the movement for neoconfessionalism also strongly opposed attempts to merge the Reformed and Lutheran churches in parts of Germany, especially in Prussia. Leaders in the neoconfessionalist movement in the German university theology faculties divided into two movements, the Repristination theologians and the Erlangen school, both of which attempted, with some success, to bring traditional Lutheran theology into the contemporary world. Formal theological education of candidates for ordination, then, varied from one university to the next, depending on the positions of the various faculty. Toward the end of the nineteenth century, new forms of religious liberalism were developed, most notably with the German theologian Albrecht Ritschl and the historian Adolf von Harnack. These theological developments, especially the forms of neoconfessionalism, were also very influential in Lutheran theological education and the training of pastors among Lutherans in North America as they established their own schools there.

The nineteenth century was also a period of great expansion of Christianity by means of mission activities around the world, especially in Africa and Asia. Groups of Lutherans developed voluntary mission societies to identify candidates for mission service overseas and to provide for their education and ongoing support. Judging that candidates for foreign missions needed a type of theological education different from those who were to serve in established European congregations, a number of mission societies developed their own schools. Often influenced by pietist models, such as the University of Halle, the theological education in these mission schools was more oriented toward practical ministerial aims. The idea was that candidates for overseas mission needed a less formal, dogmatic theological education and more instruction in biblical subjects, practical theology, mission languages, and apologetics. A number of mission schools were organized in Germany, first at Berlin (1800) and Basel (1816), then Barmen (1827), Leipzig (1832), and the Gossner Mission Institute (1836). Similar schools were developed in Scandinavia, including Stavanger (1847), Johannelund (1863), and a number of other similar schools in Sweden, Finland, and Denmark.

Another set of similar schools in Germany was generally oriented toward supplying mission pastors to serve immigrant Lutheran congregations in, most noticeably, the United States but also Eastern Europe, Australia, South Africa, and other areas of Lutheran immigration. These "preachers seminaries," such as Hermannsburg, Breklum, and Neuendettelsau, sent hundreds of Lutheran pastors to serve immigrant Lutherans around the world. These mission schools and preachers seminaries were also important models of ways theological education could be done outside the traditional university system. For mission churches, where university-trained pastors were not an option, or for Lutherans who were distrustful of the rationalism and liberalism of the European universities, these institutions were an influential alternative to the classical Lutheran pattern. In early twentieth-century Europe, theological conservatives also developed their own "free" theological schools in opposition to the university model of theological and ministerial education.

These patterns of theological education, and the various "streams" within this tradition, were carried over the Atlantic with the immigrants and were deeply influential in the development of theological education among Lutherans in North America. The European tensions also appeared in the United States: should the education and training[7] of Christian leaders be primarily based on a formal educational model, or should these processes be more focused on the spiritual development of candidates for the ministry? What about the role of the general Western intellectual tradition as compared to the historical elements of the Christian faith? How open should theological education be to new intellectual and cultural elements? And what are the relative roles of formal learning and practical training for pastoral candidates? The competing models of modern European theological education needed to be assessed and balanced. Were the American seminaries to be modeled after the European universities, the preacher seminaries, the mission schools, or some combination of all three?

THE DEVELOPMENT OF THEOLOGICAL EDUCATION IN NORTH AMERICA

When Europeans began to settle in North America in the seventeenth and eighteenth centuries, they brought with them their tradition of Protestantism, especially Reformed (Calvinist) Protestantism from England and Scotland. There were three main lines of this Protestant tradition: the Anglicanism of the Church of England, the dissenting (or nonconformist) Protestantism typified in the Congregationalists and the Presbyterians (and later the Methodists), and finally the separatist, free-church traditions, such as the Baptists and Quakers. Whatever their differences, all these groups found that the situation in North America presented them with a distinctively new context for establishing and growing their religious traditions, one where the state was much less available to support any form of organized Christianity. With the exception of the free-church groups, these Protestants generally supported the ideals of Western European Christendom and the state-church system, where church and state cooperated to form a society that was unified and uniform and where the state financially supported (and thus controlled) organized Protestantism.

The context in North America, however, militated against the development of a unified state-church system (or establishment of religion). Initially, there was some form of establishment in eleven of the thirteen British colonies (not in Quaker Pennsylvania or Baptist Rhode Island), but these establishments varied in their effectiveness. The strongest colonial establishments were in Puritan New England and, to a lesser extent, Anglican Virginia; in other colonies the establishments were more theoretical than actually realized. The weakness of colonial governments meant that they could spare little money or resources for organized religion. As well, the practical pluralism of the colonial situation complicated any form of establishment, as immigrants of varying religious backgrounds were liable to settle wherever they pleased, militating against any religious uniformity. The British model of Protestantism envisioned a dominant state-church Anglicanism with a minority of Protestant dissenting groups, but in British North America it was the dissenters themselves who tended to be in the majority.

Whatever the denominational complexion of a particular colony, the overall situation of organized religion in British North America was weak; it is estimated that by 1776, only 17 percent of the colonists had a formal membership in a Christian congregation.[8] Even correcting for the often stringent standards concerning qualifications for church membership, it seems clear that organized religion in colonial America was much weaker than today. Much of this weakness can be traced directly to the scarcity of local Christian congregations and the even more pressing lack of Protestant clergy to staff them. Because of limited funds and low population densities, it was hard to establish and support congregations. And even where congregations were established, it was difficult for them to attract and maintain resident clergy; congregations could go years, even decades, without a pastor.

The shortage of resident clergy in colonial America can be attributed to a number of factors. Almost all the clergy at this time had to be imported from Europe, as there were very limited means of educating clergy in colonial America. There were few material incentives for European clergy to immigrate to the colonies; money was lacking, and the living conditions were often difficult. As well, religious leaders were an ocean apart from their superiors in Europe, which meant that if a pastor came into conflict with his congregation, he was virtually on his own. In colonial America the clergy were, overall, a very mixed lot; North America got the best and the worst of European pastors. The best were those mission-minded clergy who came out of call and need; the worst were those clerical imposters and failed clergy who had reasons to leave Europe. There were all too many rogues and imposters who presented themselves in the colonies as pastors who had neither the education nor the ordination to the ministry, let alone the temperament to be successful Christian leaders.

The situation in New England was perhaps better than elsewhere in British North America. The Congregational church was established in Massachusetts and Connecticut and received relatively adequate state support. Equally important here was the establishment of a good educational system, including colleges such as Harvard (1636) and Yale (1701), whose function was to provide educated men for the clergy.[9] Protestant groups elsewhere in the colonies were progressively less successful in raising up indigenous clergy. The foundations of Presbyterian Princeton (1746), Baptist Brown (1765), and Dutch Reformed Rutgers (1765) were attempts by these denominations to provide a high education for candidates for ordination. Though the Anglicans founded William and Mary (1693) and Kings (now Columbia, 1754) for similar purposes, the colonial Anglicans were under a distinct disadvantage when it came to providing local, colonial clergy. The necessity for examination and ordination of Anglican priests by a bishop meant that the whole process had to take place in England, for there were no resident bishops in North America until after the Revolutionary War (1775–1783).

Although these early institutions were developed, at least in part, with the intention of preparing candidates for the Christian ministry, they were equivalent to neither the European universities nor the European Protestant seminaries or mission schools. These schools provided a foundational education, to be sure, heavily weighted toward the classical languages and other traditional, general subjects, but they did not provide the specific theological and practical training for the Christian ministry. Rather, pastors were trained through an apprenticeship system, where students who had received their education in the colonies then studied theology and practiced the arts of ministry under the supervision of a resident pastor. Students "read" theology and studied ministry in a process much like prospective lawyers read law with an established lawyer. They also provided clerical leadership for some of the smaller local congregations under the guidance of their supervisor and, when they were deemed prepared for the ministry, stood for examination by a panel of denominational pastors. With the exception of the Anglicans, ordination to the ministry was the prerogative of either the ministerium or the local congregation, depending on the system.

Even though some institutions of higher education were established in colonial North America, large numbers of potential pastors did not have the means or opportunity to study there. For many colonial pastors, the apprenticeship experience was the main means by which they received the knowledge and experience for ministry, in many ways harkening back to the historical ways that Christian leaders had been educated and trained in early and medieval Christianity. The apprentice system was in some ways a very good model for the education of Christian leaders (in a modern sense, it was very "contextual"), but it was subject to a number of limitations. The quality of education varied widely depending on the education and inclination of the local supervisor. The urgent need for pastors meant that some candidates were rushed into the ministry before they could complete their training (a perennial problem). But beyond this, the apprenticeship model was inefficient and inadequate to meet the needs of pastors for a growing Christian population, especially as people streamed out into new western territories after the Revolutionary War.

THE RISE OF PROTESTANT SEMINARIES

The establishment of Protestant seminaries, of the kind that are now very familiar, began in the United States in the early nineteenth century.[10] The first was Andover (1808) in Massachusetts, founded by orthodox Congregationalists as a reaction to the Unitarian takeover of Harvard. This new seminary was followed by many others, including independent educational institutions, such as Bangor (1814), Auburn (1818), Union (1824), Lancaster (1825), and Newton (1825), and seminaries attached to existing colleges such as those at Princeton (1812), Harvard (1819), and Yale (1822). There were a number of other seminaries quickly formed in the subsequent decades (including Lutheran ones, which will be covered later), and by 1860 there were two thousand students at sixty Protestant seminaries in the United States.[11]

Even with this expansion of Protestant theological education, many of these schools were institutionally weak, and programs of study varied widely from one place to another. Due to their own lack of resources and the pressing need for pastors, many students did not even complete the full educational process before they were ordained to the ministry. The westward expansion meant an almost total lack of pastors and congregations in these areas, and the poverty and rough conditions on the frontier provided little incentive pastors to go there. Missionary pastors occasionally traveled the frontier, but the scattered groups of Christians living there might not see a pastor for years.

The period of religious revival and ferment known as the Second Great Awakening (from the 1790s to the 1820s) initially began on the frontier, where camp meetings and revivalism brought Christianity to the scattered population. But this revival, and especially its new techniques to reach unchurched persons, soon made its way to more established eastern parts of the United States. Overall, it created a new, large demand for Christian congregations and for pastors to lead them. Into this situation came the Baptists and the Methodists; both groups were suspicious of formally trained and educated clergy and sought candidates for the ministry who demonstrated personal piety and practical skills over formal education. These two groups raised up thousands of pastors for the new country. With flexible ministry patterns, they began the process of "churching" the United States,[12] and by doing so, became numerically the largest two denominations in nineteenth-century America. They looked down on what they saw as the "unconverted" ministry of other Protestant denominations and sometimes suggested that "a seminary was a cemetery where faith went to die." Many Baptist and Methodist clergy had little in the way of formal education beyond the ability to read the Bible in English and the skills to preach extemporaneously. They were also often bivocational, supporting themselves with secular occupations, along the lines of the modern "tent-making" pastors.

The growth of American theological education continued after the Civil War (1861–1865), spurred by continuing westward expansion and the great wave of immigration from Europe. Many existing seminaries were able to solidify their finances and curriculum, while newer immigrant groups (including many Lutherans) opened their own seminaries, usually with instruction in the immigrant languages.

A significant feature of this period was the standardization of the seminary process as a three-year program. Although many candidates still did not complete the entire course, this pattern remained the norm for ministerial education into the twenty-first century. Equally important, given their numbers, was the Methodists' shift on the question of formal academic training for the ministry. Earlier they had generally rejected the need for seminaries, but as they grew (and became more socially established) they began to form seminaries, the first one in 1847. By 1880 there were eleven.

The influence of the awakening movement and revivalism of the early nineteenth century meant that the seminary education of this time stressed the formation of a candidate's own personal faith, quite along the line of the earlier European pietism. This focus was maintained through the rest of the century, but new intellectual currents within American Protestantism, especially the newer liberal and "scientific" theology from the European universities, also began to influence seminary education. The established, "mainline" Protestant seminaries began hiring faculties with the professional PhD degree, sometimes earned at a European university, and many of these new faculty began to teach along liberal lines, including the use of higher biblical criticism as a method for understanding the Bible.[13]

The twin lines of the conservative piety of the revivals and the new liberal theology of the universities maintained an uneasy relationship in the late nineteenth-century Protestant seminaries before diverging and erupting into open conflict. A series of high-profile heresy trials were brought by conservatives against liberal professors, but these were generally unsuccessful in stemming the liberal tide. These conflicts soon led to all-out battles—the so-called fundamentalist-modernist controversies, especially within the northern Protestant denominations—which were generally settled by the 1920s with the defeat of the conservative factions.

Conservative dissatisfaction with the course of Protestant denominations led to the formation of new institutions of theological education, often known as Bible schools or institutes, beginning with the formation of Moody Bible Institute in 1887 in Chicago. This pattern was quickly copied around the United States by conservative evangelical, Holiness, and Pentecostal leaders. Usually organized as independent and nondenominational, these schools did not initially require a secondary-school education or grant degrees, and they educated Christians for a wide range of ministries, be it lay or ordained. These Bible schools were found among diverse Protestant denominational traditions, even among the Lutherans. Some Bible school alumni might eventually go to seminary, but among many conservative groups, such formal training was seen as unnecessary or even suspect. Other Bible school alumni served as evangelists, lay pastors, missionaries, or lay leaders in their congregations. In the twentieth century, many of the conservative Protestant denominations eventually did establish their own theological seminaries, but a number of these seminaries maintained the traditional piety and theology of the Bible schools for quite a period of time.

In the mainline Protestant seminaries, the twentieth century saw the continued growth of theological liberalism as their main focus. However, the neoorthodox theology of Karl Barth, H. Richard Niebuhr, and Reinhold Niebuhr was also quite influential. Although many seminary faculty members were professionally trained in the European doctoral system, these American seminaries were not copies of the theological faculties of the European universities. Even at the most accomplished American divinity schools (Harvard, Yale, Chicago, and others), the emphasis remained the professional education of candidates for the ordained ministry, including teaching the practical elements of preaching and pastoral care. Instead of the European model, these Protestant seminaries rather adopted the example of the American professional schools, such as those for doctors and lawyers. Their attempt was to establish the ministry as a white-collar, professional career, equivalent to that of other professions. The new seminary curriculums followed this model of education, including, for many, a parish internship and later a clinical pastoral education unit. The Association of Theological Schools (ATS) was founded in 1918 as an accrediting agency for theological education, another move in the direction of professionalization.

POSTWAR EXPANSION

There was a steady expansion of Protestant seminary education after the end of World War II in 1945, much of which came as conservative Protestant denominations began to establish their own seminaries. Their growth numerically eclipsed the mainline Protestant seminaries, with the evangelical seminary enrollments outnumbering their mainline counterparts. Even groups like the Pentecostal and Holiness denominations, which traditionally had shunned seminary-style education for their pastors, established their own seminaries, sometimes built on the base of existing Bible schools. These new evangelical seminaries also served as the theological hubs for the growth of American conservative and evangelical denominations after the 1960s.

The social turmoil and developments after 1960 brought dramatic demographic changes in American seminaries. In the mainline Protestant denominations, the ordination of women to the ministry became possible, leading to the admission of women to once all-male institutions, quite a culture change for them. These seminaries were also influenced by the social upheavals of the decade, including the civil rights and antiwar movements, a greater interest in ecology, and the expansion of the rights of women. Professionalization continued, as parish internships and clinical pastoral education became more the norm. Another sign of this professionalization was seminaries' shift in degree status, when the primary seminary degree was moved from being a bachelor of divinity to a master of divinity in the 1970s.

Since the 1980s, a number of these trends have continued, including the enrollment of more women and a large influx of older, "second-career" students seeking a new career in their midlife (or later). Membership in the mainline Protestant denominations, which had peaked in the mid-1960s, began to decline, in some cases dramatically. This led to two problems for the mainline seminaries: less demand for congregational pastors and declining financial support from their parent denomination. Compounding these financial pressures were additional demands of a more professionalized faculty, who having sacrificed to attain a high-cost graduate education sought higher salaries and benefits. Since 2000 there has been a general, across-the-board decrease in candidates for ministry of 20 to 40 percent, especially in the mainline seminaries but also to a lesser extent in evangelical institutions, a decrease that has wreaked havoc with institutional budgets. Declining enrollments, combined with financial pressure and changes such as online and distance education, has dramatically changed the face of American Protestant seminaries across the theological spectrum. Some have gone out of operation, while a number of others have closed campuses, reduced faculties, and sought mergers with other seminaries or local colleges. Demographic and financial trends indicate that these pressures will continue to affect seminaries and pressure them to reinvent themselves and their programs for the twenty-first century and beyond.

THEOLOGICAL EDUCATION AMONG AMERICAN LUTHERANS

The most immediate context for the history of Luther Seminary is the larger history of theological education among Lutherans in North America, as they sought to establish schools for the training of pastors in the colonies. Certainly, the Lutherans who emigrated from Europe brought with them the various strains of theological education enumerated earlier, but they also faced a new context in which to establish their own institutions and programs.[14] Most importantly, there was a lack of Lutheran universities in North America, and most of the educational system, though tinged by Protestantism, was officially nonsectarian. Without Lutheran or Protestant university faculties, North American Lutherans had to establish new models and means of theological education.

Lutheran immigration to North America began in the seventeenth century, with a short-lived Swedish colony along the Delaware River. Though this colony was rather small and soon taken over by the Dutch, the congregations founded there were served by Lutheran priests from Sweden until the beginning of the eighteenth century. But the Swedish settlers never developed any of their own pastors, and with their transition to English, these congregations affiliated with the Protestant Episcopal Church. A much larger immigration was that of the colonial German Lutherans, who immigrated in small groups and families, settling mainly in the middle colonies from New York to Virginia, but principally in Pennsylvania. Scattered groups of Lutherans began to form congregations in the seventeenth and eighteenth centuries, which were served by immigrant clergy from Germany. As with the general situation of colonial pastors, these immigrant Lutheran clergy were a very mixed group, including a number of clerical imposters who were not officially ordained by any Lutheran authorities. Congregations appealed to Lutheran consistories in Europe, and to Halle University, for pastors. Some of the pastors who were sent from Europe were very good, but a number of others could not adjust to the colonial situation. One of the best of these missionary pastors was Henry Melchior Muhlenberg, who in 1748 organized the first Lutheran synod, the Pennsylvania Ministerium. Most of the colonial Lutheran pastors were trained in apprenticeship with established Lutheran pastors and then examined by a synod or ministerium before being ordained. Muhlenberg also had the hard task of rooting out the rogue pastors and ejecting them from the Lutheran congregations.

One major problem for the preparation of colonial Lutheran candidates for the ministry was the lack of adequate schools to prepare them for theological study, especially the foundational courses of classical subjects and languages. Several abortive attempts were undertaken to provide something akin to a classical education along the lines of a German gymnasium, but these schools did not flourish, and the general educational preparedness of Lutheran ordinands declined through the eighteenth century.

The development of Lutheran seminaries paralleled that of other American Protestant groups, beginning in the early decades of the nineteenth century. These early seminaries were generally just an elaboration of the older apprenticeship system. Usually they consisted of one or two Lutheran pastors with some formal education who gathered a group of candidates for the ministry around them, with the whole group living in a single building. Though there usually was a formal course of study, many of the students came and went as their financial resources allowed, and few lasted for the entire course. Early seminary faculty had more formal education than most, but their preparation was also often inadequate. Faculty spent much of their time in remedial education, giving their students the background in classics and languages. In some cases they actually founded parallel schools, known as academies, which offered a formal course of pre-seminary instruction, and some of these academies eventually became independent liberal arts colleges of their own.

The first American Lutheran seminary was Hartwick Seminary, founded in 1797 through a bequest from a colonial Lutheran pastor, J. C. Hartwick.[15] This institution was originally intended to train missionaries for outreach to the Native Americans but soon was refocused on general pastoral education. This school was never very large and closed in 1940. Of more lasting importance was the foundation in 1826 of Gettysburg Seminary in Gettysburg, Pennsylvania.[16] Organized by a group of Lutheran synods that had banded together into the General Synod, this new institution was operated largely through the efforts of one Lutheran leader, Samuel Simon Schmucker. Having received some formal education at Princeton, Schmucker was Gettysburg's president and leading faculty member for over forty years, during which time he taught over five hundred future Lutheran pastors. Like many others, this seminary struggled with the lack of adequate resources, also needing to develop a pre-seminary academy, which eventually became Gettysburg College.

Other American Lutheran seminaries were founded shortly thereafter, as the geographical expansion of the country occasioned the need for other, regional institutions. In 1830, a Lutheran synod in Ohio opened the Evangelical Lutheran Seminary in Columbus. In that same year, Lutherans in the American South opened the Lutheran Theological Southern Seminary in South Carolina. Both institutions also struggled during their early existence. Southern Seminary, which had led peripatetic preachers through much of the antebellum period, suffered greatly during the Civil War, and finally relocated to Columbia, South Carolina.[17]

THE FORMATION OF AMERICAN LUTHERANISM

As American Lutherans began the transition to the use of English in the early nineteenth century, they began to dispute among themselves how Lutheran theology and worship should be developed and defined in this new country and in a new language. The dominant form of religion in America was Reformed (or Calvinist) Protestantism, modified in the early nineteenth century by the new, theologically Arminian revivalism from the frontier. This new religious consensus, most typically found among Methodists and Baptists, deeply affected all the American Protestant groups, including the Lutherans. The influence of this new Protestant consensus on the Lutherans is seen in many different forms, including (among other things) a decline in a distinctive Lutheran confessional theology (especially concerning the sacraments), the increased emphasis on conversion and sanctification, and the popularity of revivalistic worship among many Lutherans.

This new form of Lutheranism, sometimes known as "American Lutheranism," created divisions among the Lutherans in North America. Some, like Schmucker, were willing to at least partially adapt their Lutheranism in the direction of the prevailing American Protestant consensus. But other Lutherans voiced their dissent from this trend and sought to return to a traditional Lutheran confessional position on theology and worship, in contrast to the general Protestantism around them. Early voices in this latter direction included a theological family in the South, the Henkels, who formed a staunchly confessional Tennessee Synod and a publishing operation to print works of traditional Lutheran confessional theology. This was a growing controversy and strongly divided Lutherans through much of the nineteenth century.

The controversy was, as might be expected, centered in the Lutheran seminaries in America. Under the influence of Schmucker, Gettysburg Seminary was the leading institution of "American Lutheranism." The Lutheran seminary in Columbus, Ohio, moved more in the direction of the confessionalist wing, prompting the "American Lutherans" in Ohio to develop their own school, Wittenberg College, in 1845, whose theological department eventually was named Hamma Divinity School.[18] But the major division over this issue came in the east within the Pennsylvania Ministerium. Confessionalists within eastern Lutheranism had been growing increasingly dissatisfied with Schmucker and Gettysburg Seminary, especially when Schmucker proposed the American edition of the *Augsburg Confession*, with modifications in the direction of the general Protestant consensus in the 1850s. The resulting controversy led the confessionalists in the Pennsylvania Ministerium (and elsewhere) to form the Lutheran Theological Seminary in Philadelphia in 1864.[19] So by the 1860s, there was a three-way division of the English-speaking Lutherans; southern Lutheran synods formed their own association, while the northern Lutheran synods either remained in the General Synod or joined the new General Council, formed in 1869.

American Lutherans whose roots went back to eighteenth-century immigration were joined in the nineteenth century by large numbers of new immigrants from Germany, Scandinavia, and other parts of Europe. Between 1840 and 1920, millions of immigrants from these countries, officially (or nominally) members of the state Lutheran churches, came to North America. Rather than joining the existing Lutheran denominations, whose language and theology the newcomers did not recognize, these new immigrant Lutherans formed dozens of new Lutheran synods, splitting along linguistic, ethnic, or theological lines. Of course, each of these new denominations had to provide pastors for their new congregations, and so the number of Lutheran seminaries proliferated through the nineteenth century.

Though the vast majority of immigrants came to the United States primarily for economic reasons, there were some Lutherans who came for religious reasons. Chief among these were the immigrants who formed the Evangelical Lutheran Synod of Missouri (now the Lutheran Church—Missouri Synod). The genesis of this group was the nineteenth-century Lutheran revival of Lutheran confessionalism in Germany and participants' opposition to an enforced union of the Lutheran and Reformed Protestants in Prussia. This group organized a large immigration to Missouri and, under the leadership of Carl Ferdinand Wilhelm Walther, gathered many other Lutheran immigrants into the new Missouri Synod, which was formed in 1847. In 1839, these Lutherans formed a seminary for their own congregations, Concordia Seminary, located in St. Louis, Missouri. Under the leadership of Walther, this new seminary was modeled along the lines of the classical German Lutheran theological education and became the leading institution of the synod.[20] Other German confessionalists, influenced by Wilhelm Löhe in Germany, formed their own seminary, which eventually became a part of the Missouri Synod as well. This seminary, also called Concordia Seminary, was located for many years in Springfield, Illinois, and was eventually moved to Fort

Wayne, Indiana, in 1976. This latter institution was considered the Missouri Synod's "practical" seminary, with a less rigorous academic program.

Other groups of immigrant confessional German Lutherans formed additional synods (independent of the Missouri Synod) in the United States. One group related to Wilhelm Löhe in Germany had theological reservations about the Missouri Synod and formed its own Iowa Synod instead. The Iowa Synod organized Wartburg Seminary in 1853, which after several moves was settled in Dubuque, Iowa. A smaller group, the Buffalo Synod, operated its own seminary for a number of years. Still another group formed the Wisconsin Synod, whose own seminary, Wisconsin Lutheran Seminary, traces its origins to 1863. These groups, as well as the Ohio Synod's seminary in Columbus, Ohio, represented the most strictly confessional wing of nineteenth-century American Lutheranism and alternatively cooperated with and fought with the Missouri Synod, competing to reach the masses of German Lutheran immigrants.

In the nineteenth century there were also large numbers of Scandinavian Lutheran immigrants to North America, and clerical leaders within this population formed their own national synodical bodies, again along linguistic or theological lines. Swedish immigrants formed the Augustana Synod in 1860 and in the same year began their own seminary, which in 1875 was moved to share a campus with Augustana College in Rock Island, Illinois.[21] This seminary was the only theological school among the Swedish American Lutherans, although other non-Lutheran Swedish Americans formed their own seminaries. Danish Lutherans split into two distinct groups, the Inner Mission pietists and the Grundtvigians, both of which formed small colleges and seminaries—the Inner Mission at Blair, Nebraska, and the Grundtvigians at Des Moines, Iowa. Finnish American Lutherans had their theological seminary at Hancock, Michigan, while some Finnish revival groups had their own seminary in the same area.

The situation of theological education among the Norwegian American denominations of the most immediate relevance to Luther Seminary was quite complicated.[22] The two polar ends of the Norwegian American Lutheran spectrum were the Norwegian Synod and the Hauge Synod. The Norwegian Synod represented the conservative confessionalists, organized by leaders closely related to the state Church of Norway in 1853. This group initially decided to locate a Norwegian theological professor at Concordia Seminary in St. Louis, and this arrangement for their theological education lasted from 1859 to 1876, when the Norwegian Synod opened its own institution, Luther Seminary, in Saint Paul, Minnesota. The Hauge Synod, on the other hand, represented the theology of the nineteenth-century revivals under the leadership of Hans Nielsen Hauge. Initially distrustful of an educated clergy, this group eventually did establish its own institution, Red Wing Seminary in Red Wing, Minnesota, in 1879.

In between these two groups were a rotating cast of other Norwegian American church bodies. There was a group of Norwegians and Danes who were initially in the Swedish American Augustana Synod. When they withdrew from this body, they formed their own seminary, Augsburg Seminary in Marshall, Wisconsin, in 1869, which was moved to Minneapolis in 1872. A smaller group of Norwegians and Danes formed a seminary in Beloit, Wisconsin, which was eventually merged into Augsburg Seminary in 1890. Theological turmoil among the Norwegian Synod in the 1880s, partially over the close relationship between this synod and the Missouri Synod, led to the formation of a faction known as the Anti-Missouri Brotherhood, who formed their own seminary in 1886 in conjunction with St. Olaf College in Northfield, Minnesota. In 1890, these three groups merged together to form the United Norwegian Lutheran Church, and the three seminaries were combined at the Augsburg campus in Minneapolis.

The merger of these seminaries did not go well, and the board of Augsburg refused to relinquish control of the seminary to the new United Church, occasioning a court battle. In 1893 the United Church opened its own seminary in Minneapolis, and the supporters of Augsburg eventually formed their own new denomination, the Lutheran Free Church in 1897. By 1917, the Norwegian Synod, the United Norwegian Lutheran Church, and the Hauge Synod reached an agreement to form a single denomination, the Norwegian Lutheran Church in America. Their three seminaries, Luther, United, and Red Wing, were merged together on the site of the United

Church seminary in Saint Paul, Minnesota. A smaller group from the Norwegian Synod, objecting to the merger, formed their own new denomination, the Evangelical Lutheran Synod, with a college and seminary in Mankato, Minnesota.

As Lutherans moved further into the American Midwest and West during the nineteenth century, they formed new synods in these regions, and naturally new seminaries. The General Council formed the Chicago Lutheran Theological Seminary (Maywood, Illinois) in 1891, and there were also new seminaries formed in Kansas and Nebraska. Due to a theological conflict within the faculty of the Chicago seminary, a group of faculty and students split off from this institution in 1921 to form a new seminary, Northwestern Lutheran Theological Seminary, which was eventually located in Minneapolis, Minnesota. After some initial unsuccessful attempts at founding a Lutheran seminary on the West Coast, Pacific Lutheran Seminary was organized in 1952 in Berkeley, California.

Although there were some substantial theological institutions among them, notably Gettysburg, Philadelphia, Luther, and Concordia St. Louis, many of these nineteenth-century American Lutheran seminaries were rather modest institutions. Often these seminaries consisted of a single building housing a small group of faculty and students. Faculty struggled with the demands of teaching and monitoring the students, along with a heavy load of church work. Many students were ill-prepared academically for theological study, and the faculty had to provide for remedial education in the basics, as well. Students were often extremely impoverished and could not stay at the seminary for a full course of study. The overwhelming need for pastors led to a situation where academic standards had to be relaxed in order to get students into the field as soon as possible. Although some of these pressures were reduced after the early twentieth century, workloads remained heavy, and the crying need for pastors remained a constant until the 1960s. These Lutheran seminaries were torn between the two models of theological education that they had inherited from European Lutheranism: the academically oriented university model and the more practical (and pious) mission schools. With their modest means, these seminaries could not maintain the kind of academic rigor of the universities, although this remained for some an aspirational goal. There was some degree of professionalization through the middle of the twentieth century, and new academic and professional programs were introduced, but many of the same shortcomings persisted. As a protest of the movement toward liberalism and academic theology in many Lutheran seminaries, a group of Lutheran Bible institutes was formed, beginning in the early twentieth century. Some of their graduates eventually studied at Lutheran seminaries, while other graduates went directly into congregational service.

POSTWAR CONSOLIDATIONS

After World War II ended in 1945, there was a renewed push for mergers and consolidations among Lutherans in America, leading to the formation of two large national Lutheran denominations, the American Lutheran Church (1960) and the Lutheran Church in America (1962). Along with this came a consolidation of seminaries, including the inclusion of Augsburg into Luther in 1963; of Augustana, Chicago, and several other smaller ones into the Lutheran School of Theology at Chicago (LSTC) in 1966;[23] and a merger of Evangelical (Ohio) and Hamma to form Trinity Lutheran Seminary at Columbus in 1978. A group of faculty and students walked out of Concordia Seminary, St. Louis, to form Christ Seminary in Exile (Seminex) in 1974, which later combined with LSTC.[24] After a number of years of cooperation, Northwestern and Luther merged in 1982.

With the formation of the Evangelical Lutheran Church in America (ELCA) in 1988, the number of major Lutheran denominations was reduced to two, the ELCA and Lutheran Church—Missouri Synod. The ELCA had eight seminaries, while the Lutheran Church—Missouri Synod had two. The religious shifts of the late twentieth century had major impacts on the situation of these seminaries. Concordia St. Louis lost a large portion of its students and faculty in 1974 and had to be rebuilt. The ELCA has paralleled the decline of other mainline Protestant denominations, with a concurrent decline in congregational membership. These trends, and battles since the 1990s over topics such as ecumenism and human sexuality, led to the formation of two new centrist Lutheran denominations, the Lutheran Congregations in Mission for Christ (2001) and the North American Lutheran Church (2010). These new denominations have been served by new seminaries, including the Institute for Lutheran Theology and the North American Lutheran Seminary, among others.

Since the late twentieth century, the Lutheran seminaries in America have dealt with social and theological changes that had serious impacts on their missions. Lutheran denominations (but not Missouri and Wisconsin) have allowed the ordination of women since 1970, a development of great importance for seminary education. There has also been a great trend since then of older, "second-career" students entering seminary, which has occasioned further changes. With the rise of the internet, distance education has become more feasible, meaning that physical campuses are less crucial than they used to be.

Declining membership in both the ELCA and in Missouri has meant financial pressures on the Lutheran seminaries, which now receive much less support from their parent denominations than they have in the past. Raising tuition on students was possible for a time, but students have finite resources, and many come to seminary with substantial student loan burdens. Several of the ELCA seminaries have merged, either with other seminaries or with local Lutheran colleges and universities. Budgets and resources are often tight, and some institutions have sold buildings or properties. The early twenty-first century has been a time of considerable challenge to the Lutheran seminaries in North America, which have been challenged to reinvent themselves yet again for new contexts and new kinds of theological education.

Notes

1. For a good recent survey of the history of theological education, see Justo L. Gonzales, *The History of Theological Education* (Nashville: Abingdon, 2015).

2. See *Didache* 15:1–2. It is interesting that in this second-century work, the bishops are seemingly ranked below the prophets and teacher. A

higher view of the office of bishop can be seen in the Letters of Ignatius, an early sign of the monarchical episcopate.

3. William C. Placher and Derek R. Nelson, *A History of Christian Theology: An Introduction* (Philadelphia: Westminster, 1983), 15.

4. See for example the preface to the *Small Catechism* (1529) and Luther's *Instructions to Visitors* (1527), LW 40:313–20.

5. Charles B. Foelsch, "Ministerial Education," in *The Encyclopedia of the Lutheran Church*, 3 vols., ed. Julius Bodensieck (Minneapolis: Augsburg, 1965), 2:1565.

6. For a survey of the Lutheran universities in Europe, see Carl F. Wisoff, "Theological Schools, IV: In Europe," in Bodensieck, *Encyclopedia*, 3:2353–71.

7. Words such as *education*, *training*, and *formation*, among others, have their own ideological position within theological education, and the choice of one or another of these terms has significance in how one views this process. This volume, however, uses these words interchangeably.

8. Roger Finke and Rodney Stark, *The Churching of America, 1776–2005: Winners and Losers in Our Religious Economy* (New Brunswick, NJ: Rutgers University Press, 2005), esp. 25–35.

9. For a brief overview of Protestant theological education in America, see W. C. Ringenberg, "Education, Protestant Theological," in *Dictionary of Christianity in America*, ed. Daniel C. Reid (Downers Grove, IL: InterVarsity, 1990), 379–80.

10. There is a comprehensive, three-volume history of Protestant theological education in the United States by Glenn T. Miller. *Piety and Intellect: The Aims and Purposes of Ante-Bellum Theological Education* (Atlanta: Scholars, 1990); *Piety and Profession: American Protestant Theological Education, 1870–1970* (Grand Rapids: Eerdmans, 2007); and *Piety and Plurality: Theological Education Since 1960* (Eugene, OR: Cascade, 2014).

11. Ringenberg, "Education, Protestant Theological," 379.

12. Finke and Stark, *Churching of America*, esp. ch. 1.

13. For a survey of this, see Conrad Cherry, *Hurrying toward Zion: Universities, Divinity Schools, and American Protestantism* (Bloomington: Indiana University Press, 1995).

14. For a general history of Lutherans in North America, see Granquist, *Lutherans in America*; L. DeAne Lagerquist, *The Lutherans* (Westport, CT: Greenwood Press, 1999); or E. Clifford Nelson, ed., *The Lutherans*

in North America (Philadelphia: Fortress Press, 1975).

15. There are generally histories of the various Lutheran seminaries, but they cannot all be listed here. For a historical overview of these Lutheran seminaries, see "Ministerial Education, VI: North America," in Bodensieck, *Encyclopedia*, 3:2373–84.

16. On Gettysburg Seminary, see Abdel Ross Wentz, *Gettysburg Lutheran Theological Seminary*, vol. 1, *History 1826–1965* (Harrisburg, PA: Evangelical Press, 1965).

17. For a history, see Susan Wilds McArver and Scott H. Hendrix, *A Goodly Heritage: The Story of Lutheran Theological Southern Seminary, 1830–2005* (Columbia, SC: Lutheran Theological Southern Seminary, 2006).

18. On the situation in Ohio, see Donald L. Huber, *Educating Lutheran Pastors in Ohio, 1830–1930: A History of Trinity Lutheran Seminary and Its Predecessors* (Lewiston, NY: Edwin Mellen, 1989).

19. Theodore G. Tappert, *A History of the Lutheran Theological Seminary at Philadelphia, 1864–1964* (Philadelphia: Lutheran Theological Seminary, 1964).

20. Carl S. Meyer, *Log Cabin to Luther Tower: Concordia Seminary during 125 Years toward a More Excellent Ministry, 1839–1965* (St. Louis: Concordia Publishing House, 1965).

21. G. Everett Arden, *School of the Prophets: The Background and History of Augustana Theological Seminary, 1860–1960* (Rock Island, IL: Augustana Theological Seminary, 1960).

22. On the general history of the Norwegian American Lutheran groups and their seminaries, see E. Clifford Nelson and Eugene Fevold, *The Lutheran Church among the Norwegian-Americans*, 2 vols. (Minneapolis: Augsburg, 1960).

23. Harold Skillrud, *LSTC: Decade of Decision* (Chicago: Lutheran School of Theology at Chicago, 1969).

24. James C. Burkee, *Power, Politics, and the Missouri Synod* (Minneapolis: Fortress Press, 2011).

2

The Beginnings of Norwegian American Theological Education

The most immediate context for the history of Luther Seminary is the Lutheran traditions that developed in Norway and among Norwegian immigrants to North America. Of the numerous institutional strands that eventually came together to form Luther Seminary, only one was not rooted in Norwegian American Lutheranism, Northwestern Lutheran Theological Seminary, which will be covered in chapter 6. To understand this background, it is necessary to first examine the varieties of Lutheranism in Norway and then to see how these traditions were transplanted to the United States. This chapter will then focus on two distinctive strands of the Norwegian American Lutheran tradition, the Norwegian Synod and the Hauge Synod, and their experiences of theological education. These two synods formed the "bookends" of Norwegian American Lutheranism, the Norwegian Synod being closest to the Lutheranism of the state Church of Norway, while the Hauge Synod represented the revival movements in nineteenth-century Norway. There were additional Norwegian American Lutheran groups in between these two bookends, and their history will be examined in chapter 3.

LUTHERANISM IN NORWAY

Christianity was brought to Norway from England and Germany during the ninth and tenth centuries but officially took hold in the country in the eleventh century through the efforts of two kings, Olaf Tryggvason and Olaf Haraldsson (Saint Olaf), who made Christianity the religion of the kingdom. The process of converting the Norwegian people to the new religion took time, but by the late Middle Ages most of the country was officially Christian, although older forms of pre-Christian traditions also continued to be observed in folk culture. The fortunes of the kingdom declined in the later Middle Ages. In the late fourteenth century, Norway lost its independence when it became a part of the Union of Kalmar, which combined all three Scandinavian kingdoms under the rule of the Danish royal house. It was ruled by the Danish monarchy until 1814. The Protestant Reformation was introduced to Norway in 1537 when the Danish king, Christian III, declared Lutheranism to be the official religion of both Denmark and Norway. The actual transition to Lutheran doctrine and practice proceeded slowly in Norway, with pockets of folk religion and Catholicism remaining until the eighteenth century. In 1687, Norwegian law declared the ecumenical creeds, the *Augsburg Confession*, and Luther's Small Catechism to be the official theological foundations of the Church of Norway. Significantly, the Norwegians did not place the rest of the *Book of Concord* on this same official level.

By the eighteenth century, Lutheranism had taken deep root in Norway and developed a rich tradition of popular devotion, piety, and hymnody among the people. Bishop Eric Pontoppidan (1698–1746) wrote an explanation of Luther's Small Catechism that was very influential in Norway and among Norwegian Americans well into the twentieth century.[1] The Church of Norway was a state-supported church and enjoyed an enforced monopoly in the country, with no other forms of Christianity allowed. Educated in the universities in Norway and Denmark, the Lutheran clergy became virtually a hereditary class within the country. Though Norway had no class of nobility, the educated elites (including the clergy) formed a separate social group, the "conditioned" class (*conditionert*), whose members led the local governments and the parishes of the Church of Norway. Among the common people in Norway, the ordinary landowners (*bonde*) had historically remained free (feudalism was not a factor) and guarded their own freedom and privileges. Below them were the landless poor (*husman* or *crofters*). These social distinctions remained important into the nineteenth century and were also a factor in the divisions among the early Norwegian American denominations.

Lutheran Orthodoxy and then Enlightenment rationalism had some impact on the clergy of the Church of Norway, especially as the church became more centralized in the eighteenth century. The pietism of this age also arrived in Norway from Germany through Denmark and found a place among laypeople and some of the clergy, especially through hymnody, the writings of Pontoppidan, and the efforts of Moravian missionaries to the country. Although some elements within the Church of Norway opposed it, this pietism deeply influenced the religious life of the country. The officials of the church sought to maintain a firm control over the religious life of the country, but the lay-oriented pietism movements resisted this clericalism, resulting in ongoing conflict.

THE INFLUENCE OF PIETISM

The strong nineteenth-century pietist awakenings, or revivals, of Christianity in Norway began with the great Norwegian lay preacher Hans Nielsen Hauge, who had a strong conversion experience in 1796 that led him to an intense period of revival preaching and writing (1796–1804). Hauge's awakening shaped his preaching, and he challenged people to seriously examine themselves and their sins, to seek forgiveness and awakening from God, and to live lives of personal seriousness and holiness (sanctification). The Hauge movement was also very lay-oriented, championing Luther's idea of the "priesthood of all believers" against the prerogatives of the state-church clergy. This movement has often been wrongly characterized as solely dour and legalistic. Although at times it did devolve into such traits, they were not of the essence of the Haugean movement, which emphasized a warm personal piety. Hauge himself attracted the wrath of church and governmental officials and was imprisoned in 1804 for violating a state law against lay preaching. When released in 1814, Hauge's health did not allow him to travel or preach, but through the impact of his writings and the efforts of his followers, the Haugean revival continued to spread throughout Norway. Though the Haugeans (at his urging) did not withdraw officially from the Church of Norway, in many places they founded separate "prayer houses" (*bedehuset*) for their preaching and religious activities. Hauge himself was of the common people and was very much interested not only in their spiritual development but also in their economic improvement. The Haugean movement also contained elements of resurgent Norwegian nationalism (after 1814) and efforts to broaden the rights of the common people through an expansion of Norwegian democracy. Although Hauge died relatively young in 1824, this movement continued after his death. Many of the religious and cultural elements of the Haugean movement were influential among Norwegian Americans, as well.

These revivals in Norway in the early nineteenth century had a profound effect on the Church of Norway and on the country as a whole. Eventually, laws limiting lay preaching and the devotional gatherings of laypeople (conventicles) were relaxed, and even some of the state church clergy embraced the revivals. Along with the Haugean movement, older forms of pietism (especially the Moravians) were also present, including, beginning in the 1820s, the influence of the Danish theologian and hymnwriter N. F. S. Grundtvig. This latter influence came into Norway through the efforts of a number of Norwegian theological students who studied in Copenhagen. Grundtvig's theology was a distinctive blend of religious renewal and "folk" Christianity that stressed the nationalist and cultural roots of Christianity in the life of the Danish people. Though Grundtvigianism was adopted for a time among certain pastors and church leaders, it did not have a lasting influence in Norway.[2]

Beginning in the 1850s, and in opposition to the Grundtvigian clergy, new revivals of Christianity swept through Norway, revivals of a rather different sort. The foundation of various Norwegian mission societies in the 1840s had occasioned some revival of religious life, but the real leader of this new awakening was a theological professor at the university in Christiana (Oslo) named Gisle Johnson. As distinct from Hauge, Johnson was an ordained pastor, a rather quiet and reserved person, an intellectual, and a staunch Lutheran confessionalist, but these traits were combined with the same concern for personal piety and profession of faith that characterized the faith of Hauge. Johnson ignited this new awakening, the "Johnsonian revivals" of the 1850s and 1860s, through his preaching tours of the country. Johnson also educated and influenced a generation of Norwegian pastors who carried on the themes of this revival in their parish work. This Johnsonian revival also had great influence on a number of the Norwegian American Lutheran church leaders, some of whom were trained in Christiana at Norway's sole university during this period.

While the Haugeans in America had their own denomination, the influence of Johnson was found in several other Norwegian American groups, especially in the "center" between the Hauge and Norwegian synods.[3] Because Johnsonianism was more closely tied to the historic Lutheran confessions of faith, and because Johnson himself was a professor and a pastor, his revival of religion was more appealing to Norwegian American pastors and church leaders, and thus more acceptable to some than the lay-oriented revivals of the Haugeans. Another aspect of this later revival was the influence of the Swedish revival leader Carl Olof Rosenius, who was also active about the same time as Johnson. Rosenius, himself a layperson, was a prolific writer of spiritual and devotional materials and sermons, disseminated through his periodical, *Pietisten*. Rosenius emphasized the joy and freedom of the new life in Christ, and thus Rosenian piety has been characterized as "freer" and less dour than that of Hauge. This piety soon found proponents in Norway and among the Norwegian Americans, who translated Rosenian works into Norwegian and printed them quite regularly. These three strains of revival piety—the Haugean, the Johnsonian, and the Rosenian—were deeply influential among the Norwegian Lutherans in North America.

THE DEVELOPMENT OF NORWEGIAN AMERICAN LUTHERANISM

In the great migration of Europeans to North America from 1840 to

1920, close to one million Norwegians left their country to settle in the new world. This emigration from Norway was a substantial portion of the population of the country, perhaps upward of 25 percent. Ireland and Norway share the dubious distinction of having lost the greatest percentage of their population to emigration. Norwegians settled in a number of places in the United States and Canada but predominantly in the upper midwestern United States and the prairie provinces of Canada. In their ethnic enclaves, they eventually built thriving immigrant communities in which a leading role was played by the Norwegian American churches. While the churches gathered in only a portion of the immigrant population (probably about 30 percent), they were by far the largest and most important institutions in the ethnic community. Unlike some other Scandinavian groups, Norwegian Americans remained overwhelmingly Lutheran, although they did divide into a number of different ethnic denominations.

The initial wave of Norwegian immigrants settled in southern Wisconsin and northern Illinois during the 1840s, and subsequent immigrants moved west and north, primarily into Iowa, Minnesota, and the Dakotas. Norwegian immigrants often formed small ethnic enclaves in rural areas, scattered throughout these states. Most of the immigrants arrived individually and in small groups, seeking economic advancement initially through farming but later in the century by means of jobs in the cities. They did not come in large groups accompanied by pastors, so when they sought to establish Lutheran congregations, they often had to do so without a resident pastor.

America was a strange new religious world for these immigrants. Certainly the ethnic and religious pluralism was a huge change from the very homogenous situation in Norway, but they could manage this reality somewhat by remaining primarily in their ethnic enclaves. The major issue was the lack of a state church or any official support for religious life. Laypeople had to organize, operate, and finance their congregations directly, without any additional support. Pastors had to adjust to a new situation where they were essentially employees of the local congregation. Given their scattered locations, lack of pastors, and financial poverty, the immigrant Lutherans struggled to sustain their congregations. Certainly, most of the immigrants were not from the top level of Norwegian society; most were from the landowning class or the landless poor.

The first Norwegian American congregations were organized by a Haugean lay preacher named Elling Eielsen, who in 1846 gathered these congregations into a loose grouping that became known as the Eielsen Synod. Under the influence of the Haugean tradition, this group was strongly congregational in polity, stressed repentance and conversion, made preaching primary, and abandoned the formal liturgy and structure of the Church of Norway. In 1844, Eielsen and his group got competition within the Norwegian American community when J. W. C. Dietrichson arrived in the country from Norway. Dietrichson was the very antithesis of Eielsen; he was a university-trained pastor ordained in the Church of Norway and a strong proponent of formal Lutheran liturgy and objective theology. It was inevitable that these two would meet and that their clash would be titanic. Eielsen eventually moved to the margins, and Dietrichson returned to Norway, but in a short time they established the twin polarities of the Norwegian American Lutheran community. Dietrichson and others formed the Norwegian Evangelical Lutheran Church in America (commonly known as the Norwegian Synod) in 1853, while the Eielsen Synod (officially the Evangelical Lutheran Church in America[4]) continued its loose association. The first group was as near to the Church of Norway as was possible in America, while the second represented the pietistic Haugeanism of the Norwegian prayer houses. While the Eielsen Synod remained rather small, the Norwegian Synod grew rapidly.

Between these two poles were a number of other Norwegian American Lutheran groups. Starting in 1851, some Norwegian American pastors joined with Swedish American Lutherans in a grouping that became the Augustana Synod in 1860. This interethnic arrangement lasted for only ten years, with the two groups parting amicably in 1870. But when these centrist Norwegians left the Swedes, they quarreled among themselves and formed not one but two denominations, the smaller Norwegian Danish Augustana Synod and the larger Conference for the Norwegian Danish Evangelical Lutheran Church in America (the Conference). In 1876, a division among the Haugeans in the Eielsen Synod led to a split; a small group continued the original Eielsen Synod, while a larger group formed Hauge's Norwegian Evangelical Lutheran Synod (the Hauge Synod). So by 1876 there were five distinct Norwegian American Lutheran denominations, with more to come.

Historically, the Norwegian Synod had a close relationship with the conservative and confessional German Americans in the Missouri Synod, but this was a point of dispute within the Norwegian American community. The German American Lutheran synods began a contentious theological dispute on the doctrine of predestination (election) in the 1880s, and this battle soon spread to the Norwegians. While this conflict among the Germans was between various synods, the conflict within the Norwegian Synod was internal, dividing pastors and congregations. In 1886, about one-third of the Norwegian Synod pastors and congregations withdrew from the synod to form their own group, the Anti-Missourian Brotherhood.[5] The Anti-Missourian group intended not to form their own denomination but instead to be a catalyst for merger with other Norwegian American Lutheran groups. Though eventually the Hauge Synod decided against merger, the Anti-Missourians, the Conference, and the Norwegian Danish Augustana Synod did merge in 1890 to form the United Norwegian Lutheran Church (UNLC), which at its formation represented about one-half of the Norwegian American Lutherans. The Norwegian Synod was the next largest, followed by the Hauge Synod.

The merger that produced the United Church (as it was commonly called) ran into immediate difficulties, especially over theological education. The Conference had established Augsburg College in 1869, which provided an integrated education for pastors and laypeople. With the merger in 1890, the supporters of Augsburg worried about plans to unify the new denomination's educational institutions and the potential loss of Augsburg's distinctive educational plan. In 1893, supporters formed the Friends of Augsburg, and the school's board refused to turn over title of the school to the United Church. After a legal battle, the Friends retained the school and in 1897 broke away to form the Lutheran Free Church (LFC). Another group of pietistic Norwegian American Lutherans formed a smaller denomination in 1900, the Church of the Lutheran Brethren.

TWENTIETH-CENTURY MERGERS

As the Norwegian American Lutheran groups moved into the twentieth century, a new generation of leaders took control. This new leadership, generally second-generation Norwegian American, was less invested in the struggles of the past. They sought a way to overcome their historical divisions and reached a breakthrough of sorts in 1912 with the Madison Agreement (named for the place in Wisconsin it was negotiated) or *Opjør*. The theological divisions over election split the Norwegians into two parties; the Madison Agreement declared that within some limits, both theological positions were viable. This compromise was readily accepted in the Hauge Synod and the United Church, but it caused controversy within the Norwegian Synod. After 1912 the three denominations moved quickly toward a merger, and in 1917 they formed the Norwegian Lutheran Church in America (NLCA).[6] A disaffected minority within the Norwegian Synod refused to join the new merged organization and instead formed a new denomination, the Evangelical Lutheran Synod (ELS). But even with the schism—and the continued separate existence of the Lutheran Free Church—by 1917, 90 percent of all Norwegian American Lutherans were contained within the new NLCA.

The easy part of the merger of 1917 was the legal merger itself. Living into the new church body was something else entirely, as should be evident from the fact that the two polar traditions of Norwegian American Lutheranism were now living under one roof. The Madison Agreement was a carefully negotiated ambiguity, as ecumenical agreements of this kind usually are, but the theological tensions over the two positions on election continued to be present, especially at Luther Seminary. As it was the smallest of the three merging groups, the Hauge Synod people feared the loss of their distinctive piety and traditions, especially the free, nonliturgical worship and their tradition of lay preaching and evangelism. Those from the Norwegian Synod, on the other hand, worried that their stress on confessional Lutheran theology would be watered down by the low-church piety of the other groups. As if this were not enough, the new NLCA was entering a period of change and expansion in the twentieth century, especially the rapid transition to the use of English after the end of World War I in 1918. Lutherans of all varieties were cautiously moving into the religious mainstream of American life, while the American Protestant world was fighting and dividing into the mainline and evangelical camps. The question of how to do Lutheran theology in English, especially how to express their understanding of biblical authority, was a perennial issue.

The first great round of American Lutheran mergers took place in the first decades of the twentieth century, but by the end of this period most American Lutherans were using the English language for worship, theology, and education. The question naturally arose about whether there was still a need for separate ethnic Lutheran denominations, such as the NLCA or the LFC. Another round of merger negotiations in the 1950s resulted in two mergers, one of which, the American Lutheran Church in 1960, included the NLCA. The LFC debated whether to join the ALC until 1963, when it narrowly approved the merger. A smaller dissident group then broke away and formed a new denomination, the Association of Free Lutheran Congregations, in that same year.

By the early 1960s there were no longer separate Norwegian American Lutheran denominations, outside of the smaller dissident groups. The era of such ethnic Lutheranism was over, but many of the theological and religious currents of the Norwegian American Lutheran traditions, currents that were submerged but often not too far beneath the surface, lived on.

THE NORWEGIAN SYNOD AND LUTHER SEMINARY (1876–1917)

As outlined previously, the formation of the Norwegian Synod occurred in 1853 through the efforts of Norwegian American pastors, primarily Hans Andreas Stub, Adolph Carl Preus and Herman Amberg Preus (cousins), Nil Brandt, and Claus Lauritz Clausen,[7] among others. These men were young (in their twenties and thirties) university-trained pastors ordained in Norway who had taken up the challenge of establishing Lutheran congregations among the Norwegian Americans on the frontier of the upper Midwest of the United States. During the 1840s and 1850s, they moved into a situation on the frontier where there were few organized congregations, no church schools or educational facilities, and not much else that resembled the culture or religiosity of the country they had left behind. Even their very living conditions were tenuous, and they shared the grinding poverty of the immigrants they came to serve. These pastors were strong-willed and resilient, and their wives were, if anything, even stronger than they were, sacrificing a great deal for ministry in this new world. The only thing they had in abundance was people, a rapidly expanding population of Norwegian immigrants who they attempted to serve.

The leaders of the Norwegian Synod were also surrounded by a distinctive social and religious context that differed in many respects from that of Norway. The American system of religion centered on a voluntary and free religious life, without any support from the government. What organized religion existed was mainly Reformed, low-church, and revivalistic in nature. Voluntary religion meant that laypeople now had the upper hand in their congregations, could hire and fire their pastors as they saw fit, and expected to have their say in congregational and denominational affairs. This was less of a problem among the Haugean laypeople and pastors in the United States, as their religious ethos generally fit well into the American context, but state-church pastors from Norway had more trouble adapting to this situation. That they were able to form a successful synod in the midst of all this is attributable to both their strongly held principles and their pragmatic flexibility.

The clerical leaders of the Norwegian Synod generally held to the confessional theology and the formal liturgical worship of the Church of Norway. They recognized that their setting in America meant that they could not replicate the state-church Norwegian Lutheranism in their new synod, but they did attempt to maintain as much of this ethos as they could. Though there were no Lutheran universities in America where pastors could be trained, they insisted on a classically trained clergy as much as was possible, with a strong stress on an objective theology that held closely to the historic Lutheran confessions. Delivering a series of lectures in Norway in 1867, H. A. Preus sought to explain this situation to his audiences. Referring to the new Norwegian Synod as the "vivacious daughter" of the Church of Norway, he explained that "she may not be as demure and considerate as her mother... [and] that she has some bad habits because she feels so free and is not yet used to her freedom."[8] The leaders of the Norwegian Synod looked down on the lay-dominated, pietistic Eielsen Synod with contempt, thinking they constituted not a church but a dangerous, undisciplined rabble. There was certainly a social and cultural gap here; these pastors from the Church of Norway were literate and culturally sophisticated and attempted to maintain this ethos even in the American wilderness.

The advantage that the leaders of the Norwegian Synod had was a mindfulness and clarity of theological purpose, which, in the midst of the new American situation, gave them an edge over the lay-oriented and often fractious Eielsen Synod. Certainly, the pastors of the Norwegian Synod were often inclined to theological combat over its seventy-four-year history, but these conflicts were not unlike the theological disputes within the university in Norway. Synodical meetings and pastoral conferences could be bruising affairs, but in the end the synod usually found a way to close ranks. The pastors could generally command the respect of their congregations, who they served with commitment.[9]

Given that the Norwegian Synod was frequently at odds with the other Norwegian American Lutheran denominations, it is not surprising that the leaders of the synod looked for allies to assist the fledgling institution to grow and develop, especially in providing pastors and theological education for its pastoral candidates. The synod naturally turned first to the mother Church of Norway, with whom they felt the closest connection. The synod received the sympathy and spiritual fellowship of the Church of Norway, to be sure, but not much in the way of additional pastors or material assistance. In 1860, one of the newer leaders of the synod, Peter Laurentius Larsen, returned to Norway to seek desperately needed pastors for the expanding synod. He stiffly suggested that there were many unordained theological candidates in Norway waiting for a call (he estimated that in 1857 there were some three hundred) and that it was their duty to go to America to serve in the vacant synodical congregations. This demand did not sit well with many in the Church of Norway, who retorted that it was improper of him to lecture the

Norwegians about their duty. Larsen was "bitterly disappointed" by the failure of the Norwegians to respond.[10] Very few theological candidates or pastors from Norway took up his call.

COOPERATION WITH THE MISSOURI SYNOD

To find partners for theological education, the leaders of the Norwegian Synod decided to look next to the various German American Lutheran denominations, the English-speaking "American" Lutherans synods being judged as confessionally suspect. In 1857 a committee from the synod visited the seminaries of the Buffalo Synod, the Ohio Synod, and the Missouri Synod to examine them as possible places for Norwegian American theological candidates to study. The committee was most impressed by the Concordia Seminary in St. Louis, the school of the Missouri Synod, and by its dynamic leader, C. F. W. Walther. Thus began a long and sometimes complicated relationship between the Missouri Synod and the Norwegian Synod. In Walther, synodical leaders discovered a staunch Lutheran confessional theologian and someone who, in their minds, with vigor and without compromise had successfully transplanted a genuine and objective Lutheran theology into the religious wilds of North America. The Missouri Synod was a rapidly growing conservative Lutheran denomination with an established program of theological and ministerial education. The "theoretical" seminary in St. Louis attempted to replicate, as far as possible, the classical religious gymnasium of the church in Germany, with an integrated pre-seminary and seminary program. Though it was not a university in the classic European sense, Concordia St. Louis attempted a rigorous theological education, heavily weighted on the classical languages and dogmatic Lutheran theology. The Missouri Synod also had a "practical" seminary, which moved several times between Fort Wayne, Indiana; St. Louis; and Springfield, Illinois. The academic requirements at the practical seminary were less rigorous, designed for older candidates and those with weaker educational backgrounds.

Already in 1857, the Norwegian Synod decided to begin sending theological candidates for study at the Missouri Synod seminaries, at least until the synod could decide about forming its own seminary.

The first Norwegian students arrived in St. Louis in 1858, and joining them in 1859 was Larsen, who filled the post of Norwegian professor to oversee the education of the candidates from the Norwegian Synod. This arrangement was cut short by the beginning of the Civil War in 1861; when Concordia Seminary was temporarily closed that year, Larsen and the Norwegian students returned north. In 1861 Larsen became the president of Luther College in Decorah, Iowa, and the post of Norwegian professor at Concordia Seminary was not filled. But soon Norwegian students began studying again at both the theoretical and practical seminaries, and by 1865 eleven of the thirty-one pastors in the Norwegian Synod had been educated in the Missouri seminaries. This arrangement was not always satisfactory, however, as some of the Norwegian students felt isolated among the Germans in St. Louis. One student wrote to Larsen, temporarily away in 1860, "It is dreadfully hard to keep up with the class. . . . The worst part of it is that I understand so little German, in which all the lectures are given."[11]

The relation of the Norwegian Synod to the Missouri Synod in these early years was generally harmonious, and the Norwegian leaders appreciated Walther's assistance and advice. But with the Civil War, their relations to Missouri caused a controversy within the Norwegian Synod and between the synod and the Church of Norway over slavery. Located in a border state and generally oriented toward the states' rights position of the Democratic Party, Walther and the leaders of the Missouri Synod attempted to take a moderating position on the question of slavery. Walther insisted that though the American practice of slavery was a moral evil and a punishment for sin, in biblical terms slavery itself was not a sin. The pastoral leaders of the Norwegian Synod were convinced by Walther's argument and accepted it. However, some of the synodical pastors and the vast majority of synodical laypeople were strongly opposed to slavery and rejected the position of Walther and the Norwegian Synod leadership. Because of their aversion to slavery, the vast majority of Norwegian immigrants settled in the North. As well, young Norwegian American men were fighting and dying in the Union armies, so this was more than just a theological argument.[12]

The controversy about slavery continued within the Norwegian

Synod during and even after the Civil War ended in 1865. Though synodical leaders attempted to calm the controversy, a number of pastors, including C. L. Clausen, and congregations left the synod over the issue. More importantly, this controversy created in many areas of the Norwegian Synod lingering suspicions about Walther and the Missouri Synod, which would surface again later. The controversy also spread to Norway, where church leaders too became concerned by the close relationship of the Norwegian Synod leaders to Walther and the Missourians.[13]

When the Norwegian Synod had decided to establish a relationship with the Missourian seminaries in 1857, they had also included plans for gathering funds for a university, a place where pastoral candidates could receive a preparatory education. Over the next few years, resolutions for the new institution referred to it variously as a "university," an "educational institution," a "school," and a "gymnasium," showing the various models they envisioned for it. They avoided calling it a "college," in rejection of the American model of higher education. They instead envisioned it along the lines of the Latin schools or Cathedral schools in Norway, which prepared theological candidates for the university.[14]

Larsen and the Norwegian students' departure from St. Louis in spring 1861 accelerated plans for the founding of this new educational institution. The new institution, eventually named Luther College, began in the fall of 1861 in a vacant synodical parsonage in Wisconsin with Larsen and Friedrich Augustus Schmidt as instructors and several dozen students. The next year it was moved to Decorah, Iowa, where it resided in rented buildings for several years until a permanent building could be built. This fledgling institution provided a pre-seminary education, and synodical candidates for the ministry still attended the Concordia seminaries for further education. Though the original plans intended there to eventually be a seminary connected to the institution in Decorah, this never materialized. Instead, Luther College gradually became exactly what the synod had originally rejected, an American liberal arts college.

Beginning in 1872 the Norwegian Synod resumed the post of Norwegian professor at Concordia St. Louis, with Schmidt in this position until the arrangement was ended in 1876. Schmidt, who was born in Germany and educated at Concordia Seminary, nevertheless became a central part of theological education in the Norwegian Synod into the twentieth century. There were sizable numbers of Norwegian students at Concordia during this period, as many as thirty-six during the 1873/74 school year. Also in 1872, the Norwegian Synod joined with German American Lutheran denominations the Ohio, Wisconsin, and Missouri synods in forming a cooperative association, the Synodical Conference, representing many of the conservative confessional Lutheran synods in America. The Synodical Conference envisioned a number of common activities among its synods, including the possibility of a joint seminary. Though the Norwegian Synod did consider this, they eventually rejected the idea, as there was a growing sentiment within the Norwegian Synod during this time for their own seminary.

There were various reasons for this discontinuance. Though synodical leaders and many pastors were comfortable with the theology and ethos of the Missouri Synod, some pastors and many lay leaders were not. The tensions over the slavery issue, ironically, continued among the Norwegian Americans even after the Civil War and the emancipation of the enslaved African Americans, with a lingering resentment over the position of Walther on this and other issues. As well, there were concerns over language, and it was widely felt that many of the Norwegian students at the Concordias, being educated primarily in German, were ill-prepared for preaching and teaching in Norwegian (despite the presence of the Norwegian professors). Finally, there was a competitive aspect to this: the centrist Norwegian American denominations—the Conference and the Norwegian Augustana Synod—had already established their own seminaries, and even the Haugeans were attempting to set up their own educational institutions. Luther College was making good progress in the 1870s, and it seemed time for the Norwegian Synod to act on its own delayed plans to provide for seminary education.

BIRTHING ITS OWN SEMINARY

In the fall of 1876 the Norwegian Synod opened its own seminary not in conjunction with Luther College in Decorah but in a rented building in Madison, Wisconsin—a building that formerly had been an orphanage, and before that, the governor's mansion. The two Norwegian professors, Schmidt and Asperheim, were the initial faculty of the new seminary, called Luther Seminary, with several dozen students. In 1876, the first program at Luther Seminary was the practical seminary, consisting of men who were older and without a formal educational background. A theoretical seminary program was added in 1878, the difference being the expectation of a more rigorous course of study, including in the classical biblical languages. The overwhelming need for pastors, however, meant that few theological candidates could complete the full course; the students' own poverty and the need for pastors meant that many of them left the seminary for the ordained ministry early. The Norwegian students still studying in the Missouri seminaries were encouraged to complete their studies there, but after their completion there would be no more Norwegian students to follow them.[15]

Asperheim, who had expressed strong criticism of the Missouri Synod, was forced out of his position at Luther Seminary in 1878, and two new graduates of Luther College and Concordia Seminary, Johannes Ylvisaker and Hans Gerhard Stub, were added to the faculty. Both served as theology professors for Luther Seminary until 1917, Stub responsible for systematic theology and Old Testament, and Ylvisaker (who had additional training in European universities) for New Testament. Stub served initially as the president of the seminary, although he left for a time (1896–1900) to serve as a pastor in Decorah. The first students graduated from the practical program in 1877 and from the theoretical program in 1881.

The young seminary seemed on its way to success, as it was attracting a growing number of students and had a vigorous faculty, but this situation was seriously disrupted by an internal conflict within the Norwegian Synod in the 1880s. This conflict over the question of predestination (or election) was caused, as in earlier conflicts, by the close relationship of the leaders of the Norwegian Synod to Walther and the Missouri Synod. Walther published a theological paper in 1880 on the question of predestination in which he took a position on the doctrine that seemed to some others to be (ironically enough) too close to the Calvinist position on the question. Theological controversy erupted in the Synodical Conference around the question. This dispute divided the Missouri Synod from the Ohio and Iowa Synods, and the latter two groups left the Synodical Conference. Theological debates raged in print over the issue throughout the 1880s.

While the conflict divided these German American Lutheran synods from each other, the conflict within the Norwegian Synod over election was fiercely partisan and eventually led to a division of the synod itself and even divided congregations within the synod. This was a debate that went beyond the theology professors and the leadership; ordinary pastors and many laypeople were caught up in the conflict as well. There were two parties within the Norwegian Synod, the Missourians who supported Walther and the Anti-Missourians who opposed his position on the issue, taking their cues from Pontoppidan's *Catechism*. This debate, and its consequences, would affect Luther Seminary and successive institutions on and off for the next century.

In an attempt to calm the situation, the Norwegian Synod withdrew from the Synodical Conference in 1883. While this helped temporarily, the situation soon flared up again. Though Schmidt had come out of Concordia and had been a valued colleague of Walther, he became a staunch critic of Walther over the question of predestination and served as a leader of the Anti-Missourian party. This caused a major rift at the new Luther Seminary in Madison, because Schmidt's colleagues, Stub and Ylvisaker, were strong supporters of Walther and leaders of the Missourian group within the synod. Schmidt was forced out of Luther Seminary in 1885 and was replaced by Johannes Bjerk Frich in 1888, who served there until 1902. The conflict over election only intensified during this time. In 1886 the Anti-Missourians decided to form their own seminary, and in 1887 this group, constituting about one-third of the Norwegian Synod as a whole, formally withdrew from the synod.

This division had immediate and severe consequences for Luther Seminary in Madison during the 1885/86 school year, when the departure of sixteen students for seminaries in Ohio and Missouri left only seven students in the school itself.[16] However, enrollment at Luther Seminary began to increase after the departure of the Anti-Missourians and the reestablishment of doctrinal peace within the

Norwegian Synod. In 1888, the synod decided to move Luther Seminary from Madison to the Twin Cities (Minneapolis–Saint Paul), which was becoming the new geographical center of the Norwegian American community as it moved westward. Temporarily housed in a Lutheran congregation in Minneapolis during the 1888/89 school year, the seminary moved into a new building in the Minneapolis suburb of Robbinsdale in 1889. This situation lasted for six years until the building burned down in 1895. The seminary had to move to temporary quarters in Robbinsdale in a former hotel, where they were (unsatisfactorily) housed until a permanent location could be established.

Luther Seminary continued to grow after the resolution of the election controversy, and with the departure of the Anti-Missourians, the seminary coalesced around a distinctive theological and confessional position, which became the theological focal point for the synod. Gerhard Forde suggested that the theological position of the Norwegian Synod was a reaction to the "compromises between church and state in the state church," from which the synod

> sought refuge in the objective scriptural witness, in Luther, the Lutheran Confessions, and the Lutheran dogmaticians. . . . This was a quest for a church which is firmly established on the objective truth in God's Word, which knows whereof it speaks and can bear witness with conviction and authority.[17]

This became the distinctive ethos of the synod's seminary, especially under the leadership of Stub and Ylvisaker. The faculty was augmented by Olaf E. Brandt in 1896 and Elling Hove in 1901. These two, like Stub and Ylvisaker, had been educated at Luther College and Concordia Seminary in St. Louis. These four constituted the faculty of the seminary until the merger in 1917. In 1899, the seminary finally moved to a permanent building in the Hamline section of Saint Paul, where it flourished. Between 1876 and 1917, Luther Seminary had 475 graduates who went on to the ministry within the synod.

An important element of seminary life was a focus on music, worship, and liturgy. Valborg Hovind Stub, wife of H. G. Stub, was a cultured woman and a classically trained musician, and she took the lead in establishing the musical life of the seminary community and the Norwegian Synod. She also assisted John Dahle, the musician and cantor at Luther Seminary, with his musical and hymnological projects. Dahle himself was a very important figure in the seminary and the synod, given the synod's emphasis on the liturgical and musical expressions of congregational worship.[18]

THE HAUGE SYNOD AND RED WING SEMINARY (1879–1917)

The other distinctive wing of Norwegian American Lutheranism was Hauge's Norwegian Evangelical Lutheran Synod. This denomination was formed in 1876 and continued the main line of the Haugean revival movement in America, although a much smaller group continued with the older name of the Eielsen Synod. The Eielsen Synod was defined by a document written by Eielsen himself known as the "Old Constitution," which was actually more of a theological mission statement than a constitution in the organizational or legal sense. Other pastors and congregations joined the new synod, and in 1850 Eielsen and thirty-five others signed the Old Constitution at the Koshkonong congregation outside of Madison.

The Old Constitution gave shape to the Haugean distinctives as they were being translated into a new idiom in North America. Above all, it insisted on the central importance of pastors and congregational members being converted; although such a conversion experience was not absolutely necessary for membership in a Haugean congregation, this was strongly urged of them. The conversion experience was constituted by a deep self-examination of one's sins, an often sorrowful repentance for those sins, and an often exuberant release that flooded in when one received the assurance of God's forgiveness and grace. Haugeanism stressed that the converted individual should lead a holy and moral life after conversion; though this sometimes did lead to a rather dour legalism, this was not necessarily of the essence of the movement itself. The Haugeans rejected much of the formal practice of the Norwegian state church, especially its liturgies, vestments, and clerical privileges. For the Haugeans in

America, the congregation of believers was the primary focus of religious life and authority, and they downplayed the distinctions between the ordained pastors and the laypeople, encouraging lay preaching and witnessing.[19]

Eielsen himself was a strong-willed and often difficult person, attached to his own rather stringent version of the Haugean tradition in America. As has been seen, Eielsen clashed violently with Dietrichson, but he could also be equally difficult with those in his own synod. C. L. Clausen was initially ordained in a Haugean congregation but soon left the synod, first for the Norwegian Synod and then for the Conference. Another early leader in the Eielsen Synod was Peter Andreas Rasmussen, pastor of a sizable Lutheran congregation in Lisbon, Illinois, but he too soon ran into problems with Eielsen. In 1856, Rasmussen, his congregation, and a sizable number of others left for the Norwegian Synod. Despite these clashes, the Eielsen Synod continued on, although it was always a small movement.

One of the main problems with the synod was the Old Constitution. While it was long on Haugean principles, it was short on organizational details, such as how congregations and the synod itself should be structured, which created difficulties in managing the growth of the synod. Perhaps because he thought these details unimportant or perhaps because he wished to maintain personal control over the synod itself, Eielsen did not see the necessity of changes to the Old Constitution. But others did. The situation in Norway allowed the Haugeans to be a loosely affiliated movement under the umbrella of the Church of Norway, but in the wilds of America this looseness was problematic. There were regular attempts to bring more order and central control to the often unruly organization in 1848, 1856, and during the 1860s. While Eielsen managed to fend off these attempts, many disaffected pastors and congregations left the synod. The defenders of the Old Constitution became known as the "Old Tendency," while the reformers were known as the "New Tendency."

Through the early 1870s, it became clear that the New Tendency group was on the ascendance within the synod, led by a young pastor named Østen Hanson, the editor of the synodical publication *Bud-*

bæreren. This group first proposed an entirely new constitution for congregations and the synod, but the majority felt this was a step too far. Rather, a sweeping revision of the Old Constitution was put forth, and for a time even Eielsen was tentatively resigned to this new proposal. But Eielsen soon changed his mind and, supported by a core of adherents, was reelected as synodical president in 1876. The majority of the synod left Eielsen and formed a new organization known as Hauge's Synod in Red Wing, Minnesota, within the year. Elling Eielsen died in 1883, but a small group of supporters continued to keep the tiny Eielsen Synod alive.

The attitude of Eielsen and the Haugean movement in America toward education in general, and theological education in particular, is complicated. Among this group there was a deep suspicion of education, especially higher education that had roots in the social and religious culture of Norway. Given the class system in eighteenth- and nineteenth-century Norway, it was very difficult or even impossible for any of the common people to attend the university, even if they had the requisite educational achievements to do so. Access to higher education in Norway was a self-perpetuating loop reserved for the office-holding or "conditioned" class. A university education was necessary for positions in the church or government, but candidates for the university were almost exclusively drawn from those families who had positions in the church or the government. Until the development of the mission schools in Norway in the middle of the nineteenth century, there was no access to theological education outside of the university at Christiana (Oslo).

THE STRUGGLE TO ESTABLISH A SEMINARY

Given the tendencies of the university-trained Norwegian clergy to adopt religious rationalism and their often harsh opposition to Hauge and his awakening movement, it is not surprising that the Haugeans had a deep antipathy to formal theological education for both social and religious reasons. One historian of this movement in America suggests that many Haugeans considered institutions of higher education the "open doors to hell."[20] This attitude was eventually modified after the 1850s, especially in Norway, because the Johnsonian revivals originated in the university and were led by university professors such as Gisle Johnson and Carl Caspari, but among the Haugeans in America this shift had less effect. It did not help matters any that the leaders of the Norwegian Synod, their chief opponents, were constantly criticizing the Haugeans for their lack of an educated clergy. If the result of a formal theological education was typified by the "unconverted" pastors of the Norwegian Synod, then the Haugeans wanted nothing to do with such an education.

This is not to say, of course, that the Haugean movement promoted illiteracy or lack of education—far from it. They were literate people who read and wrote books and other printed material and educated themselves and their children. But the boundaries of what they read and considered to be spiritually proper were often narrow. One of the Haugean leaders recalled of this movement, "There were homes where only religious books were tolerated; and there were parents who would not permit their children to read, even in school, any book not distinctively religious."[21] The attitude of those in the Eielsen Synod toward a formally trained clergy was equally complicated, as they wanted pastors who had been "spiritually awakened" and, with their emphasis on lay preaching, wished to avoid formal distinctions between pastors who had been educated and called, and those spiritual laypeople who felt led to their own proclamation of the gospel message.

The irony, then, is that in 1855 the Eielsen Synod was the first Norwegian American Lutheran denomination to open its own seminary for educating pastors. Most likely this was because they needed pastors for their congregations but did not trust the other American Lutheran seminaries to produce the spiritually awakened pastors that they desired. In 1854, the synod decided that there was need of such a school for pastors and decided to establish it at one of the synod's congregations in Lisbon, Illinois, under the leadership of the resident pastor, P. A. Rasmussen. Rasmussen immigrated in 1850 and attended the practical seminary in Fort Wayne from 1852 to 1854 before coming to Lisbon. This seminary attracted a handful of students over the school year 1855/56 but was closed when Rasmussen quarreled with Eielsen and left the synod in 1856.

The Eielsen Synod continued to need pastors, however, and in

1865 they tried again. In the fall of that year they opened a "layman's college" in Deerfield, Wisconsin, taught by a theological candidate, Andreas R. Aaserød, who had already been a teacher in Wisconsin for eight years and who had attended Concordia St. Louis in 1863/64. This institution was more of an academy (or religious high school), but it did not last much longer than the first attempt, closing after two years in 1867. Undaunted, the synod tried a third time and agreed in 1868 to found a seminary in Red Wing, Minnesota, but after some efforts this project was suspended. The synod next turned to a congregation in Chicago, and in the summer of 1871 the new institution, Hauge's College and Eielsen's Seminary, was opened at the Trinity congregation. This institution was hampered by the lasting economic effects of the great Chicago fire, a national depression, and the resentment of those who had wanted the school to be in Red Wing in the first place. Eventually in 1877, after six years, this school also failed and was closed by the synod. Thus three attempts and thousands of dollars spent had brought about no lasting results. Given the attitude of many of the Haugeans toward formal education, this string of failures may have seemed to many of them evidence that the Lord was not favoring their efforts.

After the split between the Old and New Tendency parties in 1876 and the formation of the Hauge Synod in that same year, another attempt was made at education. The Hauge Synod, representing the New Tendency movement, consisted of those in the movement who had gradually become more open to the need for an educated clergy and less worried about the effects of formal education, as long as the Haugean distinctives of spiritual awakening and lay religious activities were maintained in their institution. In 1877, the Hauge Synod convention authorized the resumption of educational efforts at Red Wing, and through the efforts of a local pastor, Østen Hanson, and lay leaders Andrew Ellingson and Hans Sande, a building and site were secured on the bluffs overlooking Red Wing. The new school, named the Red Wing Seminary, opened in 1878 with Rev. Ingvald Eisteinsen as the first theological professor and layman G. O. Brohaugh as the teacher in English.

It is necessary to clarify the term *seminary* in the title of the new institution. In nineteenth-century America, the term *seminary* was not limited to a school providing theological education for the ministry. Rather, seminary could refer to any number of different kinds of education beyond the primary schools; there were even quite a number of "ladies seminaries." In this sense, then, Red Wing Seminary was an institution that provided a number of different educational paths for both ministerial candidates and laypeople, consistent with the Haugean tradition of not making a large distinction between the two groups. Thus during its history, the Red Wing Seminary included not only a theological program for the education of pastoral candidates but also a preparatory academy, a junior college (which later became a four-year bachelor degree–granting institution), commercial (business) and music departments, and eventually a ladies seminary.

What these different parts of the school had in common was a commitment to the distinctive religious vision of the Haugean tradition. Hauge himself was not averse to useful secular education, and he was greatly concerned with any learning or training that would improve the lives of the common people. He was influential in Norway for his advocacy of economic and democratic improvements, and the Haugeans in America tended to share these sentiments. But the Hauge Seminary education, in all departments, shared a primary stress on a "living" and personal Christian faith for all students, no matter their course of study. The institution's catalog described the basic instructional philosophy of the seminary as providing "sufficient knowledge" for the ministerial vocation "but especially this most necessary of all the prerequisites for profitable theological study . . . a conscious life of faith in communion with God."[22] This could be said of all sections of the institution, regardless of vocational goals.

This fourth attempt at a synodical educational institution was finally a success. The academy, the secular music and commercial courses, and the junior college were fairly popular, especially with residents of Minnesota and Wisconsin. The seminary's original purchased building was supplemented with the completion of two additional structures, the Summer Hall in 1892 and its signature Main Building in 1904. The junior college was implemented in 1904 and was converted to a four-year college in 1910, granting the bachelor of arts degree. Women were admitted to the seminary in 1914.

Theological education for the ministry was an important focus from its beginning in 1879.[23] The Hauge Synod had few other options for obtaining pastors for its congregations, and the New Tendency party was less worried about the possibility of a clerical elite within the synod drawing power away from the laypeople. Since they did not have a ready pool of educated clergy and teachers to draw from within the synod, finding qualified instructors who were sympathetic to the aims and religious ethos of the Hauge Synod, especially those to serve in the theological education of ministerial candidates, was a continual problem. Professors in the theological department included Hans Bergsland (1887–1907), Martin Hanson (1886–1887 and 1898–1911), Mons O. Wee (1908–1917), and Gustav Bruce (1911–1917). Wee and Bruce continued on at Luther Theological Seminary after the merger in 1917.

Initially the limited educational background of the ministerial candidates, their relative poverty, and the immediate need for pastors in the synod resulted in few candidates completing the full course of study, limited as it was. As time went along, the situation improved, and more students could complete a full course of academic instruction. The school urged at least two years of work in the academy or college for admission to theological studies, though that requirement could be waived for older students. When the collegiate program was upgraded to a four-year college in 1910, this full course became a requirement for theological education, and students who took the classic biblical languages (Hebrew and Greek) could graduate with the bachelor of divinity degree; those without would receive a certificate of studies. This arrangement was fairly common among the Lutheran seminaries at the time. From 1879 to 1917 an average of five men a year graduated from the theological program at Red Wing Seminary, for a total of 182.

FORMING A NEW DENOMINATION

The Hauge Synod was relatively untouched by the theological conflicts of the 1880s over election that split the Norwegian Synod. In the late 1880s, the Anti-Missourian faction of that synod extended an offer to the Conference, the Norwegian Augustana Synod, and the

Hauge Synod to consider a merger of these groups, and negotiations commenced. The lay leaders in the Hauge Synod were initially open to the idea of a larger Norwegian American Lutheran denomination, though the pastors were generally more cautious about it. There were concerns that their traditional emphasis on lay preaching, low-church worship, and a converted clergy would be lost in the new, merged group. The Hauge Synod was a small part of this larger group and worried about the loss of its identity. They also worried about the fate of the Red Wing Seminary in the new church. The other parties to the merger negotiations attempted to convince the Hauge Synod that their concerns would be addressed, but by the 1889 convention of the synod it became clear that they would not approve a merger. When the United Norwegian Lutheran Church was formed in 1890, the Hauge Synod was not a part of it.

Still, many Norwegian American Lutherans dreamed of an eventual merger that would unite all of them in a single denomination, from the Norwegian Synod to the Hauge Synod. This became more of a reality with the Madison Agreement in 1912. The Haugeans still had reservations, but eventually their concerns were addressed, and the Hauge Synod entered into the new Norwegian Lutheran Church in America in 1917. This merger, however, meant the dismantling of Red Wing Seminary. Professors Bruce and Wee joined the new Luther Seminary in Saint Paul as the Hauge Synod representatives to its faculty. The collegiate and other departments remained in Red Wing for the time being, but fifteen years later, in the midst of the depression, the rest of Red Wing Seminary was closed; the collegiate department merged into St. Olaf College in Northfield, Minnesota, and the ladies seminary was moved down to Luther College in Decorah, making that institution coeducational for the first time. The closure of Red Wing Seminary in 1932 was a bitter pill for the Haugeans, who had trusted assurances in the merger negotiations that their distinctive concerns and institutions would be adequately supported in the newly merged NLCA. But the financial pressure of the depression had hit Red Wing Seminary hard, and the decision was made that this institution was no longer financially viable. With the closure in 1932, the Haugean movement lost its last distinctive institution within the NLCA. The Haugean movement would remain a force within the Norwegian American Lutheran community during the twentieth century but predominantly in parachurch organizations outside the official confines of the NLCA. In all probability, Eielsen and the old Haugean leaders would have wanted it that way.

Notes

1. Pontoppidan's *Explanation*, especially his definition of predestination, was to be very important in the theological battles among Norwegian Americans in the late nineteenth century.
2. Grundtvigianism was more of an issue in Denmark and among the Danish Americans; the latter developed two different Lutheran denominations in North America, one supportive of Grundtvig and the other strongly opposed to his theology.
3. Actually, what has sometimes been described as Haugeanism in America is in fact rather closer to Johnsonianism.
4. Imagine the surprise of the officials of the merging Lutheran churches in 1986/87 when they came to realize that their preferred name for the new church, the Evangelical Lutheran Church in America, was legally the possession of a handful of small rural congregations in Wisconsin! Church officials had to first locate these small congregations and then negotiate with them for the rights to use the title.
5. The name stems from ongoing tensions within the Norwegian Synod over those who generally supported the Missourian positions and appreciated the relationship, and others who distrusted the Missouri Synod and rejected their theological position on election. This dispute will be examined in length later.
6. This title was changed in 1946 to the Evangelical Lutheran Church.
7. For some reason, the convention popular in the nineteenth century was that men would be professionally known by the initials of their first and middle names, so Hans Andreas Stub was known at H. A. Stub. This history will follow this convention for their subsequent appearances.
8. Herman Amberg Preus, *Vivacious Daughter: Seven Lectures on the Religious Situation among the Norwegians in America*, ed. and trans. Todd W. Nichol (Northfield, MN: Norwegian-American Historical Association, 1990), 34.
9. On the theological confessionalism and search for objectivity in the

Norwegian Synod, see Gerhard O. Forde, "The 'Old Synod': A Search for Objectivity," in *Striving for Ministry: Centennial Essays Interpreting the Heritage of Luther Theological Seminary*, ed. Warren A. Quanbeck, Eugene L. Fevold, and Gerhard E. Frost (Minneapolis: Augsburg, 1977), 67–80.

10. On Larsen's trip, see David T. Nelson, *Luther College, 1861–1961* (Decorah, IA: Luther College Press, 1961), 40–42. Some in the Church of Norway, in fact, were opposed to the immigration of Norwegians to America, and this may have added to the response. Subsequent visitors from the synod to Norway did not produce any better results.

11. "Letter from a student to L. Larsen," Laur. Larsen papers, 1860, quoted in Gerhard Lee Belgum, "The Old Norwegian Synod in America, 1853–1890" (PhD diss., Yale University, 1957), 206.

12. The slavery controversy within the Norwegian Synod is examined in Nelson and Fevold, *Lutheran Church*, 1:169–80.

13. There was an ongoing debate during the 1860s between the leaders of the Norwegian Synod and the theological faculty at the University in Christiana (Oslo) in which the latter took the side of Clausen and the synodical laypeople and rejected the Norwegian Synod's official position on the issue. See J. Magnus Rohne, *Norwegian American Lutheranism up to 1872* (New York: Macmillan, 1926), 213–17.

14. Nelson, *Luther College*, 47–48.

15. Eugene Fevold, "Laying Foundations in a New Land," in Quanbeck, Fevold, and Frost, *Striving for Ministry*, 22.

16. Nelson and Fevold, *Lutheran Church*, 1:268.

17. Forde, "The 'Old Synod,'" 76.

18. Gracia Grindal, "The Role of Women in Seminary Life," in *Thanksgiving and Hope: A Collection of Essays Chronicling 125 Years of ... Luther Seminary*, ed. Frederick H. Gonnerman (Saint Paul: Luther Seminary, 1998), 85.

19. Lowell J. Satre, "The Hauge Synod," in Quanbeck, Fevold, and Frost, *Striving for Ministry*, 81–96.

20. N. N. Rønning, *Festskrift udgivet I Anledning af Red Wing Seminariums Femogtyve Aars Jubiläum* (Red Wing, MN: n.p., 1904), 55, quoted in Rohne, *Norwegian American Lutheranism*, 187.

21. M. O. Wee, *Haugeanism: A Brief Sketch of the Movement and Some of Its Chief Exponents* (Saint Paul: n.p., 1919), 55.

22. "Statement of Purpose," *Red Wing Seminary Catalog, 1917–18*, 14.

23. For the theological education at the seminary, see G. M. Bruce, "The Theological Department of Red Wing Seminary," in *Red Wing Seminary, Fifty Years of Service*, ed. Arthur Rholl (Red Wing, MN: Red Wing Seminary, 1930), 34–42.

3

The Center of Norwegian American Lutheranism

Between the two well-defined poles of the Norwegian Synod and the Hauge Synod were a number of centrist Norwegian American Lutheran denominations. While it must be said that all of the Norwegian American denominations were affected and shaped by the revivals and awakenings in nineteenth-century Norway, even to some extent the Norwegian Synod, these centrist denominations particularly represented the Johnsonian revivals of the 1850s and 1860s, as well as the adoption of Rosenian piety from Sweden a bit later. It might be helpful to label these strains of religious piety "churchly pietism," groups that were deeply influenced by the awakenings but wanted to stay within the Church of Norway and the historical traditions of Lutheranism. Gisle Johnson himself was an insider, a pastor and university professor in Christiana (Oslo), and in his revival preaching envisioned his movement as a leavening agent within the Church of Norway. Through the pastors he influenced and educated, Johnson was in a strong position to do just that.

This churchly pietism was easier to maintain in Norway than it was among the Norwegian Americans. Without the umbrella of the state church in America, separation and schism were much more likely, and the fluid situation of the frontier added to these divisions.

Even though the Norwegian Synod sought to be the church for all Norwegian Americans, this simply was not going to be the case. The Hauge Synod did remain Lutheran, but given its roots in the separate prayer houses of Norway and its advocacy for a converted clergy and membership, it had a tendency toward separatism, or the formation of congregations made up of only converted individuals. In the 1870s, the Hauge Synod pulled back from this separatism somewhat, but the Eielsen Synod maintained it, as did another Norwegian pietist denomination, the Church of the Lutheran Brethren, formed in 1900. To be sure, these groups remained officially Lutheran but maintained a separatistic posture.[1]

THE NORWEGIAN AUGUSTANA SYNOD

At the beginnings of Norwegian American Lutheranism in the 1840s and 1850s, some pastors and congregations were not satisfied with the alternative posed by either Eielsen or Dietrichson. One of the earliest leaders in this middle group was Paul Andersen, who led a group of Norwegian pastors and congregations to join with a larger group of Swedish American Lutherans altogether affiliated with an "American Lutheran" group, the Synod of Northern Illinois, in 1851. Other early leaders included pastors Ole Andrewson, Andrew Scheie, and O. J. Hatlestad. Because of language concerns, the Scandinavians formed one conference of this synod, while the English-speaking American Lutherans formed a second conference. The Synod of Northern Illinois itself established an educational institution, Illinois State University, to train its pastors.[2] From 1858 there was a Scandinavian professor at this school, a Swede named Lars Paul Esbjörn, and it was hoped that a Norwegian professor could be added later.

The arrangement in the Synod of Northern Illinois soon became untenable for the Scandinavians. This synod belonged to the eastern General Synod, whose adherence to the Lutheran confessions and traditions was not as strong as the Scandinavians thought it should be. Andersen and his Norwegian group came under withering attack from the Norwegian Synod especially for what the Norwegian Synod saw as their affiliation with a denomination that was Lutheran in name only. Both the Norwegians and the Swedes eventually determined that their initial affiliation was a mistake, and in 1860, the Scandinavian conference withdrew from the Synod of Northern Illinois and formed an independent denomination, the Scandinavian Augustana Synod. With the formation of the Augustana Synod, the Scandinavian professor and students at the Illinois State University withdrew to constitute a new seminary, Augustana Seminary, in 1860.

Augustana Seminary led a precarious life in the first decade of its existence. Initially located in Chicago, it moved several times in its first years, including a time in Paxton, Illinois.[3] The seminary had both Swedish and Norwegian students, but the professor was a Swede, as were a majority of the students. The Norwegian pastors and congregations fretted about this situation and soon decided to call a Norwegian professor to the Augustana Seminary. This was easier said than done. It took several years to locate a suitable teacher and bring him from Norway to Illinois. But eventually they found August Weenaas, a university-trained pastor and teacher from Norway, who arrived at Augustana Seminary in 1868 and soon also became a leader in the Norwegian-language section of the Augustana Synod.

Although the attempt at forming a pan-Scandinavian Augustana Synod was begun with good intentions, the subsequent mass immigration of Scandinavians to North America created an impetus toward ethnic separatism.[4] The situation in the Augustana Synod was characterized not by confrontation between the groups but rather by a growing wish on the part of the Norwegian group for its own separate denomination and identity. The Norwegians thought their students were at a disadvantage at Augustana Seminary, as they were not educated in Norwegian and were not able to fully understand Swedish. Weenaas sympathized with the movement to separate from the Augustana Synod, which was accomplished in 1870, peacefully and by mutual consent. Some Swedes in the synod urged the Norwegians to remain, but there was no dispute when they decided to leave. From this point on, the Augustana Synod and Augustana Seminary would become entirely Swedish in composition. The assets of the seminary were divided proportionately between the two denominations.

Even before the final separation between the Swedes and Norwegians, the Norwegian section of the synod had decided in 1869 to remove the Norwegian professor and theological students from Augustana Seminary, and on September 1, 1869, the new Norwegian American seminary began its existence.[5] To distinguish itself from the Swedish institution, but to still claim its Lutheran confessional roots, the new institution was named Augsburg Seminary—Augsburg being the German term behind the Latin word *Augustana*. Weenaas and the Norwegian students moved to Marshall, Wisconsin, where the Norwegian faction had purchased a private secondary school called the Marshall Academy. The plan was that Weenaas would continue to operate Marshall Academy as an American secondary school for men and women, as well as to conduct Augsburg Seminary for Norwegian American theological candidates. The school floundered for several years, with the arrangement being unworkable and financial assistance minimal. Weenaas nearly closed the entire operation in despair, but his Norwegian students persuaded him to continue.

THE DIVISION OF THE CENTRIST NORWEGIANS

The complication in this separation of the Augustana Synod was that members of the Norwegian side of the group, few as they were, became further divided among themselves. Weenaas, pioneer pastor C. L. Clausen, and other Norwegian pastors recently arrived from Norway had one vision for the group, while the older pastors in the group, mostly Haugean lay pastors, had quite another. Weenaas and the newer arrivals had more of a connection to the Lutheran confessional tradition and the Church of Norway, while the older pastors, led by O. J. Hatlestad, were more attracted by the American models of congregation and synod they had found in the Synod of Northern Illinois. A major constitutional struggle, the details of which are more exhausting than enlightening, led to a situation whereby two different groups were formed; the Norwegian Danish Augustana Synod, and the Conference for the Norwegian Danish Evangelical Lutheran Church in America (commonly known as the Conference).[6] Thus the "center" of Norwegian American Lutheranism was further divided. One historian of the Norwegian Americans describes the situation:

> Thus in 1870 there existed in the "middle way" the anomaly of a relatively churchly group (Weenaas-Clausen) advocating for a low-church, free congregational type of polity. On the other hand an essentially Haugean group (Hatlestad) advocated a rather tightly knit ecclesiastical organization not unlike that of the Norwegian Synod.[7]

Certainly in fluid situations like this, the personalities and experiences of these denominational leaders, and their relations, played a major role, too.

Constitutionally and legally, the Norwegian Danish Augustanans held the property of the school in Marshall, Wisconsin, but the loyalty of Weenaas and many of the students was to the Conference. In October 1870, Weenaas was presented with a letter from the Augustanans, who claimed their rights to the property and ordered Weenaas to vacate the property. Weenaas chose not to contest the demand, and he and his students struggled to maintain the fledgling school in makeshift accommodations in and around Marshall. During the 1870/71 school year, the seminary was located in a ten-by-eighteen-foot rented loft; some of the students boarded with Weenaas, while others found living situations in Marshall. Money was extremely scarce, and Weenaas himself received only a small fraction of his salary. The Conference prevailed upon Weenaas to continue as they sought a new home for the Augsburg Seminary.

The Norwegian Danish Augustana Synod was by far the smaller of the two groups, and by 1890 it consisted of thirty-two pastors, eighty congregations, and perhaps about nine thousand members. Its theological position was quite strongly influenced by Haugeanism, and in its general life it would have been hard to distinguish it from the Hauge Synod, except perhaps that the Augustanans were said to be much more open to the use of English and the American religious world.[8] This group was by far the smallest of the three Norwegian American Lutheran denominations that would come together in 1890 to form the United Norwegian Lutheran Church in America (UNLC).

In the 1870 dispute, the Augustanans had won a pyrrhic victory in that though they maintained possession of the Marshall, Wisconsin, academy, they lost its theological professor (Weenaas) and most of the theological students. The synod continued to operate the Marshall Academy as an "American" (English-language) school under the leadership of a series of American teachers. Though the residents of Marshall strongly wished to retain the academy in their village, in 1881 the synod moved the academy to Beloit, Iowa, where it became more of a Norwegian school. The academy grew and soon needed more room, which it found in 1884 across the border in Canton, South Dakota. There it remained until 1918, when it moved to Sioux Falls, South Dakota.

This still left the synod without a seminary. In 1874, the synod prevailed on Pastor David Lysnes to conduct a small seminary program out of his parsonage in rural northeastern Iowa. In 1876, Lysnes and his students were moved to Marshall to form a new seminary program, named Salem Seminary, at the Marshall Academy, with both a theological and preparatory department. Lysnes was the sole professor in both programs, which indicates the relative size of the operation and the breadth of expectations for Lysnes's teaching. In 1881, the newly moved institution was named Augustana Seminary and Academy, but this name was short-lived. When the academy moved to Canton in 1884, the seminary remained in Beloit. Lysnes continued to conduct Augustana Seminary until the UNLC merger in 1890, when it was merged into Augsburg Seminary in Minneapolis (of which we will hear more shortly); Lysnes himself died in 1890. Over the course of its sixteen-year existence, this small seminary had a total of thirty-two graduates.

THE CONFERENCE AND AUGSBURG SEMINARY

The other half of this story comes through the second group, the Conference for the Norwegian Danish Evangelical Lutheran Church in America. The Conference, as it was generally known, grew to be a much larger group than the Norwegian Danish Augustana Synod; by the 1890 merger the Conference numbered 369 congregations to the Augustanans' 41. So the Conference was the substantial middle for Norwegian American Lutheranism, between the Norwegian Synod and the Haugeans. It was consistently opposed to the "Missourianism" of the Norwegian Synod, with which it was in constant conflict. The Conference was more sympathetic to the Hauge Synod, with which it shared a common piety and religiosity. As mentioned before, the Conference substantially represented the Johnsonian revivals and later Rosenian piety from Scandinavia. But the Conference was further defined by the forceful vision of two leaders from Norway who arrived in America during the 1870s: Georg Sverdrup and Sven Oftedal. The Conference itself is a lesson in how a young and malleable religious organization can be shaped and directed by dynamic, young leaders, especially if these leaders were, shall we say, not conflict-avoidant.

As has been noted, the heroic labors of Weenaas to keep the Conference seminary together in the dark year of 1870/71 saved the fledgling institution for the time being, but it was soon clear that its future was not in the rural community of Marshall, Wisconsin. After some debate, the Conference reached the decision to relocate the seminary to Minneapolis, not only because it was a larger city but also because the mass immigration of Norwegians was shifting to Minnesota and the Dakotas. In Minneapolis, local Norwegian pastors and American civic leaders promised support for the new institution, and although economic difficulties complicated the work, the Conference erected a new building on the east side of Minneapolis, near the University of Minnesota, which was opened for a new school year on September 15, 1872. This location, in the future Cedar-Riverside area, was at the time still rather rural; a student who arrived at the school in 1875 later recalled that to "the southside [of the school] there was not a single house so far as the eye could see, except a decrepit uninhabited cabin."[9] To differentiate the school from the Norwegian Augustana institution (with which it shared a common root), the school was named Augsburg Seminary.

In spite of these difficulties, the new Augsburg Seminary began to grow. One of the immediate issues was the need for a program to prepare students for seminary, as the new seminary no longer had access to the Marshall academy. One initial idea was that the seminary would enter into an agreement with the neighboring University of Minnesota to educate the pre-seminary students. Such an agreement was reached in 1872, but the arrangement did not work well on either side and was terminated in 1874. The leaders of Augsburg decided to develop their own multilevel system of preparatory education, an eventual integrated program of education that became the hallmark of the institution.

The growth of Augsburg Seminary also meant that more teachers were needed, especially to relieve the burden on Weenaas. In 1873, Weenaas and Pastor M. Falk Gjertsen went to Norway to obtain another professor for the seminary, engaging a university-educated Norwegian pastor, Sven Oftedal, who began teaching at Augsburg in that same year. Oftedal served as theological professor at Augsburg from 1873 to 1905, and as president of its board of directors from 1873 to 1911. Through Oftedal, Augsburg secured two additional professors from Norway in 1874, Georg Sverdrup and Sven Gunnersen. It was the duo of Oftedal and Sverdrup who dramatically shaped the future course of not only Augsburg but also its denominational parent, the Conference.

Sverdrup was an ambitious and forceful personality and not afraid of conflict. He was well educated for the time; after his study at the university in Christiana, he sought additional education at the University of Erlangen in Germany and at the University of Paris. Like Weenaas, Oftedal and Sverdrup were influenced by the Johnsonian revivals, but the latter two were also members of families who were prominent in Norwegian political and ecclesiastical circles, the so-called persons of condition. They were deeply influenced by the Church Reform movement of the later nineteenth century in Norway, which sought a liberalization of both church and state in Norway. Georg Sverdrup was especially influential in bringing the ideals of the liberal *Venstre* (Left) party in Norway into Norwegian American Lutheranism.[10] As Eugene Fevold stated, "Sverdrup carried the torch for the idea of 'living, democratic congregations,' free from domination of the state church or its pastors. Only a 'free church,' he argued, could provide favorable conditions for the spiritual growth of the people."[11] Though there obviously was no state church in America, Sverdrup saw the same anti-democratic, hierarchical attitudes among some pastors and leaders of Norwegian American Lutheranism, most notably in the Norwegian Synod, of which Sverdrup became an implacable foe.

With the arrival of Oftedal and Sverdrup, the situation was ripe for a power struggle within the Conference and especially the Augsburg Seminary. The initial leaders in the Conference were August Weenaas, as the seminary professor, and Pastor C. L. Clausen, the first president of the Conference. Sverdrup and Oftedal soon came into conflict with these two, and the Conference itself became divided into two factions, the Old School (Weenaas and Clausen) and the New School (Sverdrup and Oftedal), over a very harsh attack that Oftedal leveled against the Norwegian Synod in 1874. Although the conflict within the Conference was over a number of principled issues, it seems that the main source of friction between the two groups was personal support for, or opposition to, the actions and positions of Oftedal and Sverdrup. Increasingly, the power and influence in the Conference (and at Augsburg Seminary) swung to Oftedal, Sverdrup, and the New School. Weenaas resigned from the seminary and returned to Norway in 1876, though he did return to Minnesota to teach at Red Wing Seminary between 1882 and 1885. Tensions in the seminary faculty between Sverdrup and Oftedal, on the one hand, and Gunnersen, on the other, led all three to tender their resignations in 1883. At the annual meeting of the Conference in that same year, Sverdrup and Oftedal were rehired as seminary professors, while Gunnersen was not; he then also returned to Norway. After this, Sverdrup and Oftedal were firmly in control of Augsburg.

Sverdrup and Oftedal had a new vision for Norwegian American Lutheranism, one that was democratic and based on the individual power of free congregations. They also sought a thoroughgoing reform of the seminary and its theological education to make this vision a reality. Augsburg Seminary would provide a theological education in harmony with their call for a "living Christianity," the simple and devout faith of the common people developed through catechetical and biblical instruction. It was the living Christian people who formed the free congregations, and they needed pastoral leaders who would understand and encourage such faith. Sverdrup and Oftedal viewed the older Norwegian system of Latin school and university education as developing an elite class of clerical leaders who dominated and stifled the faith of the people, something they thought was continuing in the Missouri and Norwegian synod systems. As one historian wrote, "Sverdrup maintained that a seminary must be both Christian and democratic (*folkelig*)."[12]

Two things were needed for them to bring their vision to reality at Augsburg: an integrated model of education and a new curriculum. The structural model that Sverdrup and Oftedal envisioned for Augsburg was a multilevel system of education that included a preparatory school, two advanced preparatory schools, and the seminary itself. The preparatory school eventually became the equivalent of an academy, or private high school. The first advanced program, known as the Greek department, was intended for pre-seminary education, while the second program, the practical department, would prepare students for work in the wider world. These two programs would eventually become four-year programs, granting the bachelor of arts degree, and were the forerunners of Augsburg University. The seminary itself would receive students from the lower programs and prepare them for the ministry. The entire education was seen as an organic whole, with an integrated curriculum.

This curriculum was based on a reforming model, envisioned by Sverdrup and Oftedal, that rejected the traditional model of theological education, which was heavily weighted toward the classics, Latin, and theological dogmatics. This course of study was what they believed to lead to "dead," formalistic theology and a class-ridden clericalism that separated pastors from their parishioners. The new curriculum was rather weighted heavily toward biblical study and biblical languages (especially Greek) but in a new way. The New Testament would be the core of the curriculum, and all other disciplines would be viewed in light of it, but the New Testament itself would be viewed historically, not dogmatically. Above all, the central approach was to understand Christianity as a historical, "living organism." This new curriculum had a number of different sources, including the pietist traditions of catechesis, the nineteenth-century folk school movement, and the new Erlangen school of theological education from Germany.[13]

The emphasis on piety and a "living" faith was a constant theme of

Augsburg Seminary and became the focal point of its instruction. As the school's catalog stated it:

> Spiritual life and Christian character are considered of infinitely higher importance than mere knowledge. No amount of reading, no memorizing of facts, no mental or intellectual ability are of any real value to the Christian minister without personal experience of saving grace and firm and manly conviction of the truth as it is in Jesus.[14]

Statements like these indicate the type of education and ministerial formation that Augsburg strove to accomplish. While such language is not by any means unique to Augsburg (the Haugeans would have wholeheartedly agreed), this seminary endeavored to integrate this philosophy at all levels of the institution.

THE PREDESTINATION CONTROVERSY

It may seem strange at first that predestination, the idea that God alone has determined those who would be saved, a theological controversy of the 1870s and 1880s, would be of such a great consequence to the history of Luther Seminary. Historically, predestination was not of major concern to Lutherans, and this controversy began among the German American Lutherans, not the Norwegians. Yet this controversy eventually became a bitter dispute among the Norwegian American Lutherans, dividing congregations and denominations and leading to a wholesale realignment among them. Even though a compromise on this issue was eventually reached in 1912, leading to a merger of many of these groups, the basic theological tensions raised by this controversy would continue to simmer at Luther Seminary until at least the 1960s. The dispute itself would come to center around core issues of faith and salvation and the role of God and humanity.

The background of the predestination controversy (sometimes called the election controversy) lay in the formation of the Synodical Conference in 1872 as a cooperative arrangement of midwestern conservative Lutheran synods, mainly German American but also including the Norwegian Synod. The Synodical Conference was dominated from the beginning by the rapidly expanding Missouri Synod and its forceful theological leader, C. F. W. Walther. Lutherans had some disputes over the doctrine of predestination in the sixteenth century but reached a vague compromise over the issue in article IX of the Formula of Concord in 1577. Predestination was historically more of a contentious and defining issue among the Reformed (Calvinist) Protestants than among the Lutherans, but this was about to change.

In 1877, Walther gave an address to a meeting of the Western district of the Missouri Synod on the topic of predestination that occasioned a lively discussion. When the published reports of the conference were circulated, several theologians within the Synodical Conference, including Henry Allwardt and Frederick Stellhorn of the Missouri Synod and F. A. Schmidt of the Norwegian Synod, suggested that Walther's position on the doctrine was closer to that of Calvin than Luther and even suggested that Walther was a "secret Calvinist" on the issue. These were fighting words, and the battle was joined, generally between the Missouri Synod, who supported Walther, and some of the other German American synods, who supported his critics. One historian has summarized the debate this way:

> The man who believes in Christ and his atoning merit is . . . predestined to be saved. But shall we say that God's predestination is the cause of his faith and his salvation, or shall we say that his faith is the cause of his predestination? The Missourians took the first alternative . . . [insisting] that a man cannot believe in Christ unless God causes him to do so. . . . [Missouri's opponents] took the second alternative and insisted that God elects man to salvation "in view of his faith" in the merits of Christ.[15]

The dispute raged furiously over several years and caused a number of the other German American Lutheran synods to leave the Synodical Conference.

The debate over predestination also spread to the Norwegian Synod, and there it quickly became an issue within that body. As has been seen previously, many of the leaders of the Norwegian Synod had a long and respectful relationship with Walther and the Missouri Synod and chose to support them. But there was also a strong undercurrent in the Norwegian Synod of resentment toward Walther and Missouri that had hung over from the slavery controversy and from fears of Missouri's "undue influence" over the synodical leadership. An early critic of Missouri's influence, Luther Seminary professor Ole Asperheim, was forced out of his position in 1878. But when Walther's former friend and supporter, Luther Seminary professor F. A. Schmidt, turned against him in 1880, the battle was joined within the Norwegian Synod and its congregations.

It is estimated that perhaps two-thirds of the Norwegian Synod, led by Luther Seminary professor H. A. Stub and Ulrik Koren, a prominent pastor within the synod, supported Walther and his position on the issue. Leading the opposition to Walther were Schmidt and synod president Bernt Julius Muus, the founder of St. Olaf College. The doctrine of predestination had an uncertain history among the Norwegian Lutherans. The two positions were labeled as the first and second form of the doctrine of election (the word generally preferred). The first form was "election unto faith," along Walther's formulation, and drew from parts of the Formula of Concord. The second form, the "election in view of foreseen faith," was taken from the deeply influential catechism of Bishop Eric Pontoppidan from his answer to catechism question 548. Adding to this, the Formula of Concord had an ambiguous status among the Norwegian Lutherans (it was never formally adopted by them), while Pontoppidan's catechism was widely revered and used among them.

The dispute over election spilled out of the pastors' conferences and newspapers of the synod and into the congregations, a number of which split over the issue. In 1883, in an attempt to pacify the critics of Missouri, the Norwegian Synod withdrew from the Synodical Conference, but the controversy only intensified. Tensions within Luther Seminary reflected this controversy, with the professors (and students) divided between the two positions. As the leading opponent of Missouri, seminary professor F. A. Schmidt came into open conflict with his colleagues, refusing to teach during the year 1885/86 as a protest against conditions at the seminary and resigning his position the next year. Enrollment at Luther Seminary declined sharply as a result of the controversy, dipping to only seven students.

By 1884 the conflict within the Norwegian Synod was leading

toward a schism. The anti-Missouri faction, which came to be known as the Anti-Missouri Brotherhood, represented perhaps one-third of the synod itself. It could not control the synod, so it began to set up alternative structures, especially an "alternative treasury" to fund professors and students who might be negatively affected by the controversy. They also decided in 1886 to set up their own independent seminary, which was located at St. Olaf School in Northfield, Minnesota. Finally in 1887 matters within the synod reached a breaking point; the synod meeting of that year declared the establishment of a new seminary a "schismatic act," leaving the Anti-Missourians and their congregations little choice but to withdraw from the synod. A number of congregations, including some very prominent ones, divided into two over the issue.

The new seminary was established in Northfield in the facilities of St. Olaf School in 1886, although technically independent of it, with its own faculty and board of directors. The Northfield seminary faculty included the veteran F. A. Schmidt and new professor Marcus Olaus Bøckman, who would become a leading figure in the history of Luther Seminary. These two professors gathered a somewhat mixed group of pastoral candidates and began their classes. The students varied widely in age and in the level of formal education they had achieved, which was typical of immigrant Lutheran seminaries of the time. One student later reported:

> The professors sat up on a high platform at the north end of the room, and looked down on us with warm interest in helping us, but with some misgivings as to whether any good could come from such a motley pack![16]

Thirty-two students of theology were enrolled in the first year. Since their separation from the Norwegian Synod, the Anti-Missourians also had no access to the preparatory education at Luther College, and thus they agreed with the trustees to use St. Olaf School for such a purpose. St. Olaf added a first-year collegiate class in 1886 and continued to add classes every year after that until it filled the new collegiate program, and the institution was renamed St. Olaf College. St. Olaf soon became a major organizational focus of the Anti-Missourian Brotherhood, including its president, Thorbjørn Nelson Mohn. But unlike Augsburg, the Northfield seminary remained structurally independent of the new college.

The Anti-Missouri Brotherhood decided against forming a new synod but decided to seek a merger of as many of the Norwegian American Lutheran denominations as was possible. The Brotherhood reached out to the Norwegian Augustanans and the Conference, who agreed to begin such a process. The Hauge Synod was also invited to participate, but although there was some potential interest in such an arrangement, in the end the Hauge Synod decided not to become a part of this new church, which was formed in 1890 as the United Norwegian Lutheran Church (UNLC). The United Church, as it was popularly called, was instantly the largest Norwegian American Lutheran denomination, larger than the Norwegian Synod and the Hauge Synod combined.

THEOLOGICAL EDUCATION IN THE UNITED CHURCH

Because the United Church came together so quickly, the details of the new merged church were left to be hammered out afterward, a situation that was often fraught with difficulties. One of the biggest challenges to the new United Church involved its educational institutions and how many of them the new denomination would fund. There were three seminaries in the newly merged church (Augsburg, Augustana, and the Northfield Seminary), and two collegiate institutions (St. Olaf and Augsburg). The common wisdom of the time was that the new denomination should support a single college and a single seminary, but the details of this were less than clear, and this unclarity set up the new United Church for a decade of turmoil and eventually schism.

The seminary question seemed to be rather straightforward. The three existing seminaries would be consolidated at Augsburg Seminary in Minneapolis. The new church convention voted that the two Augsburg faculty, Sverdrup and Oftedal, would be joined by Schmidt and Bøckman from Northfield, and by David Lysnes from Augustana (Lysnes died in 1890, and his place was taken by Emil Gunerius Lund). The endowment funds, physical assets, and student bodies of the seminaries would be likewise merged, and there would be a newly elected board of directors for the institution. This arrangement seemed to proceed calmly, although one can understand how the infusion of all these new elements into Augsburg could be potentially upsetting to the ethos of the school that had been so carefully nurtured by Sverdrup and Oftedal, who were by this point outnumbered by the addition of three new professors. But the main conflict, yet to come, concerned the collegiate and preparatory schools of the newly merged church.

By action of the constituting convention of the new United Church, Augsburg was to function as the seminary of the church, and St. Olaf College was to be its collegiate and preparatory institution. But this raised the question of the role of the preparatory and collegiate programs at Augsburg. Sverdrup and Oftedal, and the supporters of Augsburg, insisted that the entire nine-year program of Augsburg (preparatory, advanced, and theological programs) was an integrated unit of the seminary and must be maintained. The new church was willing to guarantee only that the preparatory programs at Augsburg would be continued for a short period of time. The supporters of Augsburg, mainly comprised of the New School wing of the Conference, refused to agree to this, and because of legal flaws in the incorporation of both Augsburg and the Conference, the old board of Augsburg was able to refuse to transfer its assets to the new United Church. Thus began at least eight years of parliamentary maneuvering, polemical attacks, back-room politics, score-settling, and legal wrangling that eventually ended up at the Minnesota State Supreme Court in 1898. This convoluted struggle occupies forty pages of dense prose in the Nelson and Fevold history of Norwegian American Lutheranism.[17]

Sverdrup and Oftedal had triumphed in the Conference and had molded Augsburg in their ideal of seminary education and the nature of the church, but this merger threatened to undo it all. They and their supporters feared that by unhitching the preparatory programs from the seminary, their distinctive view of seminary education would be destroyed. The supporters of Augsburg worried that although the Anti-Missourians had rejected Missouri, they still represented the same kind of elitist and clericalist tendencies that had dominated the Norwegian Synod from which they had come. St. Olaf and Augsburg represented two different visions of education, something that their partisans each sharply pointed out in their debates. Historian Richard Solberg summarizes these polemics:

> Friends of Augsburg assailed St. Olaf for its humanism and rationalism, its "luxurious facilities," its doctors of philosophy, its masters of arts, and [its] deficits. Supporters of St. Olaf branded Augsburg as a "humbug" institution offering piety as a substitute for intellectual rigor and scholarship.[18]

In the end, the supporters of Augsburg prevailed on the basis of the original (yet faulty) incorporation of the school in 1869 and successfully managed to maintain legal control of the school and its property, refusing to hand it over to the United Church. A settlement was eventually reached in 1898 by which the outside assets the United Church had put into Augsburg Seminary were returned to the United Church, while Augsburg maintained its independence.

This situation left the United Church without a seminary, a situation that they moved quickly to rectify in the fall of 1893 with the establishment of the United Church seminary. The new institution was initially located in Minneapolis, not too far from Augsburg, with an initial faculty of Schmidt, Bøckman, and Lund. The United Church also set up a preparatory and collegiate institution at the same location, having had to jettison its recognition of St. Olaf as its educational institution in the political mess that was the "school controversy" of the 1890s.

From 1893 to 1895, students and faculty struggled with perennial underfunding, which hampered the course of study. Though the seminary established a typical three-year curriculum, many students could attend only sporadically and did not complete the full program. One student remembered the great demand for pastors:

> There was a great difficulty in those days about the student assignments as well, because a great number of men . . . had never finished anything probably more than what we would call Normal School [up through eighth grade], but the need for men to go out into the field in the

Northwest especially . . . made a great drain as far as pastors were concerned for the growing church.[19]

Students would attend classes as long as their funds held out and then have to drop out, as this student, when in the preparatory program in 1893, recalled: "In the spring of '94 I had to leave seminary rather early on as my money ran out, and in the boarding club we had to keep some money always deposited in advance. . . . It was impossible to find a job anyplace."[20] Faculty struggled under these conditions to maintain anything coming close to a coherent program of pastoral education and formation.

As well, the initial location, at Franklin Avenue and Twenty-Sixth Street in South Minneapolis, consisted of a single three-story building, with student dormitory rooms on the lowest floor, then classrooms for the preparatory and collegiate programs on the next floor, with a chapel and classrooms for the seminary on the top floor. The building was quickly determined to be inadequate, with only a small library and a limited number of classrooms, which made for very overcrowded conditions.

In 1900 the seminary moved to temporary buildings in Minneapolis while waiting for the construction of a permanent building in the St. Anthony Park neighborhood of Saint Paul. The city of Saint Paul and railroad tycoon James J. Hill donated the parcel of land, and officials of the seminary and the United Church went out among the congregations to secure the funding to build the building.

The new seminary building, an imposing, columned structure at one of the highest points in Saint Paul, was opened and occupied by the seminary in January 1902. The building was eventually named Bockman Hall. In 1899, with the final solution of the dispute with Augsburg, St. Olaf College was once again officially recognized as the college of the United Church, and the seminary's preparatory and collegiate programs were transferred to St. Olaf. There were strong ties between St. Olaf College and the United Church seminary, and most of the theological candidates for this denomination came through the programs at St. Olaf first.

Given the size of the new United Church, this new seminary was very quickly a substantial institution, and in its twenty-four-year history, graduated 559 pastoral candidates. The United Church seminary was quite a bit larger than the Augsburg Seminary and also larger than the Luther Seminary of the Norwegian Synod and the Red Wing Seminary of the Hauge Synod. All four Norwegian American Lutheran seminaries were located in Minnesota, three in the Twin Cities, with the fourth down the way in Red Wing.

The initial three faculty members of the United Church seminary, Schmidt, Bøckman, and Lund, were soon joined by other full- and part-time teachers. Erik Kristian Johnsen came from Norway in 1900 to teach Old Testament, Carl M. Weswig joined as the English professor of church history in 1906, and Michael J. Stolee returned from the mission field in Madagascar in 1911 to teach missions and practical theology. Schmidt retired in 1913 and was replaced in 1915 by J. N. Kildahl, who also served as president of the seminary.[21] At this period of time, instruction in the seminary was bilingual, and the preference of the faculty member determined the language they used in class. Bøckman and Johnsen used Norwegian exclusively, Kildahl and Stolee used both English and Norwegian, while Weswig taught only in English.[22] Obviously at this time students were expected to be proficient in both languages, although some of the more recent immigrant students struggled with the courses taught in English. Of the seminary class of twelve in 1901, for example, only four or five could speak English fluently enough to serve an English-speaking congregation.[23] Up until the 1920s, and the dramatic shift from Norwegian to English, the primary language in the seminary, as in most congregations, was Norwegian.

Given the limitations of the faculty and the student populations, the courses in the curriculum were taught only once in a three-year period, with the entire student body taking the same courses at the same time. As one student recalled:

> You might come in at the beginning of the first year or you might land right at the beginning of your work in the second year in history, or dogmatics, or any of those major subjects. There were not enough teachers to divide up and the classes were not large enough to warrant it. So every third year the course began at the beginning of the subjects, and we were fortunate enough in our class of 1898, which finished the

seminary in 1901, to begin at the very beginning in Church History, in Dogmatics, as well as in the other subjects.[24]

As can be imagined this was a rather small and tightly knit community, where the students and faculty were together on a very regular basis, almost approximating a Protestant monastic community. (Theological students were not allowed to be married while in seminary.)

THE FRIENDS OF AUGSBURG AND THE FORMATION OF THE LUTHERAN FREE CHURCH

With the establishment of the United Church seminary in 1893, and amid the economic depression of the 1890s, Augsburg Seminary was in a difficult position. While the original board of directors eventually prevailed and kept the United Church from controlling the institution, they also lost the financial support that they had previously received from the Conference and initially from the United Church. Certainly the core faculty of Sverdrup and Oftedal were rehired by the seminary, but they lost the other three faculty members, and a portion of the student body as well, to the United Church seminary. From the beginning of the conflict in 1893 to its final settlement in 1898, the legal outcome was uncertain, and when the settlement did finally occur, it mandated that certain endowment funds that had been transferred to Augsburg in the merger (funds to support the professors' salaries) rightly belonged to the United Church and had to be handed over to them. Independence and pedagogical principle were maintained but at a cost.

However, Augsburg was certainly not wholly without support, and Sverdrup and Oftedal had deep ties with a number of the leading congregations of the old Conference, especially among the New School faction. In 1893, when it looked to some that Augsburg's distinctive program was threatened by the lukewarm support of the United Church, a group of supporting pastors, congregations, and individuals gathered to form an alliance known as the "Friends of Augsburg." The United Church set a deadline of June 30, 1893, for the board of Augsburg to hand over legal control of Augsburg, a deadline that was rebuffed. On June 14, 1893, the first meeting of the

Friends of Augsburg was held on the campus and sought guarantees from the United Church for the continuation of Augsburg's distinctive tradition. Another meeting was held in November, and in 1894 the group was formally organized, meeting annually for the next few years.

The Friends of Augsburg had as their mission a number of different tasks. The most important was, of course, to continue to resist the actions and demands of the United Church for control of the school's property, a battle that took several years and played out in several courts and in the Minnesota legislature. Another mission was the financial support of the school itself. During the 1890 to 1893 school years, enrollment in the school as a whole was between 188 and 167 (72 to 47 in the theological seminary). After the break with the United Church, school enrollments initially dipped to 113 but recovered to 201 by 1900 (seminary enrollment averaged around 30).[25] The financial position was, however, much more critical, and the Friends authorized Pastor Peter Nielsen to be the field representative for the board. Certainly, he raised much-needed funds for the struggling institution, but more broadly his task was to rally support for Augsburg among the Norwegian American congregations, something at which he was evidently very proficient.[26] The struggling institution survived in this hour because supporters and congregations rallied to its defense.

The Friends, however, had to address additional problems, which mainly concerned pressure that the United Church was placing on pastors and congregations in the midst of this dispute. In the heated 1893 convention of the United Church, it passed an ambiguous resolution (probably unwisely) directing the Missions Committee to disburse its support only to those congregations that were in "full loyalty" to the United Church. Of course this only stoked the fires of distrust among the supporters of Augsburg, who saw the resolution as a thinly veiled threat to "their" congregations and pastors dependent on mission support. To those who followed Sverdrup's vision of "free" congregations, this move smacked of the kind of ecclesiastical tyranny they had worked so hard to leave behind in Norway. A similar situation also concerned support of foreign mission workers, many of whom also had ties to Augsburg.

Of more direct concern to the theological program of Augsburg was the question of the ordination of its graduates, especially after the rupture with the United Church. In 1894 the United Church convention directed its Ordination Committee to examine candidates for ordination who came from seminaries other than the new United Church seminary to see if these candidates were fully supportive of the doctrines and constitution of the United Church. This was obviously a direct threat to the graduates of Augsburg Seminary and the congregations that supported it. In response to this "emergency" situation, the Friends took a serious (and escalating) step of ordaining pastors themselves, beginning in the fall of 1894. They justified this move on the idea that the United Church was blocking "free" congregations from obtaining pastors of their own choosing. This was a direct contravention of the constitution of the United Church, which still exercised authority over many of the pastors and congregations in the Friends.

The congregations that were a part of the Friends of Augsburg came under scrutiny from the United Church, especially for their refusal to provide support for the new United Church seminary. After the formation of this latter seminary in the summer of 1893, the Trinity Lutheran congregation in Minneapolis, the "mother" congregation of Augsburg, approved a resolution that declared that the United Church had broken its articles of union, and thus the congregation was "absolved" of any financial support of the new seminary and would instead continue to support Augsburg.[27] This action was the model for at least a dozen other congregations, and this defiance led the United Church to begin disciplinary action against the twelve recalcitrant congregations, threatening expulsion from the United Church at the beginning of 1897 if they did not reverse their stance.

Already the Friends of Augsburg, meeting in annual convention June 9–13, 1896, felt that they had little choice but to take steps to form themselves into a new and separate Lutheran denomination. A group of leaders, including Sverdrup and Oftedal, was selected to form a Free Church Committee, which began planning for the structure of the new group. This committee, following the ideological lead of the two theologians, organized the new group as an association of "free and independent congregations," banded together for the mutual work of the gospel. So at the annual meeting of the Friends of Augsburg, the proposed plan submitted by the committee was adopted, and the new Lutheran Free Church was established, with Augsburg as its theological school. Theologically there was not much difference between the United Church and the new Lutheran Free Church, but the question of polity divided them.

In 1896 and early 1897, individual congregations were already leaving the United Church or, as in the case of the twelve, were being expelled. These congregations, along with others that left the United Church, constituted the original core of the Free Church. The estimate is that perhaps about 125 congregations made up the Free Church at its beginning, with a total membership of about 6,200.[28] The initial size of the new church must have been a disappointment to its leaders, Sverdrup and Oftedal. They had commanded a clear majority of the Conference congregation, the New School party, before the merger, and at the time of the merger the Conference consisted about 450 congregations and 70,600 baptized members. So assuming that the congregations that constituted the new Lutheran Free Church were substantially from the New School wing of the Conference, the Free Church gathered in less than 30 percent of these congregations, representing less than 10 percent of its total membership. The majority of congregations from the Conference then remained in the new United Church, perhaps to the satisfaction of the Old School leaders who had been long been outmaneuvered by Sverdrup and Oftedal.

ON THE WAY TO FURTHER MERGERS, 1890–1917

The decades of the 1890s and 1900s saw a great expansion of Norwegian American Lutheranism. Immigration from Norway continued to be strong, and the rising second and third generations began to take leadership within the ethnic community, especially in the churches. Four Norwegian American seminaries (Luther, United Church, Red Wing, and Augsburg) were producing in greater and greater numbers new pastors, who were sorely needed to meet the demands from existing congregations and from new mission fields. A strong expansion of new home mission activities and church planting, especially in the Pacific Northwest and Canada (most notably in the United Church), was made possible by the increasing number of new pastors.

As well, the 1890s saw waves of spiritual renewal in many sections of the Norwegian American churches. The revivals of this time were initially occasioned by the evangelistic efforts of Lars O. Skrefsrud, a missionary of the Santal Mission in northeastern India. Skrefsrud was in the United States in 1894–1895 at the request of the Santal Mission Committee of America to visit congregations and to raise funds for the mission. An accomplished and effective preacher, Skrefsrud traveled widely among the Norwegian Americans and preached constantly, as much as two or three times a day. Another factor in this wave of revivals was the activity of Peter Nielsen, the field representative of the Friends of Augsburg, who organized numerous multiday meetings for spiritual renewal around the country. From about 1894 to the turn of the twentieth century, this awakening of religion was very influential among the congregations of the Lutheran Free Church and the Hauge Synod, as well as in parts of the United Church. This revival is also credited with an upsurge in the numbers of young men entering seminary, especially at Augsburg.[29] Although this awakening movement generally strengthened the existing denominations, it did occasion a small group to leave the United Church and form the Church of the Lutheran Brethren in 1900. This group sought "pure" congregations of only converted individuals, something that even the Hauge Synod had not demanded.

The initial success of the formation of the United Norwegian Lutheran Church in 1890 produced an enthusiasm for a greater merger that was not dampened by the withdrawal of the Lutheran Free Church and the eventual decision of the Hauge Synod not to enter the merger. Although this enthusiasm was perhaps the strongest in the United Church, there were stirrings of interest among elements of the Hauge Synod and the Norwegian Synod, as well. Some began to envision a united Norwegian American denomination that would include the vast majority of ethnic congregations. The relative success of the United Church merger was one factor, while another was a wave of Norwegian American ethnic sentiment, which saw during this time the establishment of important pan-Norwegian social and cultural societies around North America. Though these ethnic societies were not religiously based, they did bring together individuals from across the denominational spectrum and often became the vehicles for discussion of further church union.[30]

However influential past merger success, religious awakening, and growing ethnic solidarity were, they could not mask the fact that there remained significant theological and ecclesiastical disputes between the denominations. The election controversy and the withdrawal of the Anti-Missourians remained a difficult factor, as was the cool relationship between the Hauge Synod and the Norwegian Synod. Other contentious issues included the questions of the bases of church fellowship (the question of unionism) and a new development, disputes over how to express the nature of biblical authority and the inspiration of Scripture. Personal wounds remained as well, as the disputes of the 1880s and 1890s were fresh in many minds. The sentiment of the large majority was that there ought to be one united Norwegian Lutheran church in North America, but sentiment alone could not make it happen.

It is not necessary for our purposes to rehearse the twenty-seven years of activities, debates, and negotiations that led to the eventual formation of the Norwegian Lutheran Church in America in 1917, a merger of the United Church, the Hauge Synod, and the Norwegian Synod (the Lutheran Free Church did not participate).[31] But a number of the issues from this period had a direct impact on seminary education within the merging churches and on the future of the merged seminary that came together in 1917. As is usually the case, carefully crafted compromises had to be made to enable the eventual merger of both church and seminary, but these compromises did not completely resolve the underlying questions going forward.

The Hauge Synod had not entered the 1890 merger not out of any major doctrinal disputes with the new United Church but because of their longstanding concerns about maintaining their distinctive practices, especially lay preaching, free worship practices, and their openness to working with other Christian denominations. As formal and informal discussions happened among the three denominations, it appeared that most of these issues could be overcome, although the

Norwegian Synod remained worried about the question of "unionism" (church cooperation without first achieving complete theological agreement between the parties). The Norwegian Synod raised a new and serious theological issue, namely the precise theological formulation of the nature of biblical authority and the inspiration of the Scriptures. It is abundantly clear that all three of these churches had a deep regard for the authority of the Bible, but the Norwegian Synod, led by veteran theologian Ulrik Koren, wanted a strong, formal, and detailed agreement on the issue. This topic was a rising issue within the wider world of American Protestantism at the beginning of the twentieth century and led to the rise of fundamentalism and its split from mainline Protestantism. Eventually the issue would be addressed by the three denominations, at least enough to make the merger work. But this issue and these formulations would continue to be a cause of concern and conflict going forward.

The most serious point of contention continued to be the doctrine of election, and there would be no way to merge without a resolution on this issue. The theological debates over this question seemed insoluble, especially as the main combatants were the seminary professors, principally F. A. Schmidt of the United Church seminary and Hans G. Stub of Luther Seminary. Eventually these old foes were replaced on the negotiating committees by a new generation of parish pastors and church leaders who were eager to overcome the entrenched positions of the past. After many twists and turns, and times when it appeared that all hope was lost, the negotiators reached a compromise on the issue in the Madison Agreement of 1912. This formulation reaffirmed the primacy of the Formula of Concord article IX on the issue of election and said that, within certain limits, both positions on the issue (first form and second form) were permissible and that the issue was not church dividing. After thirty years of theological contention, the controversy was called a draw. But like the question of biblical authority, it would remain contentious below the surface and would rise time and time again.

The Madison Agreement made it possible to complete the merger of the United Church, the Hauge Synod, and the Norwegian Synod into the Norwegian Lutheran Church of America (NLCA) in 1917.[32] The merger was fully embraced by the United Church and generally (with reservations) by the Hauge Synod, especially by the majority of laypeople and parish pastors who desired the union. The situation in the Norwegian Synod was more complicated; the majority of the Norwegian Synod, including most of its leaders, accepted the Madison Agreement, but a vocal minority did not. This minority kept up its opposition until the end but could not derail the process; in the end, most of the pastors and congregations of the Norwegian Synod entered into the new NLCA, but a minority of the minority withdrew in 1917 to form a small separate denomination, eventually known as the Evangelical Lutheran Synod.[33]

One major negotiation concerned the future of seminary education in the new NLCA. It was widely accepted that there should be a single seminary in the new denomination, but it would have to be constituted in a way that was agreeable to all parties. The campus of the United Church seminary in Saint Paul was selected as the physical location of the new seminary; the Norwegian Synod's Luther Seminary, as well as the theology department of the Red Wing Seminary, were to be transferred there. The faculty would consist of four professors from the Norwegian Synod (Ylvisaker, Brandt, Hove, and Stub), four from the United Church (Bøckman, Kildahl, Johnsen, and Weswig), and two from the Hauge Synod (Wee and Bruce). Since Stub was subsequently elected president of the NLCA, Professor Stolee from the United Church was selected to replace him. Bøckman was elected as president of the new seminary, with Ylvisaker as the vice president. The new institution was called Luther Theological Seminary.

Notes

1. The parallel experiences of the Swedish American denominations show a contrast to this, where the separatist-leaning pietists eventually dropped any formal adherence to the Lutheran confessions, forming groups such as the Swedish Covenant, the Swedish Evangelical Free, as well as ethnic Methodist and Baptist groups. For the contrast see Mark Granquist, "A Comparison of Swedish- and Norwegian-American Religious Traditions, 1860–1920," *Lutheran Quarterly* 8, no. 3 (Autumn 1994): 299–320.

2. This institution does not have any direct ties to the current institution of the same name. After the collapse of the first ISU, the Missouri Synod eventually bought the buildings for its practical seminary.
3. On the history of the Augustana Seminary, which eventually located in Rock Island, Illinois, see Arden, *School of the Prophets*.
4. Since there were no organized Danish American denominations or many congregations at this time, many Danish immigrants became members of Norwegian American congregations. The historical ties between the two lands and the similarity in languages made this possible.
5. It is from the formation of Augsburg Seminary in 1869 that the present Luther Seminary determines its founding date. Although, as has been seen, there were older attempts at theological education among the Norwegian Americans, the line of continuous operation goes back here to 1869, although it could be traced back to 1860 or earlier.
6. Most of the Danish congregations and pastors left these two denominations in the 1880s, with the formation of Danish American Lutheran denominations.
7. Nelson and Fevold, *Lutheran Church*, 1:210.
8. Nelson and Fevold, *Lutheran Church*, 1:212.
9. John H. Blegen, "Biografiske optegnelser for mine Barn," handwritten manuscript, Minnesota Historical Society, quoted in Carl H. Chrislock, *From Fjord to Freeway: 100 Years, Augsburg College* (Minneapolis: Augsburg College, 1969), 8.
10. Georg Sverdrup and Sven Oftedal both had family members who were leaders in the Norwegian Liberal party and were closely tied to its religious and political aims. Georg's older brother Jakob was Minister for Church Affairs.
11. Nelson and Fevold, *Lutheran Church*, 1:222.
12. James S. Hamre, "Augsburg Theological Seminary, 1869–1963," in Gonnerman, *Thanksgiving and Hope*, 23.
13. The later point was made in 1910 by Professor John O. Evjen, quoted in Hamre, "Augsburg Theological Seminary," 17.
14. *Catalog of Augsburg Seminary, 1899–1900*.
15. Abdel Ross Wentz, *A Basic History of Lutheranism in America*, rev. ed. (Philadelphia: Fortress Press, 1964), 206.
16. K. O. Lundeberg, "Luthersk Presteschole, 1886–1890," unpublished memoir, 1940, quoted in Joseph M. Shaw, *A History of St. Olaf College, 1874–1974* (Northfield, MN: St. Olaf College Press, 1974), 78.

17. See Nelson and Fevold, *Lutheran Church*, 2:38–78.
18. Richard W. Solberg, *Lutheran Higher Education in North America* (Minneapolis: Augsburg, 1985), 232.
19. Johan Arnd Aasgaard, "Unpublished Autobiographical Interview," in the Region 3 Archives of the Evangelical Lutheran Church in America, 1957, 32–33. Aasgaard himself became a leading pastor in the church and eventually president of the Norwegian Lutheran Church in America in 1925.
20. Aasgaard, "Unpublished Autobiographical Interview," 13.
21. Fevold, "Laying Foundations," 30–31. See also Joseph M. Shaw, *John Nathan Kildahl* (Northfield, MN: Highland Books, 2014).
22. Nelson and Fevold, *Lutheran Church*, 2:247.
23. Aasgaard, "Unpublished Autobiographical Interview," 33.
24. Aasgaard, "Unpublished Autobiographical Interview," 28.
25. Hamre, "Augsburg Theological Seminary," 23.
26. Eugene L. Fevold, *The Lutheran Free Church: A Fellowship of American Lutheran Congregations, 1897–1963* (Minneapolis: Augsburg, 1969), 82.
27. Fevold, *Lutheran Free Church*, 92. This action, approved by a two-to-one margin, caused the dissenting minority of the congregation to withdraw from Trinity and form a new and separate congregation.
28. Clarence J. Carlsen, *The Years of Our Church* (Minneapolis: Lutheran Free Church, 1942), 167.
29. Fevold, *Lutheran Free Church*, 88–91.
30. Nelson and Fevold, *Lutheran Church*, 2:152–54.
31. For the complete details of this process, see Nelson and Fevold, *Lutheran Church*, 2:129–225.
32. The NLCA would eventually change its name to the Evangelical Lutheran Church (ELC) in 1946. For the purposes of this work, NLCA will be used to refer to the denomination until 1946, and ELC will be used afterward. But they are the same church body.
33. See Nelson and Fevold, *Lutheran Church*, 2:219–20, and Theodore A. Aaberg, *A City Set on a Hill* (Mankato, MN: Board of Publication of the Evangelical Lutheran Synod, 1968).

4

Luther Theological Seminary, 1917–1963

The merger in 1917 brought together the three major Norwegian American Lutheran denominations: the United Church, the Norwegian Synod, and the Hauge Synod.[1] For the first time in North America, the vast majority of Norwegian American Lutherans were united in a single Christian denomination. Of course, there were several much smaller denominations, but close to 95 percent of all Norwegian American Lutherans were in the new church.[2] The three merging denominations were of unequal sizes; the United Church had 257,000 baptized members, the Norwegian Synod about 161,000 baptized members, and the Hauge Synod about 42,000 baptized members, meaning that the new Norwegian Lutheran Church in America (NLCA; as it was known until 1946) consisted of approximately 460,000 baptized members, with almost 1,200 ordained pastors. This new church was, at the time, the third largest Lutheran denomination in North America, trailing only the United Lutheran Church in America (ULCA) and the Evangelical Lutheran Synod of Missouri and Other States (the Missouri Synod), and because of its size it became a major factor in North American Lutheranism.

The size of the new denomination, however, belied the significant internal tensions that were present at its beginning. The Madison Agreement of 1912 was a thinly padded peace treaty that did not address the still-existing tensions over the doctrine of election.[3]

Though the heated events of the 1880s were somewhat mitigated by the passage of thirty years, many of the original participants of that controversy were still in power. Divisions within the Norwegian Synod over the merger caused some within the minority to leave, but most of those opposed to the merger remained (unhappily?) within the new NLCA. The lingering fondness of the Norwegian Synod leadership for the Missouri Synod still rankled many in the United Church group, especially the former members of the Anti-Missouri Brotherhood. The Haugeans, who were a smaller percentage of the new denomination, worried that their theological distinctives and low-church worship style would not be honored in the new denomination and that the Red Wing Seminary would not be adequately supported.[4]

The new denomination needed careful tending to make sure that these tensions, among others, would not seriously disrupt its development. Fortunately, in its forty-three-year history the NLCA had a cadre of wise leaders, including presidents Hans G. Stub (1917–1925) and Johan A. Aasgaard (1925–1954), who were extremely adept at balancing the internal tensions and conflicting loyalties that continued to exist. At the constituting convention of the NLCA in 1917, the newly elected president, Stub, was from the Norwegian Synod; the vice-president, J. N. Kildahl, was from the United Church; and the secretary, H. J. Løhre, was from the Hauge Synod, in a carefully balanced slate to represent the three merging denominations. But despite careful attention to the internal parties, the old issues would erupt from time to time.

LUTHER SEMINARY, 1917-1930

As one of the most important institutions of the new NLCA, the newly formed Luther Seminary also contained all the tensions and factionalism that were to be found in the new denomination. The question of the "first form" and "second form" of the doctrine of election would be a continuing issue throughout the history of the seminary, as would be questions of intra-Lutheran and ecumenical strategy, the nature of biblical authority, evangelism and worship styles, and the kinds of piety represented in the church. As the theological professors in the seminary itself were elected by the annual church convention, the theological composition of the seminary was a matter of church politics and had to be carefully handled by the administration of the seminary and church leaders.

The assumption of most involved at the time was that there would be a single seminary for the newly merged denomination, and of course at the time of the merger there were three. The smallest was Red Wing Seminary, which consisted of a pre-seminary academy and collegiate and theological divisions, but its location and limited facilities ruled it out as the home of the new seminary. The theological division was moved to Saint Paul and the collegiate program to St. Olaf College, while the academy remained in Red Wing for the time being.[5] This left the two seminaries in Saint Paul: the United Church Seminary in the St. Anthony Park area and the Norwegian Synod Luther Seminary in the Hamline area. The initial decision was that the buildings of both former seminaries would be used for the new institution, but it did not take long before the realization set in that not only was this an awkward situation, it also cost too much money to run. When the decision was made for consolidation, the St. Anthony Park facility was chosen, and the Hamline campus was shuttered and eventually sold.

FORMATION OF THE FACULTY AND THE ORGANIZATION OF THE SEMINARY

The merging church decided that, at the beginning, there would be ten professors at the new seminary, four from the United Church Seminary, four from Luther Seminary, and two from Red Wing Seminary, roughly matching the numbers of permanent professors at the former institutions. There was a bit of a problem to begin with, as there were actually five professors at the United Church Seminary, but this problem was eased when Stub, one of the four Luther Seminary faculty, was elected president of the NLCA. Stub proposed that his position, one of the four allotted to the Norwegian Synod, be instead filled by the fifth professor from the United Church Seminary. So the initial ten faculty lined up this way:

United Church: Marcus Bøckman, Erik Johnsen, Carl Weswig, M. J. Stolee, J. N. Kildahl

Norwegian Synod: Johan T. Ylvisaker, Olaf Brandt, Elling Hove

Hauge Synod: Mons Wee, Gustav Bruce

John Dahle, of the United Church Seminary, continued his role as instructor of hymnody and chanting. Bøckman was selected as the president of the new institution and Ylvisaker as the vice president. But the academic year had barely begun when Ylvisaker died and was replaced by Brandt.

Many of the faculty of the new seminary had been teaching for decades by the time of the merger. Ylvisaker was eighty-five and had been teaching since 1879; Bøckman was sixty-six and had been teaching since 1886. Many of the other faculty had been teaching for several decades. Weswig (1906), Wee (1908), Stolee (1911), and Bruce (1911) were the newest of the faculty. As a whole, the faculty had been primarily educated within the Norwegian or Norwegian American world, although many had taken further education in European universities. Some had taken postgraduate work in the United States, including Brandt, Bruce, Stolee, and Wee. Weswig was an exception to this; having consciously avoided the Norwegian American seminaries, he received his theological education at Chicago Lutheran Seminary and the University of Chicago. Of the original ten, only two had been born in America.

The death of Johan Ylvisaker in 1917 was the first change in the faculty but not the last. J. N. Kildahl died in 1920, followed by Erik Johnsen in 1923, and Elling Hove in 1927. These losses severely taxed the remaining faculty, who had to cover the remaining courses. In 1925, Jacob Tanner was added to the faculty from Concordia College in Moorhead, Minnesota, but when he came to the seminary, he was already sixty years old. A series of temporary professors were added in the late 1920s: Rasmus Malmin (1928–1929), Magnus Nodtvedt (1929–1930), and Herman Preus (1930–1936). Preus was elected to a permanent position in 1936. But it is clear that through the 1920s the faculty was older, overtaxed, and represented a much older world than the students who were coming to study at the new seminary. As Roy Harrisville Jr. later recalled:

For however erudite and devout, [the faculty] almost all spoke with a brogue, affected the style of another era (the Prince Albert, wing collar, white bow tie and piping around the vest, the cross of the Order of St. Olav dangling from the neck) and wore facial hair reminiscent of Vienna in the period of the Hapsburgs.[6]

This generation gap was particularly apparent to the students, who were known to complain about their much older professors (some things have not changed). Yet as Harrisville also observed, ironically the older faculty insisted that these students had to encounter and understand the new world of the twentieth century, for the sake of the church and their own ministries. It must be remembered that these older faculty members were highly intelligent men who had given their lives to the Christian ministry; they were not narrow thinkers though they represented an older, immigrant world. There would not be a mandatory retirement age for the seminary professors until 1934, when the NLCA annual convention instituted a retirement age of seventy, to be effective in 1936. As a result, Bøckman and Brandt had to retire in that year, aged eighty-seven and seventy-two, respectively.

As could be imagined, there were bound to be theological tensions within the faculty itself, built as it was from the seminary faculties of three formerly competing denominations. Bøckman and Kildahl had led the Anti-Missouri Brotherhood out of the Norwegian Synod, while Stub, Ylvisaker, and Hove had been leaders of the Synod. The Madison Agreement was maintained, but tensions persisted nonetheless. Wee and Bruce carried the Haugean banner into the new seminary and fought a continuing minority battle to ensure that Haugean theology and traditions would be honored. Wee observed these tensions in 1936, suggesting that some of them were of "a quite serious nature," both from within the seminary and from outside. But, he insisted:

> Not once did the spirit of Christian fellowship fail to function. If we failed to reach a unanimous decision, the voice of the majority prevailed. This spirit of mutual respect and brotherly love has really been very

remarkable in view of the fact that we did, individually, represent quite different church traditions.[7]

Perhaps faculty members were attempting to be peaceful or to present a public united front, but it does seem for all their differences, they did indeed greatly honor the spirit of compromise that brought the NLCA together in 1917.

To a great extent, the faculty were the only employees that the seminary had, and they functioned in a myriad of roles beyond teaching. The faculty rotated the administrative duties among themselves. Beyond the president and vice president of the institution, faculty functioned as secretary, registrar, and librarian. The faculty also spent a great deal of time supervising the students, counseling them, and evaluating them as to their readiness and suitability for the ordained ministry in the NLCA. Work in the denomination itself, as well as among its congregations, was a constant demand, as were duties on various intra-Lutheran organizations, especially the National Lutheran Council (founded in 1918). An informal system for faculty leaves was converted into a regular sabbatical program in 1926, but this was eliminated in 1931 for budgetary reasons during the Depression. There was no dedicated treasurer for the seminary, whose financial business was handled at the NLCA national offices. There was an employee in charge of the buildings and grounds, but not until 1926 were the faculty granted a part-time stenographer, whose work was moved to full-time in 1931, a development for which the faculty declared itself "duly grateful."[8]

THE SEMINARY CURRICULUM AND DEGREE PROGRAMS

There were two main tracks through seminary to ordination, initially labeled the "theoretical" and the "practical" divisions. The theoretical department was for students with a college degree and demonstrated competence in the classical languages, Greek, Hebrew, and Latin. The practical department was for students whose formal educational backgrounds were less complete. The names of these two tracks were changed in 1931 to the "degree" course and the "diploma" course.

All graduates of both programs received a certificate naming them as *Candidatus Theologiae*, but only those in the theoretical/degree course received the bachelor of theology (BTh) degree. The relative size of the two groups can be noted from these statistics: by 1936 some 646 students graduated *Candidatus Theologiae*, but only 185 of these were given the BTh degree.[9] On rare occasions, a student might receive a less formal "certificate of graduation." The seminary also offered a postgraduate bachelor of divinity (BD), later known as the master of theology (MTh), for further theological work. This was granted primarily to students who graduated and then completed a thesis out of residence.

The initial curriculum and degree structure of Luther Theological Seminary did not change much from that of the predecessor seminaries, focusing quite heavily on biblical languages, exegesis, dogmatic theology, history, and preaching. Of the 138 hours initially required for graduation, some 50 of these hours were in Old and New Testament study and exegesis, and this number could be increased if the homiletics courses, which were primarily biblical, were counted. There were six major subjects in the curriculum: Old Testament exegesis, New Testament exegesis, dogmatics, church history, missions, and homiletics, and each of these subjects was taught three hours a week during both semesters. There were enough students that each seminary cohort class was supposed to have its own dedicated courses, although fluctuations in the number of faculty sometimes dictated a modification of this arrangement. Almost immediately this curriculum had to be modified. During the 1920s, additional required subjects were added, including ethics, Christian education, symbolics, and English Bible. The number of minor subjects and electives was actually quite small, with most of the curricular courses being required. Elementary Greek and Hebrew were electives, as it was assumed that students would arrive at the seminary already proficient in these languages and enter the degree program; those without this background were usually destined for the diploma program.

One of the huge problems involving the seminary, especially the curriculum, during the 1920s was the language question. Up to World War I the Norwegian language was widely and primarily used in the Norwegian American congregations as the language of worship, preaching, and instruction. But younger members were pushing hard for greater use of English, and many congregations had English-language worship services as a secondary alternative. In some urban areas, younger Norwegian Americans established "English" Lutheran congregations, and the generational push for the use of English was strong. The transition was rapid: by the middle of the 1920s English had supplanted Norwegian as the primary language of the NLCA, and by 1930 the immigrant language was in steep decline. Of course this transition occasioned quite a bit of tension in the NLCA and its congregations, but it also meant a huge demand for new pastors who were fluent in English.

The language tensions and transitions were very evident in the seminary community. Many of the older professors, especially Bøckman, Ylvisaker, and Johnsen, lectured primarily or exclusively in Norwegian, and in the biblical exegesis courses the immigrant language was the primary language of instruction, at least at first. But from the beginning in 1917, it was recognized that pastoral candidates had to be proficient in English and that no one would be admitted to the seminary who did not have at least a working knowledge of English. It appears that the initial hope was bilingualism, where students would use both Norwegian and English in their studies. But this was fighting against the seemingly inexorable tide of the language transition. In the spring of 1919, the first-year (junior) class of the seminary petitioned that an all-English course of study be implemented by the following year. Given the composition of the faculty at hand this was unworkable, but professors were required to translate their lecture notes into English for their students. Norwegian-language courses and bilingualism soon died, and by 1924 the seminary *Catalog* was reduced to suggesting that students consider the bilingual courses, which were rapidly disappearing. As Wee observed in 1936:

> The faculty has made an earnest effort to encourage students to attend classes in Norse [Norwegian], but with comparatively little success, as many students have either no knowledge of Norse at all, or are very deficient in it. In an effort to increase interest, special Norse evenings have been arranged for once a week.[10]

Increasingly the Norwegian language was becoming a romantic sliver of the past, used for occasional heritage services of the past or for worship with the elderly.

SEMINARY LIFE AND COMMUNITY

The formation of the new seminary came at a pivotal and sometimes difficult time for Lutherans in North America; the years surrounding World War I were some of the most eventful for this denominational family. By the early twentieth century, Lutherans had become the fourth largest denominational family in the United States and were planning the celebration of the four hundredth anniversary of the Reformation in 1917 to publicly mark their arrival on the American scene. The entry of the United States into the European war in April 1917 derailed these plans, as a wave of anti-German and anti-foreign xenophobia swept the country. Still mainly operating in their European languages, immigrant Lutheran groups (including the NLCA) were targets of suspicion and hostility. Though they hurried to declare their loyalty to the war effort and made public professions of their support by buying war bonds, these Lutherans faced public pressure and legislative efforts to disenfranchise them, especially over their continued use of the Norwegian language. Though the German-ethnic denominations fared the worst, all Lutherans were suspect by extension. On top of all this came the great influenza epidemic of 1918–1919, which further added to social instability.

American Lutherans mobilized to meet the wartime challenge, especially to provide ministry to the troops at training bases in the United States and in camps in Europe. In 1917 Lutherans formed their first cooperative organization to meet this challenge, the National Lutheran Commission on Soldiers and Sailors Welfare (NLCSSW). Luther Seminary was directly touched by the war, as seminarians were drafted or joined the effort. Twenty-three of the incoming students in 1917 entered into military service, and subsequent classes contained numbers of returning veterans. Many of them never did get overseas, but a few saw combat: John Erickson, Sten Severtson, and Enoch Tetlie fought in France, while others served in the navy or in the postwar occupation of Germany. The faculty also did their part. Carl Weswig was a camp pastor at the Great Lakes Naval Training Station 1917–1918, and M. J. Stolee was sent by the NLCSSW to France in 1919 and later did relief work in Eastern Europe under the auspices of the newly formed National Lutheran Council (NLC).

Back at home the new seminary attempted to consolidate its life on the St. Anthony Park campus. The Main building (later to be named Bockman Hall) contained the vast majority of the campus—the classrooms, offices, chapel, dorm rooms, and dining facilities were all contained in this single building. Unmarried students, at this time the vast majority of the community, lived in rooms in the Main building. The president and a number of the professors lived in houses that ringed the campus. The decision to abandon the Hamline building, along with the growth of the student body, meant that the Main building was overcrowded. The student body, initially at around 100 students, grew by the end of the decade to 150 students. The number of classrooms was inadequate, for example, and courses had to be staggered to accommodate them. There was no dedicated space for the library and no librarian (the position rotated among the faculty), so the library books were scattered across six different rooms in the building. Later, students were employed as assistant librarians. During the 1920s, a third story was added to the center wing of the Main building to allow for more living and dining space, but this was the only addition to the size of the campus. Repeatedly the seminary requested the NLCA for funds to build a library building. In 1930 the denomination finally allowed a campaign to fund a new building, but the Depression scuttled these plans, and the library-classroom building (now Gullixson Hall) was not built until after World War II.

In spite of the fact that the new seminary was short of both space and faculty, the students who lived on campus, and the faculty who educated and supervised them, seemed to create a vibrant and energetic community. The student body as a whole was mainly drawn from the colleges of the NLCA, which then included Luther, St. Olaf, Concordia, Augustana (Sioux Falls), Pacific Lutheran, and Waldorf. There was no shortage of college rivalries, and sometimes even theological rivalries, among the alumni of these institutions, which certainly enlivened the life of the institution. Right after World War I, there were a number of returning veterans among the student body, older and more experienced than the usual students entering right out of college. Given that at this time there was a significant shortage of pastors in the growing NLCA, many students were employed by congregations on a temporary or part-time basis, especially over the summers and during school breaks. Some students regularly traveled significant distances on the train to serve congregations on the weekends, providing continual pastoral leadership for smaller or struggling congregations.

As was typical in academic communities during this period, the students formed a rich social and cultural life at Luther Seminary. There were no dining facilities operated by the seminary itself, so students ran and took their meals from a cooperative boarding club. If the meals were not *haute cuisine*, they were at least adequate to sustain life. There was also a cooperative laundry and bookstore. Students formed various academic and vocational groups, focusing on theological and missiological subjects and enlivening the campus. The spiritual life of the community revolved around daily chapel, along with various formal and informal prayer groups. Special weeks of spiritual emphasis were regularly a part of the school year. But the students also had fun—sometimes too much fun in the minds of their faculty guardians, who tried to keep a watchful eye on the spiritual development of the students. There were two campus musical organizations, formed by Professor Dahle and directed by students, including a Seminary Choir that toured to NLCA congregations around the upper Midwest.

LUTHER SEMINARY, 1930–1945

The next chapter of the history of Luther Seminary begins with the election of a new president and faculty member for the institution in 1930, Thaddeus Franke Gullixson. He replaced the then eighty-one-year-old Marcus Bøckman as president, although Bøckman continued to teach at the seminary until 1936. Gullixson served as president of the seminary from 1930 to 1954, overseeing an eventful quarter-century defined by the Depression, World War II, and the postwar boom. During Gullixson's tenure, the seminary faculty was completely replaced by a newer generation of teachers and scholars, and the school's transition to a fully American seminary was completed. Gullixson himself was a theological conservative out of the old Norwegian Synod confessional tradition. It is reputed that in 1917 he almost left the synod for the new breakaway group but that later he came to firmly identify with the NLCA and the theological compromise that was forged in that denomination. He was characterized by a later faculty member as being a remarkable leader with "an overriding theological conservatism and churchly pietism."[11] But despite his innate conservatism he was not bound to the past and brought in new faculty from a range of theological traditions and backgrounds, including the first non–Norwegian Americans to become faculty members. He was also a representative of the NLCA at the meetings of American and international Lutherans, and to the larger merger negotiations of the mid-twentieth century.

Once in office, Gullixson faced an aging and depleted faculty and a denomination weakened by economic depression. The NLCA had expanded its congregational base numerically and geographically during the 1920s, but most of these new congregations (and many others) were dependent on financial support from the Home Missions committee. Though the Great Depression is traditionally reckoned to have begun in October 1929, there had been a serious economic depression in rural America all through the 1920s, with a crash in commodity prices after the expansions of World War I. The NLCA was heavily rural in nature, so this financial weakness put serious strains on the denominational budget, which the stock market crash and general Depression made even worse. Many of the departments of the NLCA ran substantial deficits during the 1920s, and the denomination relied on lines of credit from Minneapolis banks to maintain its programs. When the crash hit and income from the congregations declined drastically, the NLCA was in a perilous financial condition that required substantial budget reductions. In 1934, for example, the Home Missions board had an accumulated deficit of $261,000.[12] Although Luther Seminary itself was in decent financial condition, it was dependent on the NLCA for almost all of its funding and saw a decline in funding during the 1930s. There was also a decline in student enrollment during the Depression, though this had less of a financial impact, as students at the time paid very little (if anything) for their seminary education.

Including Gullixson, there were eight faculty members at Luther Seminary in 1930, six of whom were original faculty. A series of retirements caused a turnover in faculty during the 1930s and 1940s.

RETIRED	NEW FACULTY
Marcus Bøckman (1936)	Herman A. Preus (1936)
Olaf Brandt (1936)	George Aus (1938)
Jacob Tanner (1938)	John Milton (1941)
Mons Wee (1941)	Rolf Syrdal (1941)
Carl Weswig (1946)	Iver Iversen (1944)
Gustav Bruce (1949)	Robert Boyd (1946)

Thus by the end of the 1940s the faculty had been completely replaced, and Gullixson, who began in 1930, was now the longest-serving professor.

These new faculty were of the next generation in outlook and temperament. They were mostly born in America (Iversen was the exception) and educated in American educational institutions, with some additional study abroad. In choosing John Milton for the Bible position in 1941, Gullixson made a controversial choice; Milton was a Swedish American and educated in the Augustana Synod. This choice caused considerable grumbling within the NLCA, and some asked whether there was not some competent Norwegian American to fill the position.[13] But Gullixson was not afraid of reaching out for distinctive persons for his faculty, something that was evident in the selections of Herman Preus and George Aus, who came to represent new variations on some old theological controversies; in them, the old "first form, second form" debate was reborn for a new century.

Herman Preus was a descendant of the original founders of the Norwegian Synod and a well-educated scholar, having taken a law degree before studying at universities in Edinburgh, Oslo, Paris, and Tübingen. He represented not only the confessional tradition of the Norwegian Synod but also the passion with which correct theology was conducted and appreciated. He came to Luther Seminary in 1936 as professor of New Testament, symbolics, and liturgy. He was a champion of the "first form" of the question of election. George Aus represented the broad theological tradition of the United Church, was equally well educated but mainly in American institutions, including General Theological Seminary and Biblical Seminary in New York, and had a doctoral degree in education from New York University. Equally intense, Aus was quite interested in both the Lutheran confessional tradition and the new twentieth-century theologians, such as Aulén, Barth, and the Niebuhrs, among others. Appointed as professor of dogmatics in 1938, he was a partisan of the "second form." Almost immediately, these two very distinctive men with different theological positions came into conflict, and this conflict soon roiled the seminary. As one history recalls this situation in the 1940s:

> The hostilities reached to the students who gleefully engaged, urging Aus against Preus, and vice versa, tacking their own bulletin boards with arguments pro and con, up to the wee hours preparing for the next morning's melee—until Gullixson, aghast at the carnage, summoned the chief protagonists and ordered them to cease and desist.[14]

The conflict between these two professors and their partisans continued during the 1940s, until NLCA president J. A. Aasgaard had to appoint a committee to examine the fracas. This group returned a report reaffirming the 1912 Madison Agreement and found that there was "no essential disagreement" between the two.[15] Though the conflict subsided somewhat, it was a constant tension at Luther Seminary for the next several decades; Preus taught at Luther until 1967 and Aus remained there until 1973.

The other major question within the faculty, and within the NLCA as a whole, involved the question of biblical interpretation and the authority of Scripture. As has been seen, the Luther Seminary curriculum was heavily weighted toward the study of the Bible, and so these questions were at the front and center of seminary life. They also arose in the context of the larger debate on the Bible and biblical authority that was raging among American Protestants in the first half of the twentieth century, with the concurrent rise of higher biblical criticism and the fundamentalist rebuke to this method. During the 1920s and 1930s the fundamentalist-modernist controversy was being fought within the mainline Protestant denominations, causing conflicts and schisms. In no way were American Lutherans, and the NLCA in particular, theological modernists, nor did they practice higher biblical criticism. Yet for the most part, perhaps aside from the Missouri Synod, American Lutherans were also not fundamentalists in the classic sense; they were trying to maintain a classic and conservative Lutheran understanding of the authority of Scripture and trying to render this into the English language.[16] The trouble was in their choice of language and terminology to express their views on biblical authority, especially the English-language terms *inerrancy* and *infallibility*. It is not clear that they used these terms with the same meaning as the fundamentalists, for whom these words were crucial.

Hans Stub and others in the NLCA urged the use of the terms *inerrant* and *infallible* in the Chicago-Minneapolis theses (1919–1925), and they were employed in a number of other documents. The wider use of these terms implied that the Bible was free from any error whatsoever (historical, geographical, scientific, etc.) and not just theological or doctrinal error. But it appears that many American Lutherans would in fact limit the inerrancy of the Bible solely to theological and doctrinal matters. The faculty at Luther Seminary, nearly all of whom taught the Bible in some form or another, were conservative and cautious in their understanding of the truth and authority of Scripture, and there was a long tradition of influence among them from the Princeton School (Hodge and Warfield), which held that God's direct verbal and plenary inspiration ensured that the Bible was inerrant, at least in its original writings.[17] There was some contention among the various Luther faculty on elements of this; some tried to avoid the more mechanistic elements of this theory, allowing for variant readings and for the human personality of the writers to have a place in the Scripture writing. The question of whether the inerrancy of Scripture extended beyond its theological and doctrinal elements was also a source of contention. Roy Harrisville observes of the faculty:

> If Luther's biblical faculty never applied to itself the epithet "fundamen-

talist," seeking to steer its little bark clear of the rocks and reefs of a rationalistic interpretation of faith, whether to the right or left, its defense of the satisfaction theory, or Christ's bodily resurrection, and its animus toward Darwinism gave it a cast reminiscent of fundamentalism—at least to those for whom the term "Lutheran" suggested no distinctive ethos.[18]

Two things seem very apparent in all this: first, that they held to a high view of biblical authority in a classic Lutheran sense, and second, that they struggled to find the correct terms in English to express this. Change in the biblical area came slowly at Luther Seminary, and the new insights about the biblical texts brought about by higher biblical criticism were only very slowly and cautiously entertained. The arrival of John Milton in 1941 provided a transition of sorts; at the beginning of his career he was opposed to the new biblical criticism, but later in life he was somewhat more open to it. Milton eventually provided the cautious opening to higher biblical criticism that others would continue in the 1960s.

THE DEVELOPMENT OF SEMINARY LIFE

The educational life of a seminarian in the 1930s was generally laid out in fairly rigid schedule. Students were sent to Luther Seminary with the endorsement of their local pastor and with the approval of the faculty. The students showed up at the seminary in the fall (or whenever they could make it), found a vacant bed in the Main building, and located friends and acquaintances from college. Students usually arrived at seminary the fall after they graduated from college and moved through seminary as a cohort; if things went well (and sometimes they did not) they graduated three years later. There was no agonizing over course selection, as the curriculum was almost entirely prescribed, and there was little room for elective subjects. Students paid no tuition, as their education was provided by the NLCA, but they were responsible for the costs of room and board and other miscellaneous fees. During these hard economic times, students would stay in seminary as long as their money held out, and as long as they could find work to support themselves, usually summer employment in congregations if they could find it. Some students had to withdraw for periods of time because their funds ran out. Life in the Main building was rather spartan, and students tried to stretch their limited resources as best they could.

This is not to say that life at the seminary was dull; students found ways of both taking their education seriously and still finding enjoyment in the process. The theological disputes among the faculty and within the NLCA filtered down into the seminarians, some of whom became partisans of one position or another. Students also developed many community groups, especially formal and informal organizations to consider the theological, missiological, and spiritual aspects of their intended calling. It was quite literally a brotherhood. All the students were men, virtually all unmarried, and they slept and ate, studied, and went to class in a single building. Married students were a rarity, usually older men who were going to seminary after working out in the world for a number of years. Formal engagements to be married were frowned upon, but breaking an engagement was cause for dismissal from the seminary. Some seminarians had "understandings" with young women about future marriage plans but generally kept these arrangements private. Toward the end of their educational career, students were expected to find a call, graduate, and find a wife in rather short order, for it was expected that a pastor would have a wife who would be an (unpaid) extension of his congregational ministry.

A major change to the rhythms of seminary life came during the depths of the Depression, in the middle of the 1930s: the addition of an internship year between the second and last year of coursework. The internship experience originated in another American Lutheran seminary, the Swedish American Augustana Seminary in Rock Island, Illinois. Titled the Bergendoff plan after its originator, seminary president Conrad Bergendoff, this plan entailed the seminarians leaving seminary after the first two years of study, working in a Lutheran parish during the third year, and then returning for a fourth and final year of classes. The pedagogical explanation for this change was that it was necessary for students, most of whom had come to seminary directly from college, to have a sustained experience working as a pastor in a congregation. But there was another reason for this change at this time: in the depths of the Great Depression, many congregations were without pastors (and the funds to pay them), and too many graduating seminarians could not find a call. This internship year provided pastoral leadership to vacant congregations and stretched out the seminary process, thus reducing the number of students who graduated without call. In 1934, the NLCA annual convention voted to require this change in the seminary process, and the internship requirement was instituted for the 1935/36 academic year.

Of course, this male-dominated community of faculty and students was supported by the efforts of the women who were linked to the community.[19] Most important were the wives of the faculty, who marshaled their efforts to assist the "boys" living in the Main building. The faculty wives provided support and aid to the seminarians as best they could, beginning an informal group of "friends" of Luther Seminary that would later become a formal organization. The congregational women's mission societies of the Norwegian American denominations, and later the NLCA, provided material support for the seminary and the seminarians. A group of younger NLCA women gathered in 1928 to form the Lutheran Daughters of the Reformation (LDR), with the purpose of supporting home and foreign missions. Their important contribution to Luther Seminary was the eventual purchase of buildings adjacent to the seminary for the use of furloughed and returning foreign missionaries. The presence of these missionaries in the wider seminary community widened the scope of the ministry of the school itself and was an additional spur to students to consider calls to the overseas missions of the NLCA.

A strong emphasis on missions was characteristic of the NLCA, a focus that it had inherited from the three denominations that constituted it in 1917. Each of the three had denominational mission societies and separate (usually larger) women's mission societies, as well as independent mission groups, such as the China Mission Society and the Zion Society for Israel. When the NLCA was formed in 1917 it consolidated these efforts, and the women of the church founded their own unified Women's Missionary Fellowship. Norwegian Americans had already been active in home missions, establishing new congregations in an ever-widening geographical circle of North America as immigrants moved to new areas. In the late nineteenth century, Norwegian Americans also began to enter foreign mission work in China, Madagascar, and South Africa, at first in cooperation with groups in Norway and then independently.

This emphasis on missions was also a hallmark of Luther Seminary as an extension of efforts in the NLCA community. Seminary students were naturally involved in home mission expansion efforts, both in their summers and in part-time employment during the academic year. Many of the first calls extended to seminarians were in mission congregations around the country, both because the young men were energetic and enthusiastic and because they were relatively less expensive to employ. Students organized a mission society of their own at Luther Seminary, chiefly to learn more about mission work and to make it a priority within the community.

One of the key proponents of foreign missions at Luther was Professor M. J. Stolee, who had joined the United Church faculty in 1911 and taught at Luther Seminary until 1941. Stolee was a missionary in Madagascar between 1901 and 1909, and the work of foreign missions was near and dear to his heart. During his thirty years of seminary teaching, Stolee taught courses on missions of all kind and was the central advocate for foreign mission activity within the seminary community, along with his wife, Martha, who was similarly committed to this work. When Stolee retired in 1941, the NLCA annual convention recognized the importance of this work to the life of the seminary and selected Pastor Rolf Syrdal to succeed him. Syrdal had been a missionary in China between 1929 and 1936 and had also taught at St. Olaf College. Syrdal taught at Luther Seminary until 1946, when he was called to the denominational headquarters as the executive in charge of world missions. Stolee and Syrdal formed a continuing tradition of teaching missions at Luther Seminary that continued through the rest of the twentieth century.

The difficulties of the Depression years were replaced by a new and different set of difficulties during the American participation in World War II (1941–1945). The seminary process, which had been lengthened during the depression by the addition of the internship year, now needed to be compressed to meet wartime necessities. Pastors were urgently needed for congregations, in part because NLCA pastors were entering military service as chaplains and also because there was a continuing shortage of pastors. The seminary students also had to justify to themselves, and to a skeptical public, why they should be allowed to stay at home and study while other young men of their age were serving in the military. The course of instruction continued throughout the whole twelve months of the year, with no time off in the summers. Students went to school continuously, both to get them out into the parishes as soon as possible but also to enable them to maintain their exemption from the draft. The internship requirement was actually suspended 1944–1945, and a large class (eighty-five students) was graduated in January 1945. A number of seminarians did leave for military service, and many others postponed their seminary studies for the duration of the war.

LUTHER SEMINARY, 1945–1963

From 1930 to 1945, the situation at Luther Seminary had been anything but normal, with the economic difficulties of the Great Depression followed by the wartime issues of 1941–1945. During this generation in seminary life, challenges pushed the seminary and its people to adapt. People had put many parts of their lives on hold "for the duration." At the end of the war in 1945, there was a strong desire in the country for things to return to normal. But the postwar era brought with it a whole new set of challenges and opportunities. Normal, it seems, would have to wait a bit longer.

One of the biggest challenges for the seminary was the flood of new students who wanted to enter theological study after World War II. Enrollment in the seminary had dipped during the middle of the Depression but had rebounded to around 150 students on the eve of World War II. By the end of Gullixson's presidency in 1954, the total enrollment had surged to around four hundred students a year. Although these numbers were an issue unto themselves, the composition of the student body was also changing. Many of the new students were older—men who had served in the armed forces during the war or who had worked in defense plants. Not only were they older, but many of them were married or soon to be married. The predominant "bachelor days" of the seminary were now a thing of the past. Housing for married students and even families was now a pressing issue. These men were often very serious students and in quite a rush to get through seminary and out into the parishes.

Pastors were also very much needed in the parishes of the church, renamed the Evangelical Lutheran Church (ELC) in 1946. Dropping the word *Norwegian* from the name of the denomination was a bit controversial and had to be finessed by church leaders, but it represented the truth: this was no longer an immigrant or even a hyphenated denomination but a wholly American church body in the Lutheran tradition. And it was an expanding denomination, growing rapidly and moving outside of its traditional upper-midwestern territory. After the war Americans were on the move, with great numbers moving to the southern and western states or leaving cities for fast-growing new suburban areas. Like many of its Lutheran denominational partners, the ELC was founding mission congregations in these new areas as fast as they could. Together, the American Lutheran denominations were establishing hundreds of new congregations to serve the new "baby boom" (1946–1964), and existing congregations grew as well. There was an incredible need for pastors to serve these congregations and to replace the older generation of pastors, many of whom had extended their ministries because of the Depression and war and now needed to retire.

Of course, all this growth put a huge strain on the personnel and facilities of Luther Seminary, which had operated so long on an economy of scarcity. One of the first things to do was to replace older faculty members and expand the faculty as a whole. Although six new professors had been added to the faculty in the period 1938–1946, there was a desperate need for more faculty members. Andrew Burgess replaced Rolf Syrdal in 1947, and Warren Quanbeck was added in New Testament and systematics. Gullixson welcomed two displaced Latvian professors, Edmund Smits and Janis Rozentals, in 1950, and in 1952 the church convention agreed to expand the faculty to twelve permanent positions. Added soon thereafter was Laurence Field (practical theology), E. Clifford Nelson (church history), and John Victor Halvorson (Old Testament). More permanent and temporary faculty would be added through the 1950s as the student body expanded, from fifteen faculty in 1954 to twenty-one in 1959. This faculty expansion was also necessary because of outside pressure from accrediting agencies that warned that the postwar student-faculty ratio (then thirty to one) was jeopardizing the seminary's accreditation. But in addition to increasing the number of faculty, the seminary enhanced the quality of the education offered. These new teachers were well trained in the leading graduate schools of North America and Europe, most of them with the PhD degree, and they expanded the seminary's contact with Christian communities around the world. Even so, however, they had been raised in the denomination itself and knew its people and its ways.

With the expansion of the student body and the faculty came a need for a more formal structure of administration. Initially a faculty member had served as registrar of the school, which was a relatively easy task because almost all the courses were sequential and required. But as the curriculum became more complex, additional assistance was needed in this office. A growing faculty needed additional tending, and E. Clifford Nelson was selected as the first dean of the faculty in 1961. Faculty also later served in the positions of dean of students and dean of graduate education. A separate business office was established in 1956, as was another new expectation, tuition, which was initially $200 a year. The old simplicity of a community of scholars and students was giving way to a professionalized educational institution.

The man who led this transition was the new seminary president, Alvin N. Rogness, who was elected in 1955 at the church convention in a contested election, winning over faculty member George Aus.[20] Rogness was an experienced pastor serving one of the largest congregations in the ELC and widely known as a preacher and denominational leader. He was also known as a skillful and diplomatic administrator whose talents were sorely needed in the periods of growth and turmoil of the 1950s and 1960s. (He served as president for twenty years, until 1974.) As someone quite in touch with the rank-and-file pastors of the ELC, Rogness was able to preside over the transformation of the seminary while smoothing the ruffled feathers of those who were worried about the changes at the seminary of the denomination.

It would take all of his skills to get the ELC to approve (and pay for) the dramatic expansion of the seminary, both in terms of faculty and administration, as well as its physical plant. There was no question that the old Main building, initially occupied in 1902, was wholly inadequate to house the seminary. In 1930 President Gullixson had gotten initial approval for a fund drive to construct a library-classroom building, but this was shelved indefinitely through the Depression and war. In 1943, as a part of the NLCA's Centennial Drive, funds were finally dedicated to this new building, which opened in 1949, just in time for the postwar boom. But this was just the beginning of the expansion of the campus. In 1954, ELC president J. A. Aasgaard (soon to be retired) pushed the denomination to approve another fund drive to renovate the Main building, with the balance of funds remaining to be applied to other building projects. The churchwide appeal raised $1.5 million, and renovations on the Main building began.

The money arrived just in time for a golden opportunity, and a bargain one at that. Just down the hill from Luther Seminary, at Como and Hendon Avenues, was the campus of Breck School, a private secondary school affiliated with the Protestant Episcopal Church. Breck was also flourishing at the time, had outgrown its present campus, and was seeking to build a new and larger facility in Minneapolis. In 1955, Luther Seminary acquired two buildings and thirty-seven acres of land from the Breck School at a cost of $800,000. The buildings would be used for additional dormitory and chapel space; perhaps more importantly, the land allowed for further expansion. The buildings became named after prominent leaders in the Norwegian American denominations: the Main building became Bockman Hall; the library, Gullixson Hall; the Breck dormitory, Stub Hall; and the Breck Chapel, Aasgaard Hall. Eventually a cluster of ninety-six apartments were built on the land, and the complex was named after T. O. Burntvedt, president of the Lutheran Free Church. Almost overnight, the size of the seminary campus had dramatically expanded. A much larger administration was now needed to care for such a campus.

A DIVERSIFYING SEMINARY COMMUNITY

One significant aspect of the expanding seminary community and faculty was the diversification and specialization of the instructional curriculum. Along with the professionalization of the faculty, with their graduate school PhD degrees, came a parallel emphasis on the professionalization of the clergy, especially by means of the seminary curriculum. The postwar push in American theological education was to train and position parish clergy as professionals, on par with the doctors and lawyers in the community. To achieve this, seminary students had to have specialized and professional instruction in areas such as pastoral care, educational theory, homiletics and public speaking, and church leadership and management, among other disciplines. The social scientific disciplines took their place alongside Bible, theology, apologetics, and history, to the chagrin of those who championed the classical seminary curriculum. In the late 1950s, new faculty in the field of practical theology were added, including Frederic Norstad in pastoral care, Gerhard Frost in Christian education, and Arndt Halvorson in homiletics. The faculty increasingly specialized, teaching in specific areas of the curriculum and organizing into divisions. As valuable as these changes might have been, there was a danger in them as well. As Rogness later reflected:

> The gap between the professional language of theology and the language of the people widened. The students, better equipped with the professional language of modern scholarship than an earlier generation, nonetheless faced as pastors a more difficult task of translating the language of the "fraternity" into the language of the people.[21]

The education was certainly technically better and addressed contemporary issues, but some wondered aloud if the theological and biblical core of the seminary education was losing ground.

One important traditional area that grew in strength during the 1950s was that of missions, and especially world missions, under the energetic leadership of faculty member Andrew Burgess. This had always been a special emphasis of the NLCA, but now in the 1950s it had its own place in the seminary curriculum with additional and specific courses in the curriculum dedicated to this field. This was equally an expansive time for world missions in American Lutheranism in general, as North Americans were taking the lead in world missions from the European Lutherans, who, after World War II, did not have the money or personnel to continue the mission activities that they had previously begun. There had long been a mission society among the seminary students, but now its activities were augmented by the presence of furloughed missionaries and mission leaders from overseas. Burgess led student mission trips to countries in Latin America, so seminarians could see the mission fields for themselves. There is no specific count of the number of Luther Seminary students who took calls in the mission fields abroad, but in the 1950s the ELC was sending out considerable numbers of new missionaries every year.

More than this, the world was coming to Luther Seminary, in the persons of Latin American, African, and Asian Lutheran students and pastors who came to study in Saint Paul each year. There were, for example, twelve such international students in 1956/57 and sixteen in 1961/62, bringing an increasing diversity to the student body and to seminary life.[22] International students from Luther returned to their home countries to provide leadership to their churches and built a continuing relationship between those countries and Luther Seminary. This tradition of interchange became a hallmark of Luther Seminary in the postwar years and a continuing tradition into the twenty-first century.

Another source of increasing diversity among the seminary community was the presence of women on campus, not yet as students but as the wives of seminarians. The presence of married students on campus transformed the institution; if it was not yet a coeducational institution, then neither was it the bachelor, quasi-monastic community of the prewar era. These young seminary wives were capable and often well-educated women, and many of them were equally dedicated to the ministries to which their husbands were being called. After the war, these young women began the Seminary Wives Organization at Luther Seminary to network among themselves and to learn about how they could assist in the future ministry of their husbands, guided by the wives of the faculty members. Though it may seem old-fashioned, at this period of time pastors' wives played an important role in their husbands' ministries, and the experience of the faculty wives was crucial to helping these young women in dealing with such expectations. This organization also was instrumental in planning social events for the entire seminary community, including a Christmas party and fall and spring activities.[23] The women of the Friends of Luther Seminary and the Lutheran Daughters of the Reformation continued to make very important contributions to the life and ethos of the seminary.

THE 1960 MERGER AND THE FORMATION OF THE AMERICAN LUTHERAN CHURCH

Almost as soon as the various ethnic Lutheran denominations made the transition to the use of the English language in the 1920s, the question arose as to the continuing need for so many separate American Lutheran denominations. By 1930, the number of such denominations had been reduced to about ten, eight of which were in the National Lutheran Council (NLC); the other two, the Missouri Synod and Wisconsin Synod, in the Synodical Conference. But the path to further mergers and unification was a complicated one, involving complex theological and organizational challenges. In essence, there were two larger denominations among the ten, the United Lutheran Church in America (ULCA) and the Missouri Synod, each at about 1.5 million members. These two represented the ends of a theological spectrum. In between were seven American Lutheran denominations, all a part of the NLC, and together they represented approximately an additional 1.5 million members. The ELC was one of these seven denominations.

The ULCA and the Missouri Synod each represented distinctive and very different theological positions and approaches to church fellowship and merger. The ULCA was very open to the American religious world and held that as long as there were agreements in theological essentials, denominations could work together in ministry. The Missouri Synod, on the other hand, insisted that before there could be any cooperation or fellowship (let alone merger), there had to be complete theological agreement between the groups. Missouri did not trust the ULCA and felt that its theological claims to being Lutheran were suspect; the ULCA rejected the preconditions for fellowship and merger that were established by Missouri.

For the groups in the middle, including the ELC, the question was which direction to head. In any merger process that included the ULCA, Missouri would probably not participate. But to exclude the ULCA seemed uncharitable and might not result in agreement with Missouri anyway. When the merger negotiations among the American Lutherans began in earnest toward the end of World War II, this basic conundrum split the seven denominations and resulted in not one but two merger processes. The Augustana Synod held out for including the ULCA, and thus walked out of merger negotiations with the ELC and others in 1952. Augustana and the ULCA, along with a Danish and Finnish group, formed the Lutheran Church in America (1962–1988).

The ELC, Luther Seminary's denomination, continued the older merger negotiations with another Danish group, the Lutheran Free Church, and the American Lutheran Church (ALC, 1930–1960), the latter representing Midwestern German Lutherans of the old Ohio, Iowa, Buffalo, and Texas synods. The merger of these groups into the American Lutheran Church occurred in 1960, although it was not until 1963 that the Free Church officially joined. In this merger, then, the tradition of a singular and ethnic Norwegian American Lutheranism came to an end. Luther Seminary, born in the Norwegian merger of 1917 and the sole seminary of that merged church, now found itself as one of several seminaries of the newly formed ALC. Luther's identity was still predominantly tied to its traditional constituency, the Norwegian American Lutheran congregations, especially in the upper Midwest, but now it was a part of a bigger American Lutheran world.

Notes

1. Officially, the United Norwegian Lutheran Church (1890–1917), the Synod for the Norwegian Evangelical Lutheran Church in America (1853–1917), and Hauge's Norwegian Evangelical Lutheran Church in America (1846–1917).

2. The smaller groups included the Lutheran Free Church, formed out of the United Church in 1897; the Church of the Lutheran Brethren,

formed in 1900; the Norwegian Synod of the American Evangelical Lutheran Church, formed in 1918 out of the Norwegian Synod; and the Evangelical Lutheran Church in America, the original Eielsen group from 1843. The Free Church was the largest of these four groups but still rather small.

3. As the distinguished historian of Norwegian American Lutheranism E. Clifford Nelson explained the Madison Agreement, it "can best be described as the instrument of an ecclesiastical rapprochement rather than as an astute and flawless display of theological finality . . . the victory of heart over head. " Nelson and Fevold, *Lutheran Church*, 2:181.

4. On the continuation of the Haugean tradition in the new NLCA and at Luther Seminary, see Thomas Jacobson, "Hauge's Norwegian Evangelical Lutheran Synod in America and the Continuation of the Haugean Spirit in Twentieth-Century American Lutheranism" (PhD diss., Luther Seminary, 2018). To a reasonable extent, their fears were justified.

5. The Haugeans assumed that there was an understanding that the academy in Red Wing would continue to be supported by the NLCA and would serve as a continuing institutional center for the Haugean movement in America. This was the case for the first fifteen years, but in 1932, during the Depression, the NLCA cut off this funding and merged it into Augustana College in Sioux Falls, South Dakota. Many in the Haugean wing of the church saw this as a betrayal. See *Shall Red Wing Seminary Be Closed?* (Red Wing, MN: Red Wing Printing Company, [1932?]).

6. Roy Harrisville Jr., "Interpreting the Scriptures," in Quanbeck, Fevold, and Frost, *Striving for Ministry*, 127.

7. M. O. Wee, "Along the Years Together," in *Luther Theological Seminary St. Paul, Minnesota, 1876–1936.* Sixtieth Anniversary Service at the Twelfth General Convention of the Norwegian Lutheran Church of America, June 6, 1936, 31.

8. Wee, "Along the Years Together," 30.

9. Wee, "Along the Years Together," 47.

10. Wee, "Along the Years Together," 26.

11. E. Clifford Nelson, *Lutheranism in North America, 1914–1970* (Minneapolis: Augsburg, 1972), 86.

12. Nelson and Fevold, *Lutheran Church*, 2:261.

13. The debate over this appointment were summarized by the editor of the NLCA periodical. *Lutheran Herald* 24, no. 26 (June 25, 1940): 669. Milton had, however, been already teaching at Augsburg Seminary, so

apparently he carried some sort of ethnic credentials.

14. Roy Harrisville Jr., "Luther Theological Seminary, 1876–1976," in Gonnerman, *Thanksgiving and Hope*, 47.
15. Letter to J. A. Aasgaard from the committee, April 8, 1948, quoted in Fevold, "Laying Foundations," 39. It was the decision of this committee that reportedly led brothers J. A. O. Preus and Robert Preus to leave the NLCA for the "Little Norwegian" Synod and from there the Missouri Synod.
16. Mark Granquist, "The Scripture Controversy in American Lutheranism: Infallibility, Inerrancy, Inspiration," in *Rightly Handling the Word of Truth: Scripture, Canon, and Creed*, ed. Carl E. Braaten (Delhi, NY: ALPB Books, 2015), 71–88.
17. Harrisville, "Luther Theological Seminary," 43–45.
18. Harrisville, "Interpreting the Scriptures," 133–34.
19. Grindal, "Role of Women," 83–92.
20. The fact that Aus was one party to the ongoing theological struggle within the seminary may well have moved some in the church to support Rogness as an outsider and perhaps as a peacemaker.
21. Alvin N. Rogness, "Reflections on Theological Education in a Turbulent Time," in Quanbeck, Fevold, and Frost, *Striving for Ministry*, 57.
22. James Burtness, "Reaching Out in World Missions," in Quanbeck, Fevold, and Frost, *Striving for Ministry*, 182.
23. Grindal, "Role of Women," 87.

The so-called Octagon House was home of the Norwegian Lutheran Seminary, Madison, Wisconsin (1878–1888).

Augsburg Seminary professors Sven Oftedal (1873–1904), George Sverdrup (1874–1907), and Sven Gunnerson (1874–1883) joined the faculty soon after the school erected its building (1872–1902) in the Cedar-Riverside neighborhood of Minneapolis.

Marcus Olaus Bøckman was professor and president of United Church Seminary (1893–1917) and president of Luther Seminary (1917–1930).

Gallery

United Church Seminary students posed for a photo in a classroom of Old Main (1905/06).

Luther Seminary faculty gathered for a photo sometime after 1917.

Luther Seminary students interrupted studies for a snowball fight (1906).

After Luther Seminary's building in Robbinsdale, Minnesota, was destroyed by fire in 1895, the synod treasurer began soliciting donations using a chain letter. Each donor was asked to "give ten cents in coin . . . to get a new Seminary."

Gallery

Extracurricular activities at Luther Seminary included the Norwegian Synod Glee Club (1903/04).

United Church Seminary's Old Main, later named Bockman Hall, included classrooms, offices, a chapel, dorm rooms, and dining facilities (here in 1914). The building was made into a dormitory when it was remodeled in 1956.

A HISTORY OF LUTHER SEMINARY

From 1940 to 1967, Northwestern Seminary owned Passavant Hall, formerly the Charles S. Pillsbury home, near the Minneapolis Institute of Arts in South Minneapolis. The seminary campus included a number of additional buildings in the neighborhood.

Some of Northwestern Seminary's South Minneapolis buildings retained their original elegance, visible in the school's chapel (ca. 1950).

Gallery

Northwestern Seminary students and faculty indulged in a long-traditioned Skip Day (1931).

Decades of Luther Seminary students gathered between classes in The Diet, a coffee shop (ca. 1960).

The wives of seminarians together in front of the Wee House (later Wee Care Day Care Center and eventually Global Mission Institute) on the Luther Theological Seminary campus in 1929. Mrs. O. E. Brandt is seated in the middle.

Luther Seminary hosted an all-campus Christmas dinner in Bockman Hall after a new dining service was established in 1978. Guests included Alma Roisum, secretary to seminary presidents Alvin Rogness and Lloyd Svendsbye; Lucille Schleicher, longtime seminary bookkeeper; and Madeline Johnson, business office manager and later Contextual Education office manager.

Gallery

Central Lutheran Church in downtown Minneapolis has hosted Luther Seminary graduation ceremonies for many years (perhaps 1940s).

Luther Seminary's upper campus was once ringed by large houses used for faculty, staff, student housing, and other purposes. In 2018, some of the houses, those between Gullixson Hall and Luther Place, were replaced by a forty-nine-unit senior housing cooperative.

Frederick A. Schiotz (president of the Evangelical Lutheran Church, 1954–1960, and president of the American Lutheran Church, 1960–1970); Alvin N. Rogness (Luther Seminary president, 1954–1974); and Thaddeus F. Gullixson (Luther Seminary president, 1930–1954) assembled for a photo (1972).

In every era, seminary student have poured over books.

Gallery

Terry Boehlke (assistant manager, later manager, 1973–2013) and Jennings Mergenthal (manager, 1966–2003) presided over the Luther Seminary Bookstore when it was located in the basements of Bockman Hall, then Gullixson Hall (here in the 1980s), and later Olson Campus Center.

Generations of students have soaked up ambience and information in the Luther Seminary Library reading room (1973).

Carl A. Volz, Luther Seminary professor of church history (1974–1998), regularly led archeology digs, including a 1978 trip to Caesarea Maritima.

Faculty members Paul Sponheim (systematic theology), Don Juel (New Testament), and Rollie Martinson (pastoral theology and ministry) kneeling in "prayer" during a student/faculty basketball game in the Aasgaard Hall gymnasium (1979).

Gallery

Mary Preus, instructor of New Testament Greek, led a class in Gullixson Hall (1982).

In 1970, two groups of Lutherans in the United States authorized the ordination of women, and by the 2016/17 school year, Luther Seminary's student body was 55 percent women. Here, students practice leading worship.

Northwestern Seminary's Chapel of the Cross was used for campus worship 1967–1984 and later for more intimate worship services and worship classes.

Since the 1984 construction of Olson Campus Center, seminary chapel services and other events have been held in the Chapel of the Incarnation.

Gallery

A sign on the lawn of Bockman Hall reflected the 1982 merger of Luther and Northwestern seminaries.

By 1988 the library card catalog had been moved to computer.

Students from around the world have studied at Luther Seminary (1996/97).

5

Augsburg Seminary, 1890–1963

This chapter will return to the narrative of Augsburg Seminary in Minneapolis as it was left in chapter 3 with the merger that produced the United Norwegian Lutheran Church (1890–1917). We now trace its history from that point forward until the seminary was merged into Luther Seminary in 1963 as a part of the process that resulted in the formation of the American Lutheran Church (1960–1988).

During the 1890s the supporters of Augsburg resisted the formation of the United Norwegian Lutheran Church (UNLC) and its merger of seminaries, fearing the loss of Augsburg's distinctive pedagogical and theological approach. Through ambiguities in its founding legal documents, the Augsburg board was able to legally resist the UNLC and maintain control of Augsburg's property, with professors Sverdrup and Oftedal leading the way. But a seminary needs congregations as "consumers" of its product—that is, pastors—so inevitably the independence of Augsburg Seminary led to the formation of an association of congregations (as they would prefer to call it) that formed into the Lutheran Free Church (LFC) in 1897. Thus, Augsburg and its supporting congregations maintained their independence from the UNLC and did not join in the subsequent merger that produced the Norwegian Lutheran Church in America in 1917.

As is often the case with groups that splinter off at a time of merger, the newly formed Lutheran Free Church did not gather in nearly the number of congregations that they initially expected. The supporters of Augsburg were the main part of the New School party of the Conference,[1] which was reckoned to be the majority of that denomination in 1890. But by 1900 the UNLC had some 130,000 members to 38,000 for the LFC, which suggests that quite a number of the former supporters of Augsburg remained in the UNLC. Although the Lutheran Free Church and Augsburg Seminary remained independent until 1963, changes in both the LFC and Augsburg led to the gradual erosion of Sverdrup's original vision for Augsburg Seminary. What had been envisioned as a nine-year, seamless, integrated process of ministerial preparation could not be sustained. Augsburg eventually dropped its initial preparatory school, and the collegiate program was gradually expanded to become a liberal arts institution with a multiplicity of majors, while the actual seminary itself became an increasingly smaller portion of the institution as a whole. Augsburg Seminary remained, certainly, but Sverdrup's grand vision of the institution and its shape gradually faded away.

1890-1911: THE GEORG SVERDRUP ERA

The 1890s were difficult for Augsburg Seminary and its supporters. As has already been seen (in chapter 3), the supporters of Augsburg had to resist pressures from the newly merged UNLC to maintain control of the institution, which they did successfully. The final settlement of the legal issues in 1898 was a compromise that allowed Augsburg to remain independent yet cost the seminary a significant portion of its already meager endowment and a portion of its library books. Of greater concern, however, was the future of its graduating students. The formation of the United Church Seminary and the hostility of UNLC leaders meant graduates from Augsburg could not readily find calls from congregations in that denomination. The formation of the Lutheran Free Church in 1897 mitigated that issue somewhat, but the size of that group yielded a diminished pool of both applicants for the seminary and positions for its graduates. More importantly, the loss of financial support from the UNLC was traumatic, and only emergency appeals to friends and supporters allowed Augsburg to continue.

In the midst of this turmoil, the seminary's leaders, Georg Sverdrup and Sven Oftedal, consistently reaffirmed their original pedagogical vision of Augsburg Seminary as an integrated system of education leading to the production of pastors for "free and living" Norwegian American Lutheran congregations. Sverdrup was the leading visionary of this type of education. He identified the problem with theological education in Norway and among Norwegian Americans as being "humanism," or the classical education prevalent in the Norwegian Latin schools, which was generally a prerequisite to study for the ministry at the university in Norway. This humanistic education was founded on the intensive study of Greek and Latin, and the classical works in these languages, to form a truly "educated" person. He saw this pattern being replicated in the Norwegian American colleges, especially at Luther and St. Olaf.

To his mind, the problems with this education were that it did not create true and living Christians and that it encouraged the development of class differences between the educated clergy and their congregations. Sverdrup wrote: "Humanism and Christianity do not go together. In religious life humanism leads to rationalism and in social life it leads to aristocracy. This is why humanism is so resilient; what appeals to the baser inclinations of the natural man is always hard to dispose of."

This kind of humanistic, classical education was especially devastating as a means for pre-seminary education. It meant that the young students would absorb this worldview as they became "cultured." He quipped sarcastically, "A Christian youth could be preserved in his Christian faith through the long years of humanistic training. It may even have happened." But a pastor who is trained in this culture of humanism generally becomes an empty and class-ridden individual who has little or no faith in Christianity:

> He who keeps his humanism intact during his theological studies becomes a pastor who preaches not what he has experienced but what he has learned. He treats religion as something which is good enough

for the ordinary man, but has no importance for someone like himself who belongs to "the cultured."[2]

To Sverdrup, this kind of a pastor was the opposite of the leader needed by a free and living congregation.

This is why Sverdrup and his followers developed Augsburg Seminary as an integrated system of education leading up to study for the ministry. If candidates from the ministry were to come to Augsburg Seminary from a humanistic collegiate education (such as at St. Olaf), they would already be ruined by humanism. Rather, students needed a preparatory and collegiate education aligned with the goals of Augsburg Seminary, so the future pastor could be nurtured in the faith in ways that were consistent with Sverdrup's vision. The UNLC plan for education, which envisioned preparatory and collegiate education at St. Olaf with further ministerial training at Augsburg, was an integral threat to everything that Sverdrup and his followers stood for.

There is a statement, found in the Augsburg catalog from about 1899, that expresses the educational philosophy that characterized the school and its education:

> Spiritual life and Christian character are considered of infinitely higher importance than mere knowledge. No amount of reading, no memorizing of facts, no mental or intellectual ability are of any real value to the Christian minister without personal experience of saving grace and a firm and manly conviction of the truth as it is in Jesus.

The catalog continues: "Augsburg Seminary subordinates all its work, its whole curriculum, its management and its discipline, to these principles."[3] Thus, the continuation of Augsburg and its nine-year system of education and formation was of paramount importance, taking precedence over everything else.

The continuation of Augsburg was, however, quite a struggle. Through the heroic fundraising efforts of Pastor Peter Nielsen during the 1890s, congregations and individuals donated enough money to Augsburg to allow it to survive the loss of funding from the UNLC, but poor finances and the lack of adequate facilities continued to plague the school. The formation of the Lutheran Free Church in 1897 mitigated this somewhat, but the LFC itself struggled to find its way financially, and financial assistance to Augsburg, approved at annual conventions of the LFC, were more goals than they were reality. Making things worse was the financial depression of the 1890s, which hit hardest the rural congregations that predominated in the LFC. Still, student enrollment at Augsburg during the 1890s managed to climb from a low point of 113 in 1893 to a range of 180 to 200 students later in the decade. The number of ministerial students held steady, around thirty a year, through this period. Augsburg as an institution had survived with its distinctive pedagogy intact, but the open question was whether it could thrive.

The turn of the century was a difficult time for Augsburg. Anemic financial support led to annual deficits. There had been a longstanding need for a new building on campus, and the LFC had encouraged a drive to gather funds for such a structure, but the funds came in slowly, and the institution could not proceed without cash in hand. For some time, the new building was only an excavated pit on campus, but eventually enough funds were raised to complete construction of the "New Main," which was dedicated in 1902. This building was a major victory for the school and raised spirits on campus. But a controversy at this same time, which involved the pastor of Trinity Lutheran congregation in Minneapolis, M. Falk Gjertsen, weakened support for the school. Trinity was the congregation adjacent to the seminary, and Gjertsen and the congregation were pivotal and long-time supporters of the institution. In late 1900, Gjertsen was accused of improprieties while on a trip to Norway, and the congregation was thrown into turmoil, a conflict into which Sverdrup was drawn. The resulting split of the congregation over the issue weakened the Augsburg community even further at a time when the seminary was facing other problems.

Sverdrup and Oftedal were the heart and soul of the institution and had been since their arrival in the early 1870s. Together they had built the institution, given it a vision, and preserved it through the turmoil of the 1890s. Yet by the early twentieth century, they were aging, and the seminary faced the problem of succession. Oftedal submitted his letter of retirement in 1902 but was persuaded to stay on until 1904. Sverdrup continued until 1907, when he died suddenly and unexpectedly. Also in 1907 came the death of Ole Paulson, the Minneapolis pastor who had initially brought Augsburg to Minnesota in 1872. These three losses, along with the alienation of M. Falk Gjertsen, meant that four pivotal individuals in the seminary's life were gone. Professor Hans Urseth, who had been appointed as the English professor in the seminary, died in 1909. At the time of Sverdrup's death, Oftedal was persuaded to return briefly as president, but he was really more of a figurehead and had little to do with the daily operation of the institution. Oftedal remained tangentially involved at Augsburg until his death in 1911.

The need for new professors and leaders was strong. Professor Andreas Helland was appointed to fill Oftedal's position (mainly in New Testament) in 1905, and he served the seminary in that capacity until 1940. More importantly, Helland served as the keeper of the Sverdrup tradition at Augsburg; he edited a multivolume set of Sverdrup's writings (in Norwegian) and wrote his biography (in English). This tradition would be continued by Helland's son Melvin, who took over his father's position in 1941 and who translated and edited a volume of Sverdrup's writings in English. Another transition that also reflected continuity came in 1909 when George Sverdrup was appointed to the faculty to take up his father Georg's position as theological professor. George Sverdrup was a bit of a controversial figure; of course, he represented the Sverdrup family, but he had a wide range of academic interests outside of the world of the Lutheran Free Church. It is not apparent that he initially wanted the position, but when he did take it, he threw his energy into serving Augsburg. After several years of various interim arrangements, he was appointed the president of Augsburg Seminary in 1911, a post he maintained until his early death in 1937. Also added to the theological faculty in 1909 were Elias Harbo in systematic theology and John Evjen in church history. These four professors then provided for the period of transition in the seminary, which of course also included the linguistic transition: Helland and Harbo lectured in Norwegian, while Sverdrup and Evjen lectured in English.[4]

During this period of transition, questions naturally arose about the future direction of the institution, both organizationally and pedagogically. The most pressing questions surrounded not so much the theological seminary but rather the preparatory and "Greek" (collegiate) sections of the institution and whether Augsburg would remain an institution primarily focused, at all three levels, on the production of pastors or broaden the preparatory and collegiate sections to educate students who were not headed into the ministry. In his last address to the LFC in 1906, Georg Sverdrup seemed to signal that he might be in favor of some curricular changes that would broaden the collegiate department, but the question remained open and controversial in the LFC until at least 1923.[5] Augsburg was not accredited as an educational institution, and on the collegiate level the course offering remained fairly narrowly envisioned. This was at the same time that other Norwegian American colleges were expanding their programs, seeking (and gaining) accreditation, and doing well in attracting students. In the nontheological departments, Augsburg had 146 students in 1898 compared to 184 at St. Olaf. By 1914 the Augsburg numbers had declined to 103, while at St. Olaf the count had risen to 545.[6] If Augsburg was to remain primarily an institution for producing pastors, then broadening the nontheological departments was less necessary, but it would remain a fairly small and weak institution.

To enumerate the school's challenges is not to overlook the rich traditions and accomplishments of the school, especially among the student population. The students at Augsburg, at all levels, organized a number of organizations prevalent at the time. The students organized and independently ran a boarding club to provide meals for those who wished to join, which lasted until 1924. Besides providing meals, the club also oversaw other areas of student residential life, including operating the student post office and overseeing the distribution of firewood for the stoves that heated students' rooms (central heating was not added to the buildings until much later). As well, in 1876 students and faculty formed the Augsburg Medical Aid Society, a mutual society to which all residential students were required to belong and that provided for medicines and medical care for its members. There were a number of literary and debating societies on campus involving students, as well as the usual student-run publications. Theological students and those of the other departments together operated all these elements of student campus life. Students also independently managed at least one of the libraries on campus, raising funds and buying books, until eventually the campus libraries were merged into a unified whole after the turn of the century.

The students at Augsburg carried this same activism into their social and religious activities, both on campus and out in the local community, where they were especially active. Religious activities on campus were fairly constant, including chapel worship and formal and informal prayer fellowship, and were carefully monitored by the faculty. Given Sverdrup's philosophy that students receiving an Augsburg education should not be disconnected from the "free and living" congregations they were intended to serve, students were strongly pressed to volunteer for service in local Lutheran congregations, both while school was in session and during vacation periods. This involvement was urged on all students, whether they were preparing for ministry or not. The wave of religious revival that swept through Norwegian American Lutheranism in the 1890s and beyond was strongly felt on campus. The same Peter Nielsen who so heroically raised the funds to keep Augsburg alive after the split with the UNLC was also one of the primary preachers of these religious awakenings and was frequently on campus at Augsburg. One observer on campus in 1892 noted that the community of the time was in a near constant state of religious revival activities.[7] The Augsburg community, faculty, students, and friends prided themselves on the degree of "piety" of their institution, which they felt differentiated them from the other Norwegian American colleges and seminaries.

The interest in religious mission, which was in part a feature of many religious schools of the time, was strongly seen on the Augsburg campus and beyond. The students had already formed their own Mission Society in 1885, and soon thereafter two Augsburg graduates were ordained and sent to work with the Norwegian Mission Society in Madagascar, the first two of many Norwegian Americans who entered mission work abroad.[8] When it was formed in 1897, the Lutheran Free Church took special interest in missions overseas, both its own work and the work of independent Norwegian American mission societies, such as the China Mission Society, the Santal Mission, and others. Augsburg students were also very active in religious and social ministry activities in their local community. The location of the campus in an urban area gave students great opportunity for such efforts. Students volunteering in local LFC congregations participated in the formation of an urban outreach mission in Minneapolis called the Gateway Mission. They also participated in other religious activities with the disadvantaged population in the area, in revivals and witnessing, and in service at the Hennepin County Poor Farm.[9] Another area of intense interest for students was the then-popular agitation for the prohibition of alcohol, a sentiment shared by the large majority of the Augsburg community. Those especially interested formed the Prohibition Club of Augsburg Seminary, which participated in events on campus and in the local area. Augsburg was well known for its small traveling student vocal ensembles, which brought religious and prohibition messages to communities around the region.

The interim period between the death of Georg Sverdrup in 1907 and the final selection of his son George Sverdrup as president in 1911 was a time of some fluctuation for the seminary. The day-to-day responsibilities of running the institution were split between two newly created dean positions, one for the seminary and the other for the college. Andreas Helland took the lead in the seminary, and Hans Urseth did the same in the college, until his early death at age forty-two in 1909. This division was a bit misleading, because the four faculty who taught in the seminary program also often taught in the collegiate program. When George Sverdrup arrived on campus in 1909 to serve as a theological professor, he was named vice president of Augsburg Seminary. In this position, the younger Sverdrup was essentially the acting president of the school, and the death of Oftedal in late 1911 led finally to his formal elevation to the presidency of the institution.

The long interim between the death of the elder Sverdrup in 1907 and the formal appointment of his son as president in 1911 was both indicative of the identity crisis of the school and a contributor to that same crisis. The elder Sverdrup had personally so defined the institution for over thirty years that his shoes were hard to fill. His vision of the school from the nineteenth century was increasingly at odds with the identity and the needs of the school in the early twentieth century. Although the Lutheran Free Church, meeting in convention in 1909, had passed a resolution reaffirming the elder Sverdrup's vision for Augsburg Seminary, there were elements at the institution and in the LFC who were pushing for changes. The main agitation was for a restructuring and broadening of the collegiate program, which was then the "Greek" department of the institution, focused primarily on producing candidates for theological and ministerial education. Yet the reality of the institution was that increasing numbers of students in the collegiate program were not going on to ministerial preparation. From 1885 to 1897 a full 80 percent of collegiate students went on to study for the ordained ministry, but during the next period, from 1989 to 1910, this number had declined to 50 percent.[10] This shift was noted in the 1907 college catalog, which stated that "hundreds of men have attended Augsburg and graduated from its college department who have not pursued theological studies afterward or even intended to do so."[11] Though this seems like the institution was at least tentatively signaling changes in its vision and purpose, these changes came hard and involved both conflict and the need to dedicate many more resources to the collegiate program. The question was whether this could be done at the same time as honoring the original vision of the institution as so ably articulated by the elder Sverdrup.

1911–1937: THE GEORGE SVERDRUP ERA

Although George Sverdrup was his father's son, his education and experiences were quite different from those of his father; George represented the classic example of a second-generation immigrant religious leader. While his father had been born and educated in Norway and formed by the pietist and liberal party struggle for greater independence from the Norwegian state and state church, George was educated in the United States and was finely attuned to the needs and opportunities of the Norwegian American religious communities as they moved inexorably toward acculturation and assimilation in United States. Instead of attending the preparatory department at Augsburg, George instead received an American high school education in Minneapolis. After earning a collegiate degree at Augsburg, he took further classes at the University of Minnesota and in 1901 was admitted to the Yale University Graduate School, where he earned a master's degree in 1902 in Semitic languages and biblical studies. Like his father before him, he was not an ordained pastor, and neither of them had ever served in a congregation. He attended Yale on and off as his finances would allow and spent several years in the Middle East studying and participating in archeological excavations and even teaching at the Protestant college in Beirut, Lebanon.

Given these factors, and his desire to return to Yale and complete his PhD, it seems reasonable to conclude that he had ambitions beyond the small and confined world of Augsburg Seminary. But with the death of his father in 1907, Augsburg came calling, and George dutifully answered. George Sverdrup was emblematic of a number of bright and academically talented Lutherans of the second and third generations in these immigrant denominations who had the ability to complete doctoral degrees and gain a wider career but sacrificed these opportunities to return to church colleges like Augsburg and help transform them into modern educational institutions. He labored at Augsburg for thirty years until his untimely death in 1937 at age fifty-eight. One cannot say for certain, but surely the personal labors that were required to bring Augsburg into the twentieth century and through the rigors of the Great Depression could easily have led to his death at a relatively young age.

One thing was certain: Augsburg desperately needed his help, because the institution was directionless and in decline. The seminary program was holding its own through these years; although it was never a growing or flourishing program, there was a constant need for pastors for the Lutheran Free Church, and the seminary supplied these. But surely the narrowly defined and unaccredited collegiate department was in crisis. The decline in collegiate enrollment that had begun at the start of the twentieth century continued and threatened the very survival of the entire institution. By 1911 the number of students in the college had declined to fifty-three, and by 1918 the numbers had slipped to twenty-three, although some of this drop might be attributed to the effects of World War I.[12] Even though the primary focus of the entire institution was to produce pastors, this program of theological education also required a robust collegiate program as a feeder. As well, a substantial collegiate program was vital to support the physical plant of the institution itself.

The dilemma George Sverdrup faced was how to modernize and expand the whole institution while still maintaining the tradition of theological education envisioned by his father. Not only was this distinctive tradition deeply rooted in the essence of Augsburg Seminary, it was one of the key elements in the formation and continuation of the Lutheran Free Church itself, which, as has been seen, came into existence primarily to support Augsburg. Just to survive, let alone flourish, Augsburg would have to modernize in significant ways without seeming to abandon its reason for existence in the first place. This was not an enviable position for the younger Sverdrup, and the dilemma required his entire attention. The fact that he was his father's son might have granted him some initial credibility, but the family name would take him only so far.

At the beginning of the young Sverdrup's presidency, the theological faculty in the seminary covered the four classic disciplines: Sverdrup in Old Testament, Andreas Helland in New Testament, Elias Harbo in systematic theology, and John Evjen in church history. These four actually taught a range of courses both in the seminary and in the college, as circumstances dictated—as was often the case in an institution of such a size. Since there were few to no administrative officers in the formal sense, these faculty members also served the institution in many administrative roles, along with serving the Lutheran Free Church as necessary. As president of the institution, Sverdrup was often on the road among the congregations of the LFC, "showing the flag" and maintaining ties, raising money, and recruiting students. Faculty salaries were quite modest, even by American Lutheran standards, and a calling to teach at an institution like Augsburg was often a sacrificial one.

Some of the difficulties that Sverdrup had came from members of his own faculty who publicly disagreed with him about the direction that Augsburg and the LFC should be taking. These were not traditionalists, seeking to solidify the heritage of Augsburg and the Free Church, but rather those wanting to change the direction of both institutions. The first controversy came in 1918 with Professor John Evjen. He graduated in 1898 from the seminary and then went to Germany and earned a PhD at the University of Leipzig in 1903. After short stints teaching at the United Church Seminary (1903–1905) and Pennsylvania College (now Gettysburg College), he joined the Augsburg Seminary faculty in 1909. A brilliant scholar and a gifted linguist, Evjen was apparently not the easiest person to get along with. This temperament, combined with a series of articles he wrote for the LFC publication *Folkebladet* in 1918 questioning the validity of the denomination's stance on congregationalism (the core of LFC identity), brought criticism from leaders in the LFC and from President Sverdrup. Stung by this controversy, Sverdrup himself submitted his resignation in 1919 to the seminary board. The board rejected Sverdrup's resignation and instead notified Evjen that his career at Augsburg was at an end.[13]

A similar situation arose about a decade later with another member of the faculty, Lars Qualben. He also had attended the collegiate and theological divisions of Augsburg, graduating in 1921. Qualben earned a PhD at Hartford Theological Seminary in 1923 and joined Augsburg Seminary in 1926 as professor of New Testament. In 1928, he publicly expressed his views on the Lutheran Free Church and its future; to his mind, it had none. Surveying the changes at Augsburg—which was rapidly developing into a typical Lutheran college (something he agreed with)—Qualben suggested that these developments negated the traditional rationale for Augsburg's independent existence and that both Augsburg and the Lutheran Free Church would be better off if the LFC merged into the much larger Norwegian Lutheran Church in America. Since in his estimation the LFC could not provide the resources to strengthen and modernize Augsburg, the institution could only succeed if it was part of a larger denomination. This dispute was carried to the LFC annual convention in 1928, and although Qualben had some support in the denomination, the antimerger sentiment was much stronger, and Qualben, too, was invited not to continue at the seminary. He went to teach at, of all places, St. Olaf!

To replace Evjen and Qualben, two new faculty members were added to the seminary faculty. Lars Lillehei was another Augsburg Seminary graduate (1907) and had been professor and president at the Lutheran Bible School in Wahpeton, North Dakota, from 1909 to

1919. He replaced Evjen on the faculty in 1919 and taught church history and systematics. Karl Ermisch came from outside the Augsburg and LFC orbit, a German American who studied at Wartburg Seminary and the University of Minnesota. He was added to the seminary faculty in 1929 after the departure of Qualben.

Although Sverdrup resisted the more pronounced calls for substantive change at Augsburg and in the Lutheran Free Church, it was clear to many that there needed to be changes at Augsburg to ensure that it not only survived but flourished. These changes focused primarily on the collegiate division of the institution and would complete the evolution of that section of Augsburg from a "Greek" department mainly producing candidates for theological education to a full-fledged American college. The collegiate curriculum and its course offerings were gradually expanded. A major change for the entire campus was the admission of women to the college in 1921, which was a hard-fought battle but completely necessary to the survival of the institution. In 1933, in the midst of the Depression, the preparatory department was finally closed. It had served an important function for many years, but by the 1930s most young Norwegian Americans, even in the rural parts of the country, had access to free public high school education, and the preparatory department could not compete with free. The closing of the preparatory department was actually part of a larger trend in Norwegian American Lutheran schools; these departments either were transformed into collegiate programs or closed down entirely.

President Sverdrup walked the line between traditionalists, who resisted any change to Augsburg's configuration and mission, and those like Evjen and Qualben who sought the transformation of Augsburg into a full-fledged liberal arts college and the abandonment of its distinctive educational profile. Sverdrup mastered the art of working through the structures of the Lutheran Free Church, so he could steer incremental changes to Augsburg without appearing to be abandoning his father's legacy. In pushing for coeducation in the early 1920s, Sverdrup argued that though women were not ordained as pastors, they could serve as parish workers and missionaries, or serve congregations in other ways. Regarding the growing numbers of collegiate students who did not enter the seminary, he insisted that Augsburg was never narrowly envisioned as a *presteskole* (pastors school) and that congregations needed educated and spiritually awake lay leaders. When Qualben questioned whether Augsburg and the LFC still had a reason for separate existence, Sverdrup replied that the threat of clerical and synodical domination of congregations remained constant. The Augsburg board and the LFC seemed generally to trust Sverdrup's leadership.

The college grew to nearly four hundred students by the end of the 1930s, but of course this meant that the seminary program became an increasingly smaller part of a larger whole. Signs of this shift went back to the 1910s, when small but incremental developments suggested the seminary was no longer at the apex of the institution. In the 1916/17 Augsburg catalog, this growing split was signaled by a graphical change in the way the institution's name was punctuated. The new title looked like this: "Augsburg [College and Theological] Seminary," which seemed to signal the now distinctive natures of what had originally been a single institution. Eventually the brackets were dropped, and in 1942 the situation was made official. As one historian noted: "Both existed on the same campus and maintained close relations, but their purposes were no longer identical. Sverdrup's task was to demonstrate faithfulness to the founding principles even while working to adapt the institution to changing times."[14] Through the first six decades of its existence, the Lutheran Free Church grew only modestly, especially when compared with the Norwegian Lutheran Church in America. The explosive growth of the latter denomination meant a corresponding growth in the size of Luther Seminary, but the demand for new pastors in the LFC was modest and did not lead to an expansion of Augsburg Seminary (now a distinctive institution apart from the college).

Of course, growth in numbers of students and in financial resources to support the seminary (which from hereafter will refer particularly to that section of Augsburg concerned with theological education for pastors) was also greatly affected by the Great Depression of the 1930s. In fact, there had been a longstanding agricultural depression after World War I, lingering through the 1920s, which seriously affected the mainly rural congregations of the Lutheran Free Church. When the stock market crash of 1929 seriously damaged the rest of the American economy, the situation for small and undercapitalized institutions like Augsburg was dire. Many such schools closed (like Red Wing Seminary) or underwent dramatic retrenchment. Students in the seminary paid little or no tuition but were responsible for their own room and board, along with books and other incidentals. Even these modest costs were beyond the reach of many students, while others needed to return home and help their own families financially. The main source of funding for the seminary was the annual payments from the LFC, and as their revenues declined dramatically during the Depression, so too did financial support for the seminary itself.

Historically, one of the core missions of the LFC was the support of Augsburg, and the economic depression meant the denomination could not provide the funds the institution needed. For a small denomination like the LFC, "their" school, Augsburg, was a point of considerable pride and loyalty, and many in the denomination personally felt troubled about their inability to donate the money needed to keep the school going. In response to repeated calls for donations in the church newspaper, *The Lutheran Messenger*, one farmer noted his own desperate financial situation and observed that there were "many thousand farmers in just as bad shape as I am and many much worse." He wanted to assure denominational leaders that the lack of response to these financial appeals was not from a lack of willingness but a lack of means, and then added, "It is plain helplessness, and no one feels worse about it than the farmers themselves."[15] Economic conditions in the country, especially in the rural areas, continued to be bad through the 1930s, only to be improved by the mobilization of the country just ahead of World War II.

This decline in funding was mainly borne by the faculty and staff of Augsburg, who had to decide whether a greatly diminished salary was better than no salary at all. It seems that the employees of Augsburg, underpaid as they were even by contemporary standards, were still deeply committed to the work and the mission of the institution. In 1931 the faculty at Augsburg agreed to a voluntary 10 percent reduction in salary, but this was only the beginning. During the 1933/34 school year, the faculty had no firm salary but agreed to receive a proportional share of the school's income; during this year they went several months in a row with no payment whatsoever. In 1934 the payroll was cut by another 25 percent, and only in the later 1930s were these cuts gradually restored.[16]

Augsburg did what it could to help students affected by the Depression, but it had limited resources to assist them. The school opened up an employment service, where students could find part-time jobs and other work, often in return for housing or meals, which was at times enough for students to eke out an existence through the school year. Traditionally, theological students would do temporary work in LFC congregations during breaks and in the summer, but this source of income was also curtailed by the Depression. The situation grew rather desperate at the low point of the Depression in 1933 and 1934. One theological student remembered that on one winter day President Sverdrup announced in chapel:

> The college didn't even have enough credit to get a load of coal and he appealed to the students at that chapel service that morning to take up an offering in order to raise some money so that the college might go out and get a load of coal to keep the buildings from freezing up.[17]

But by the late 1930s things had improved enough that Augsburg launched a successful appeal to raise funds for the construction of badly needed buildings on campus. President Sverdrup spearheaded this appeal, and it seems likely that the financial pressures of the Depression, along with the strain of a major fund-drive, probably contributed to his early death in 1937.

During the inter-war period, Augsburg continued to maintain the strict moral code of its heritage in nineteenth-century pietism, something that was reinforced by many elements of American Protestantism of the time. The student handbooks reflected this morality; participating in or even attending a dance was grounds for expulsion, as was drinking or frequenting pool halls. Playing cards was greatly frowned upon, as was "indiscriminate attendance" at movies.[18] Prohibition remained a very strong emphasis on campus. Although Augsburg was in the middle of a major metropolitan area, where the culture was changing rapidly in the 1920s and 1930s, it seemed more like a cloistered island in the middle of a larger culture. Students were encouraged to be out doing the work of God in the world but certainly not of that world.

Within the theological seminary at Augsburg, the evolution of its theological program continued through the early twentieth century. The older theological tradition at Augsburg, as embodied in the teaching of Oftedal and the elder Sverdrup, was rooted in the nineteenth-century Johnsonian revival in Norway. The theology of Gisle Johnson was a form of churchly pietism that also demonstrated a moderate Lutheran confessionalism. Besides this tradition, Georg Sverdrup was also influenced by the neoconfessional Lutheranism of the Erlangen school in Germany as embodied in the teaching of J. C. K. von Hoffman and his colleagues. This school of Lutheran theology was an attempt to combat religious rationalism by returning to traditional Lutheran confessional theology while remaining responsive to the modern situation. The influence of the Erlangen theology, which was also felt at Luther Seminary, was continued at Augsburg Seminary through the work of theologians such as Elias Harbo, Lars Lillehei, and Karl Ermisch.[19] Certainly George Sverdrup inherited this tradition from his father and probably agreed with it, though as primarily a biblical scholar (and very busy president) this influence is less discernible in his writings.

As there were few faculty in the seminary, there was not much in the way of curricular changes and developments at Augsburg Seminary through the 1920s and 1930s. There were essentially four pedagogical positions in the seminary, one each in Old Testament, New Testament, systematic theology, and church history. Since it was a part of a larger educational community, the seminary could and did draw on professors from other areas of the institution for occasional instruction, including in homiletics and music, but seminary teachers also served the college. Karl Ermisch taught German, for example, as well as carrying out his duties in the seminary.

One interesting element of the seminary during the 1930s was the development of a dual degree program. Traditionally, students had graduated from Augsburg Seminary with a certificate of theology (CT). In the late 1930s an additional option was added, a bachelor of theology degree (BTh), which required as a prerequisite a bachelor of arts degree, additional competence in languages, a minimum grade-point average, and the completion of a substantial thesis.[20] This addition is noteworthy for the fact that it did not seem to be controversial; it certainly could have been seen as a move toward the kind of elitist, "humanistic" education that was so reviled by Georg Sverdrup, but apparently this change, too, seemed at the time like another natural evolution in the life of the seminary.

1937–1963: THE BERNHARD CHRISTENSEN ERA

The last period of Augsburg Seminary's independent existence was overseen by Bernhard Christensen, who served as president of the college and seminary from George Sverdrup's death in 1937 until 1962, when the Lutheran Free Church and Augsburg Seminary were about to end their independent existence and merge into the newly formed American Lutheran Church. Christensen had earned his BA at Augsburg in 1922 and, after studies at Augsburg Seminary, had received his BTh and MTh at Princeton. In the late 1920s he studied in Germany and then received his PhD at Hartford Seminary in 1929. During the late 1920s, Christensen was being prepared for an eventual teaching position at Augsburg Seminary, but this consideration came with some controversy. For a brief time, Christensen had worked in the ministry at Trinity Lutheran Church, Brooklyn, New York, with another pastor, Asmund Oftedal (Sven Oftedal's son), a member of the Augsburg board of directors. Asmund Oftedal questioned Christensen's stance on the authority of the Bible, thought he was on the road to theological "modernism," and opposed his appointment as a professor at Augsburg Seminary.[21] Of course, this concern all came in the context of the fundamentalist-modernist controversies that were convulsing American Protestantism at this time, especially concerning the authority of the Bible.

Christensen was initially inclined to withdraw his name for consideration, but Sverdrup convinced him to continue. Christensen was requested to submit to the theological faculty a statement of his understanding of the authority of the Bible and the appropriate means of biblical study and teaching. In the statement, he affirmed that the Bible contained "the historical revelation of God to the people of Israel" and was a "sufficient guide in all matters of faith and conduct." But, he continued,

> in the scientific study of theology I do not believe that we can avoid a consideration of the historico-critical research that has been carried out in the last hundred years. These critical studies I do not look upon as hindrances, but rather as helps to the true understanding of the Scripture.[22]

The theological faculty found Christensen's statement to be acceptable, and although some controversy continued, Christensen began teaching at Augsburg in 1930.

The willingness of the faculty to affirm Christensen's statement and welcome him as a colleague signals their cautious openness to some of the less controversial aspects of modern critical biblical studies. Questions about the authority of the Bible and the appropriate means to study the biblical record were lively and controversial topics for American Lutherans in the 1920s and 1930s, especially as the nineteenth-century immigrant groups began to do their theological work in English. A number of the more conservative Lutheran theologians urged the adoption of the English words *inerrant* and *infallible* to describe their understanding of biblical authority, although it is not clear exactly what they meant by these terms. American Lutherans were conservative, to be sure; they were not classic fundamentalists, but neither were they modernists or liberals.[23] From the late 1930s onward, there was a cautious openness among the faculty at Augsburg toward employing critical biblical studies in their teaching, although there was the stated intention that these studies were there to elucidate the Bible and not to undermine the normative authority of the Scripture. It is unclear, however, whether even such a cautious approach to biblical criticism was more than conservatives in the Lutheran Free Church, such as Asmund Oftedal and others, could tolerate.

Upon the death of George Sverdrup in 1937, Christensen became a leading candidate for the position of president at Augsburg, but he was not the only candidate whose name was urged for consideration. In 1936 Sverre Norborg, a theologian from Europe, joined the Augsburg College faculty, quickly became an important figure on campus, and gained the support of at least some of the students and board members. When the president's position came open, a number of them began to agitate within the LFC for Norborg to be considered instead of Christensen. In some sense, this choice involved a larger question that would dominate the next decades of the LFC—namely, whether the denomination should remain independent or fully participate in the merger discussions that were swirling among American Lutherans. Norborg gathered support from those favoring continued independence, while Christensen favored full participation in the merger discussion. In such a small and tight-knit denomination, a contested election needed to be handled with tact and subtlety, but in this instance it became a controversy instead. A majority of the Augsburg board was in favor of Christensen, but matters spilled over into the LFC convention in the summer of 1938, and although Christensen was elected, his margin of support was not decisive.[24]

Christensen quickly became an important theological voice, both in the Lutheran Free Church and in the wider sphere of American Lutheranism. He was careful to pay homage to Georg Sverdrup and the distinctive Augsburg traditions, especially the call for a "living faith" in "free and living congregations," and felt that Augsburg should continue in some form with such an emphasis. In an address to LFC pastors in 1944 he also affirmed the stance of the LFC:

> Our Church has never been willing to let itself become entangled in the network of increasingly refined theological definitions, but has sought to maintain what may be called "theological Freedom" through a single confession of faith in the authority of the Word of God, and adherence to the Unaltered Augsburg Confession and Luther's Small Catechism.

He rejected any other attempts to codify official theology beyond this, especially rejecting "various thesis-making experiments." By this, Christensen was referring to regular attempts to negotiate theological agreements as a means of achieving fellowship and union among American Lutherans.[25]

During the Christensen period, the seminary added five new faculty members, the last five who would serve in that capacity. The older faculty, including Lars Lillehei, Andreas Helland, and Karl Ermisch, gradually retired. Christensen himself was increasingly busy in the position of president of the entire institution. Melvin Helland, who had served for decades as a missionary in Madagascar, took his father's position in New Testament in the seminary in 1941. John Stensvaag, who had been a pastor in Minneapolis, took over teaching duties in Old Testament in 1942, until his election as the last president of the LFC in 1958. Iver Olson came to Augsburg in 1945 from Oak Grove Lutheran School in Fargo, North Dakota, and taught in systematic theology. Paul Sonnack joined the faculty in 1949 to teach church history, and Philip A. Quanbeck became professor of New Testament in 1957. There is a common thread among all of these seminary professors: they were all graduates of Augsburg, all had parish experience, and all had graduate degrees from American institutions, especially the Hartford Seminary Foundation. Since the size of the seminary itself was fairly modest, they often also had teaching duties within the college.

During the 1920s and 1930s, the students and faculty at Augsburg as a whole generally were isolationists, urging that the United States not be drawn into the conflicts in Europe, an attitude fairly common among American Lutherans of the time. Some of them also held degrees of pacifist convictions and were involved in the Fellowship of Reconciliation, a pacifist organization. The German invasion of Norway in 1940 and the entry of the United States into World War II in 1941 changed matters, however, and Augsburg as an institution was forced onto a wartime footing. The college felt a downturn in students because of young men entering the armed forces, a dip that was somewhat cushioned by the earlier shift to coeducation and by leasing some college facilities to the armed forces during the war. The seminary itself also saw a decline in students. After the war, the total enrollment in Augsburg increased dramatically, climbing to 966 students in 1949 and over 1,400 students by 1962. The seminary remained a "virile if small branch" of the larger institution,[26] but increasingly Augsburg's focus was on continuing its transition to becoming a Lutheran liberal-arts college. This student growth could not be fueled by the Lutheran Free Church alone, and the percentage of Augsburg College students from the LFC declined throughout this period. Despite protests to the contrary, the growth of the total institution suggested that the theological seminary had become a smaller focus of the larger institution. The seminary itself remained closely connected with the LFC and its congregations, and many activities at the seminary, especially annual conferences for pastors, brought seminary alumni back on campus and renewed ties with them.

The postwar period brought other changes to the seminary. As in other Lutheran seminaries, the normal pattern before World War II was that seminary students would not be married while in school. The war changed this, and after 1945 there was a steady growth in married students. Augsburg seminary students already had an advantage here over the students at many other Lutheran seminaries in that the seminary was located on a coeducational campus and not far from a Lutheran school of nursing. Understanding that it would be a good practice to give seminary wives some idea of what life would be like for them as pastors' wives in congregations, the seminary developed programs to assist these young women. An organization of these women called the Seminettes functioned during the postwar years. Older women, the wives of professors and local clergy, met with these women for mentoring, support, and socializing. During the annual meetings of the LFC, the pastors' wives met as a separate group, and these seminary activities were also a way to bring these new pastors' wives into the larger community of which they would be a part.[27]

The size of the student body at Augsburg Seminary recovered after World War II but never grew substantially; there were usually between twenty and thirty-five students in the seminary in any given year, with a graduating class between six and ten.[28] Seminary students at Augsburg had long maintained their own organization, the Concordia Society, which met to discuss professional and spiritual development and theological and ethical issues of the day; during the 1950s, this group maintained a publication called *Concord*. The campus also held regular religious and social events to create closer community ties. It was a fairly small place in the midst of a larger educational institution, and there was the need for differentiation so they could focus on their own distinctive educational preparation.

As the twentieth century progressed, the curriculum at other Norwegian American seminaries, especially Luther Seminary, changed substantially away from the older university model (heavy on the classical and biblical languages and dogmatic theology) and toward more emphasis on practical theology, homiletics, and other professional ministerial disciplines. The original vision for the curriculum at Augsburg Seminary articulated by Georg Sverdrup, however, had already initiated a move away from this older university model in favor of a more practical ministerial formation focused on "living Christianity" for "free and living Lutheran congregations." Thus, in a sense, Augsburg was already ahead of the seminary curricular curve and had less distance to travel. The basic shape of the seminary curriculum did not change drastically, then, during the George Sverdrup and Bernhard Christensen administrations, remaining focused on substantial biblical study, along with systematic theology and church history. During the period after World War II, however, there was a gradual broadening of instruction and focus within this standard curriculum, especially as the five new professors joined the faculty, bringing with them a new range of theological authors and approaches. Professors Stensvaag and Quanbeck were carefully exploring the results of modern biblical criticism with their students and imagining the possible advantages that such results might have for biblical studies. The whole life of postwar Lutheran seminary education was being transformed by new theological currents from neoorthodox and existential theologians such as Karl Barth, Dietrich Bonhoeffer, Reinhold and H. Richard Niebuhr, and Paul Tillich. Lutheran theological studies were being enlivened beyond the traditional Erlangen confessional school by the "Luther Renaissance" and the work of Scandinavian theologians like Gustaf Aulén, Anders Nygren, Regin Prenter, and Eivind Berggrav. Although the seminary did not institute a formal internship requirement, it had always been expected that seminary students would spend significant periods of time in congregations during their course of studies. The eventual expectation was for at least six months of such an experience, generally split up over several summers.[29]

The postwar years were also a period of intense activity among American Lutherans over the issue of the possible mergers of the numerous denominations then in existence.[30] Although most observers felt that such mergers and realignments were inevitable, there were substantial disagreements as to the nature and direction of such activities and which groups would be involved in what processes. The Lutheran Free Church was a member of several different Lutheran cooperative organizations, including the eight-member National Lutheran Council (NLC) and the centrist, five-member American Lutheran Conference (1930–1954). These two groups were a natural focus of merger activity, but there was sharp disagreement among their members as to the exact nature of the merger process and its composition. The details of this process are not necessary to recount here, but when the dust settled in the early 1960s, there were two large, newly merged Lutheran denominations, the American Lutheran Church (1960) and the Lutheran Church in America (1962). The Lutheran Free Church was a party to the negotiations that brought together the American Lutheran Church (ALC) in 1960, a development that would rejoin the LFC with the Evangelical Lutheran Church, the main group of Norwegian American Lutherans from whose antecedents the LFC had initially departed in 1897.

Obviously, this was a momentous and controversial development for the Lutheran Free Church and for Augsburg Seminary, for the loss of their separate existence was seen, at least by some in the denomination, as the betrayal and loss of everything that the LFC had stood for in its existence. Augsburg College would certainly weather the storm of the demise of the LFC, but for Augsburg Seminary, the loss of the LFC signaled the end of its independent existence and a merger of its own. As has been seen previously, the question of the merger into a large Lutheran denomination had been controversial within the LFC throughout its existence, apparent in the disputes between George Sverdrup and Lars Qualben in 1928, and was a subtext in Christensen's election in 1938. But by the postwar period, Christensen, firmly in control at Augsburg, began to signal his support for LFC participation in the American Lutheran merger negotiations. In a report to the Augsburg board in 1950, Christensen declared his support for the merger process, saying that after "long and careful thought" he had concluded that it was time that the LFC might "begin to explore the possibilities of union with other Lutheran bodies closely related to it."[31] Seminary professor John Stensvaag, later the last president of the LFC, was a proponent of merger, as were a number of the board of trustees.

There was, however, a strong sector of the Lutheran Free Church after the war who favored the continued independence of the denomination and who were vocally opposed to any merger that meant the loss of its separate identity.[32] The battle over merger was joined during the 1950s within the LFC in denominational publications, at pastors' conferences, and above all at the annual gathering of the denomination itself. This was a small denomination that operated much like an extended family, with many of the same dynamics. Most LFC pastors had attended Augsburg Seminary together and had moved in the same denomination circles for years, and there was probably even a fair amount of intermarriage between their families. The annual denominational meetings were in many ways a family reunion, so this conflict was so sharp because it was personal. There was also a fair degree of generational conflict involved, as older delegates and pastors tended to oppose merger, while younger ones were in favor of merger.

During the 1950s, delegates from the LFC regularly attended the meeting of the Joint Union Committee (JUC), the group that was planning the merger of the American Lutheran Church. Several proposals to make the LFC a distinct, nongeographical district within the ALC were rejected as being impractical, although the JUC as a whole took some pains to seriously consider the other concerns of the LFC. Eventually, three Lutheran denominations came together to form the new ALC, which began operation in the 1960s. Since it was congregationally based in its polity, the LFC had to take a more circuitous route to joining the ALC, by means of congregational referendum. The first such referendum in 1955, which had to pass by a 75 percent approval rate, failed to meet this rather high standard, with only about two-thirds of the congregations voting to approve the merger proposal. In 1957 the standard was reduced to two-thirds, but even then, the vote in the affirmative came up just short. After 1957 the question went into abeyance for several years while LFC leaders continued to work for an approval of the merger agreement. A third vote was held in 1961, and this time the merger passed with 70 percent of the votes in agreement of the resolution. This meant that the Lutheran Free Church would enter the American Lutheran Church in 1963, ending sixty-six years of independent existence.

This vote also meant the end of the independent existence of Augsburg Seminary. The ALC decided that the human and physical assets of Augsburg Seminary were to be merged into Luther Seminary in Saint Paul.[33] The faculty of those last years at Augsburg Seminary were dispersed. Philip Quanbeck remained as a teacher in the religion department at Augsburg, while John Stensvaag and Paul Sonnack went on to teach at Luther Seminary. In 1962, Bernhard Christensen surprised the Augsburg community by tendering his resignation as president, and later he, too, joined the faculty at Luther Seminary.

The fifth and final faculty member, Iver Olson, took a different path. Of those congregations that had opposed the merger, about fifty had decided to leave the LFC and not go into the ALC in 1963. These congregations formed a new denomination that they sought to name the "Lutheran Free Church (not merged)," but legal action by the ALC resulted in a ruling prohibiting them from using any variation of this name. The group renamed itself the Association of Free Lutheran Congregations (AFLC) and opened its own Bible school and seminary in the Medicine Lake area of suburban Minneapolis. Iver Olson joined the new faculty of the AFLC seminary in 1963.

Thus, after ninety-three years of separate existence, Augsburg Seminary came to an end. It had a complicated history of denominational relations, led by five dominant leaders: August Weenaas, Georg Sverdrup and Sven Oftedal, George Sverdrup, and Bernhard Christensen. In its history, it graduated 710 men for the Lutheran ministry[34] and sought to create a distinctive path for Lutheran theological education in the United States.

Notes

1. The Conference for the Norwegian-Danish Evangelical Lutheran Church in America (1869–1890).
2. Georg Sverdrup, "The Malaise of Humanism," in *The Heritage of Faith: Selections from the Writings of Georg Sverdrup*, trans. Melvin A. Helland

(Minneapolis: Augsburg, 1969), 108–9. The original is in a series of articles published in the periodical *Folkebladet* in 1891 and 1892.

3. *Catalog of Augsburg Seminary, 1899–1900*, quoted in Hamre, "Augsburg Theological Seminary," 23.
4. Hamre, "Augsburg Theological Seminary," 26.
5. Chrislock, *From Fjord to Freeway*, 89–90. Of course, the development of Augsburg as a college is not the direct interest of this chapter, but since the question involves, in some respects, the parallel development of Augsburg Seminary, these developments will be noted from time to time.
6. Chrislock, *From Fjord to Freeway*, 87.
7. Leola Nelson Bergmann, *Music Master of the Middle West: The Story of F. Melius Christiansen and the St. Olaf Choir* (Minneapolis: University of Minnesota Press, 1944), 41.
8. Hamre, "Augsburg Theological Seminary," 23.
9. Chrislock, *From Fjord to Freeway*, 113.
10. Chrislock, *From Fjord to Freeway*, 117.
11. *Augsburg Seminary Catalog, 1907–1908*, 8–9.
12. Chrislock, *From Fjord to Freeway*, 136.
13. Evjen went on to have a career at a number of different Lutheran institutions, including a term at Hamma Divinity School and Wittenberg College in Springfield, Ohio, 1924–1930, and eventually ended up at Carthage College, at the time in Carthage, Illinois.
14. Hamre, "Augsburg Theological Seminary," 28.
15. Fevold, *Lutheran Free Church*, 186.
16. Fevold, *Lutheran Free Church*, 205–6.
17. Hamre, "Augsburg Theological Seminary," 28.
18. Chrislock, *From Fjord to Freeway*, 178–79.
19. Warren A. Quanbeck, "Keeping Faith with the Reformation Heritage," in Quanbeck, Fevold, and Frost, *Striving for Ministry*, 152–53.
20. Hamre, "Augsburg Theological Seminary, 1869–1963," 29.
21. Chrislock, *From Fjord to Freeway*, 174–75.
22. Letter from Bernhard Christensen to George Sverdrup, November 28, 1928, as cited in Chrislock, *From Fjord to Freeway*, 175.
23. Granquist, "Scripture Controversy," 71–88.
24. Chrislock, *From Fjord to Freeway*, 184–88.

25. Bernhard Christensen, "An Address delivered at the Pastor's Institute at Augsburg College and Seminary in September 1944," in *Freedom and Christian Education: Addresses and Greetings at the Seventy-Fifth Anniversary of Augsburg College and Theological Seminary, 1869–1944*, ed. John Houkom (Minneapolis: Augsburg College and Seminary Board of Trustees, 1945).
26. Chrislock, *From Fjord to Freeway*, 190.
27. Grindal, "Role of Women," in *Thanksgiving and Hope*, 87.
28. Hamre, "Augsburg Theological Seminary," 34.
29. Hamre, "Augsburg Theological Seminary," 32.
30. For the details of this period of American Lutheran history, see Granquist, *Lutherans in America*, 271–73.
31. "Bernhard Christensen to the Augsburg Board of Trustees, May 4, 1950," in Chrislock, *From Fjord to Freeway*, 227. The merger was already a virtual reality in the college in the 1950s, when the number of non-LFC Lutheran students on campus was double the number of students from the LFC (Chrislock, *From Fjord to Freeway*, 223n37).
32. For the details of these developments within the LFC, see Fevold, *Lutheran Free Church*, 272–98.
33. The final revenge of Gjermund Hoyme?
34. Hamre, "Augsburg Theological Seminary," 34.

6

Northwestern Lutheran Theological Seminary, 1920–1982

To this point a reader might well ask, is the story of Luther Seminary solely about Norwegian Americans? Certainly the history up to this juncture has been primarily about the seminaries that were formed by immigrants from Norway and shaped by the second and third generations of their descendants. This chapter, however, focuses on a different stream of American Lutheranism, namely the descendants of the German Lutheran immigrants who arrived in the English-speaking colonies along the Atlantic seaboard in the eighteenth century. These Lutherans later spread into the midwestern regions of the United States and, in the late nineteenth century, founded English-language Lutheran congregations from Chicago to the Pacific Northwest. This group of American Lutherans needed a seminary on their territory, thus providing the impetus for the founding of Northwestern Lutheran Theological Seminary.

EASTERN, COLONIAL LUTHERANISM

The beginnings of the Lutheran presence in the United States go back to German Lutherans who immigrated to the British colonies during the seventeenth and eighteenth centuries, mainly to the "middle" colonies, from New York to Maryland. The epicenter of colonial Lutheranism was in Pennsylvania, which during the eighteenth century had a large and robust German immigrant population. It was in Pennsylvania that the first Lutheran synod, the Pennsylvania Ministerium, was formed in 1748, as were many of the first Lutheran educational institutions, including the first American Lutheran seminary, Gettysburg Seminary, in 1826. By the beginning of the nineteenth century, this German-immigrant population was well on its way to transitioning to the use of English and in becoming a truly Americanized religious family. As these American Lutherans spread out geographically, they formed numerous local synods, and in 1820, they made the first attempt at a national Lutheran organization, the General Synod. By the 1840s there were dozens of new Lutheran synods formed in the east, south, and midwestern parts of the United States. Most of these new synods were defined by a geographic region, usually one of the states, but some, such as the Tennessee Synod, were defined by theological differences. Additionally, the great European migration of the nineteenth century (1840–1914) brought millions of new Lutherans to the United States, most of whom formed their own synods, based primarily on ethnicity and linguistic differences.

The transition to the United States raised for these Lutherans a whole series of theological and organizational issues as they attempted to transplant their European Lutheranism to the American context. Certainly, American religious pluralism and the voluntary church system were quite different from the European state-church Lutheranism, but eventually American Lutherans figured out how to structure their congregations and organizations for this new context. More of a challenge for them was how to translate their European Lutheranism into the English language and into an American ethos dominated by reformed and revivalistic Protestantism. As these Lutherans made the transition to the use of English in the beginning of the nineteenth century, many of them were (consciously or unconsciously) incorporating many elements of this broader religious ethos into their own traditions. For Lutherans in America, this raised a series of difficult and fundamental questions about the nature of their Lutheran identity and how to establish this identity in a new culture.

The traditional foundation of Lutheranism was the theological positions of the Lutheran confessional documents, especially the Augsburg Confession (1530). Written by Philipp Melanchthon, this document was addressed to the Catholic imperial court of the Holy Roman Empire and was as conciliatory to that body as Melanchthon dared, within the bounds of the Lutheran tradition. When many American Protestants (and more than a few American Lutherans) looked at this sixteenth-century document, they judged it to be too Catholic in its positions on a number of issues, including the real presence of Christ in Holy Communion, the question of baptismal regeneration, and the Sabbath. Already by the late eighteenth century some American Lutherans were distancing themselves from the Lutheran confessional documents because of this. Samuel Simon Schmucker, the premier American Lutheran leader of the early nineteenth century, attempted to "save" the Augsburg Confession for American Lutherans by editing out these objectionable parts. Though this attempt failed, the question of confessional authority, and the theological nature of Lutheranism in America, remained an open question.[1]

THE SYNOD OF THE NORTHWEST AND A NEW SEMINARY

In 1867 this open question led to a splintering of the national Lutheran organization, the General Synod, when a group of more confessional Lutheran synods broke away to form a rival national organization, the General Council. This new organization was more formally attached to the Augsburg Confession and Lutheran confessional theology, though not strictly enough for some others, especially conservative immigrant Lutheran groups such as the Missouri Synod. As American Lutherans moved into the new territories of the midwestern United States, they formed a series of rival regional synods. As leaders from the General Council, including William Passavant, George Gerberding, and George Trabert, founded congregations stretching from Milwaukee to Montana, they eventually formed a regional synod of the General Council, the Synod of the Northwest, in 1891. When the General Council itself was reunited with the General Synod (and the United Synod, South) in 1918 to form the United Lutheran Church in America (ULCA), the Synod of the Northwest remained as one of its regional synods. It was from this synod that the Northwestern Lutheran Theological Seminary was eventually formed.

Both the General Synod and the General Council, and eventually their successor, the ULCA, were predominantly situated in the mid-Atlantic states, especially in Pennsylvania, and this was where their seminaries were located, as well. As the General Council expanded into the Midwest and Pacific Northwest, pastors and congregations in these regions pushed for a new seminary closer to these areas. As early as 1869, there were calls within the General Council for a western seminary to be located in Chicago, then the fast-growing gateway to the west. This seminary was imagined not only for the synods of the General Council but also to provide English-language theological education for the German and Scandinavian Lutheran denominations, although this vision never came to fruition. In 1874, the indefatigable William Passavant, not waiting for the General Council to take action, took matters into his own hands and purchased a two-acre section of land on the north side of Chicago for the new seminary. But funding for the new seminary was hard to obtain, and it was not until 1891 that the new Chicago Lutheran Theological Seminary was opened. In 1910 this seminary was moved to Maywood, Illinois, a western suburb of Chicago.[2]

In the General Council, as in the ULCA that succeeded it, seminaries were owned and controlled not by the national church body but by combinations of regional synods and other groups. This situation of the Chicago Lutheran Theological Seminary was even more complicated. Although it was initiated by the General Council, it was also supported by congregations and synods from the rival General Synod, and the seminary itself was controlled by an independent, self-perpetuating board of directors. For several years prior to 1920, there were theological and ecclesiastical tensions within the seminary itself, which came to a head in 1920 when the board appointed a new professor to the institution, a person whom a number of the

General Council members of the faculty considered unqualified. Subsequent protests by some students and faculty were disregarded by the board, who summarily dismissed four of the dissenting professors, G. H. Gerberding, Bertram Reed, Paul H. Roth, and Joseph Stump. That year, those four professors and a considerable number of students established their own new seminary in Chicago, with the backing of the Synod of the Northwest. This new seminary was moved to Fargo, North Dakota, in 1921, in line with the request from the ULCA Board of Education that the new seminary be no closer to Chicago than Fargo. But the location in Fargo was too far from the core area of the Synod of the Northwest (Wisconsin and Minnesota), and there were not enough local congregations for students to do field work. So in 1922 the synod moved the seminary again, this time to Minneapolis, Minnesota. These developments were expressly contrary to the wishes of the administration of the ULCA and its special "committee of fifteen" set up to examine the situation surrounding the Chicago Lutheran Theological Seminary. But given its organizational structure and the tradition of regional control over seminaries, there was little that the ULCA could do to stop the Synod of the Northwest from settling the new seminary in Minneapolis.[3] The founding constitution of the ULCA expressly prohibited its national church body from owning or legally controlling any seminaries.

NORTHWESTERN LUTHERAN THEOLOGICAL SEMINARY

The new fledgling Northwestern Lutheran Theological Seminary survived its peripatetic beginnings with the assistance of the Synod of the Northwest, which raised over $175,000 to finally settle the seminary in a building on 19th Avenue NE in Minneapolis in time for the 1922 academic year. Joseph Stump (systematics) was the seminary's first president, and the other three professors that left the Chicago seminary, George H. Gerberding (pastoral theology), Bertram Reed (Old Testament), and Paul Roth (New Testament and church history), constituted the rest of the faculty. The seminary was born of an expansive vision of providing a Lutheran theological education in English for students from all Lutheran denominations. But by the

1920s the seminaries of the "ethnic" Lutheran denominations were rapidly transitioning to the use of English, so the Northwestern seminary drew its students mainly from the ULCA synods in the Midwest and West.

However, Northwestern did meet a longstanding need for a seminary on the territory of the Synod of the Northwest. Successive presidents of this synod complained that the Chicago seminary was not attracting and producing candidates for synodical congregations; in the twenty-nine years that the synod was connected with the seminary in Chicago (1891–1920) only twelve students from the synod graduated and took calls in the synod.[4] The new location of the seminary in Minneapolis was better situated, and the hope was that more candidates would attend. Optimistically, the *Northwestern Seminary Bulletin* noted in 1924:

> In the four years, including the year at Chicago, our Synod has graduated 34 men. Of the thirteen seminaries in the U.L.C.A. only four have graduated more, and some of these institutions are very old. . . . Our classes bid to increase in size rather rapidly. There is no doubt at all about the prospects of a properly supported English Seminary in this territory.[5]

The initial optimism of the growth of the seminary was not particularly realized in the next two decades, as the numbers of students enrolled and students graduated remained steady through 1940. Seminary enrollments averaged around twenty-three students for the first twenty years of its existence, and there were an average of seven graduates every year. Given the size of the Synod of the Northwest, however, this was a relatively good result, and increasingly the seminary drew students from other midwestern ULCA synods.

The fact that the ULCA did not have any control over the seminaries of its constituent synods did not stop the ULCA Board of Education from trying to engineer various realignments of those seminaries. The problem was that the ULCA as a whole had too many seminaries, thirteen in total, which were too small and cost too much to operate. In comparison, the Lutheran Church Missouri Synod (which was nearly the same size as the ULCA) had two seminaries, and the Norwegian Lutheran Church in America had only one. At its 1924 convention, the ULCA established a special Commission on Theological Education, charged with examining this situation. As one historian noted, "From 1926 on there was continuous pressure from the top echelon of the Church that the existing seminaries be consolidated."[6] The initial pressure was that Northwestern Seminary be reunited with the seminary in Chicago, but nothing came of these suggestions. When the commission made its reports to the ULCA convention in 1932, one recommendation was that Northwestern Seminary be consolidated with two smaller seminaries in Nebraska (Martin Luther and Western) to form a new "Western" Seminary. This suggestion was ignored, as Northwestern Seminary had no interest in relocating to Nebraska, and the Nebraska seminaries had no interest in moving to Minneapolis.[7] The national administration of the ULCA continued to seek power over the seminaries and to force some consolidations, but these efforts were equally ineffective.

The Synod of the Northwest had great pride in its seminary, in spite of pressures and sometimes ridicule from other sections of the ULCA. The first several years of the seminary were fairly rocky, as a "seminary in exile." A historical sketch at the twenty-fifth anniversary of the seminary recalled:

> Our opponents accused the Synod of starting a spite seminary to humor a few willful men. They predicted that we would soon run out of funds. There were a few times when it looked like their predictions might come true. . . . On November 15, 1920, I received a letter from Dr. Stump asking for $500 by return mail. There were not that many pennies in the treasury.[8]

A "ram in the thicket" (Gen 22:13) was found, when the next day an unknown donor sent $500 for the seminary. Even though the Great Depression of the 1930s forced drastic economies on the seminary administration, they were able to weather this period and keep the seminary in operation. In 1933, the seminary reported that "the difficult conditions under which the whole Church has been suffering have fallen upon the Seminary, too, which had borne its shares of cuts and diminished income. But the work of the school has not suffered."[9] Enrollments at the seminary remained fairly stable through the 1930s, as did the graduation rate. In October 1934, the seminary reported to its constituency, "There was a deficit last year of about one thousand dollars. Considered in comparison with other seminaries, this is a mighty fine record."[10] The Synod of the Northwest historically had a definite emphasis on stewardship, and this was a continuing theme at Northwestern Seminary as well.

THE LIFE OF THE SEMINARY

The academic life of the seminary itself mirrored that of many other small seminaries of the day. There were four faculty members, including President Joseph Stump, and virtually no other staff. The faculty served to oversee student life, the library, and all other aspects of the school. When President Stump retired in 1935, he was replaced as president by Paul H. Roth. The number of faculty was increased to five by 1941, a number that remained steady until after World War II. There was a bit of controversy in 1944 when one of the tenured faculty was dismissed by the seminary board, but historian Dorris Flesner notes "the grounds for dismissal appear to have been other than a question of fidelity to the confessions of the Church."[11] The curriculum was highly structured and consisted mainly of required classes. The academic year initially consisted of six, five-week terms (a thirty-week year), and students generally took three classes per term; classes met five days a week. This calendar lasted until 1941, when the seminary went on the quarter system, consisting of three, eleven-week terms (a thirty-three-week year). The seminary offered two basic degrees: the bachelor of divinity (BD) required Hebrew and a minimum grade point of about a B plus, while the Diploma of Divinity was granted to other graduates. A limited number of STM degrees were granted through this time period. In 1938 the ULCA Board of Education urged their seminaries to apply for accreditation from the American Association of Theological Schools (AATS), something that Northwestern achieved in 1944.[12]

Student life at the seminary was typical for the time; all the seminarians were unmarried young men, and most of them lived together in the seminary building. The students were required to work in local congregations during the academic year and were urged to disperse into the congregations of the synod over the summer to assist in these congregational ministries and to earn money. Tuition and room for students from the Synod of the Northwest was free, and students paid only for their meals at a student-run boarding club (four dollars a week until 1945, when it increased to six dollars a week). By 1926, the seminary *Bulletin* noted that all the rooms in the seminary building were occupied and that they had had to find two extra rooms to accommodate the overflow of students.[13] Students were quite on top of each other, in that they lived, socialized, and went to classes together in the same building. In 1927, a student gave a rather detailed sketch of dormitory life, suggesting that it was better than he had anticipated:

> Personally, I must say that our dormitory bunch is the nicest and jolliest bunch of fellows I ever lived with under one roof, and when I say this, I say a great deal, considering the former monkish image I had of a Theological Seminary.[14]

In that year (1926/27) sixteen of the thirty students in the seminary lived in the dormitory, but this was a peak year of enrollment; after this the enrollment averaged in the low twenties for the next ten years, not rising until the late 1930s.

A NEW HOME FOR NORTHWESTERN

The rising student numbers put pressure on the physical plant of the seminary, and the need for larger facilities was evident throughout the 1930s, although the financial situation of the times meant that nothing could be done about this immediately. But in 1940 the Synod of the Northwest authorized a fund drive for a new location for the seminary and for further endowment, which gathered in $200,000. As one historian notes, "in choosing its living space, the seminary had a penchant for great old mansions,"[15] the first in Chicago in 1920, and the second in Fargo in 1921. In 1940 the seminary purchased another building in south Minneapolis, the Charles S.

Pillsbury mansion in the vicinity of the Minneapolis Institute of Art, and renamed the building Passavant Hall, in honor of William Passavant. Eventually the seminary bought the adjacent Alfred Pillsbury mansion and two other local mansions from the Crosby family.[16]

The Charles S. Pillsbury mansion became the headquarters of the seminary and retained an elegant air from its former occupants. President Roth's daughter, Amalie Roth Shannon, described the building:

> A carved oak grand staircase, hand-riven English paneling, pegged teak floors, molded plaster ceilings, dozens of leaded-glass windows with 17th century glass Flemish medallions. There were seven fireplaces. One, of sculpted stone dating from London's 1660 fire, graced the president's office; the living room fireplace was of carved oak.[17]

Of course not all the seminary buildings were so grand, but the main building gave the seminary a grand and gracious space as its focal point. The Alfred Pillsbury house, later Jensen Hall, served as the seminary library. This complex of buildings also included space for the offices of the Synod of the Northwest.

THE PRESSURES OF WORLD WAR II

The new and expanded physical space for the seminary came just in time, because the seminary saw a jump in enrollments during the 1940s; from a low of twenty students in 1940, the numbers doubled by 1944 to forty students and remained steady until the postwar boom of the 1950s. This is despite the pressures and hardships of the war period, during which resources were squeezed and the academic program was accelerated. In the summer of 1942, the *Bulletin* noted that despite positive indications, there were concerns:

> Several students were prevented from entering by the military draft. The prospects for a large entering class this fall are at this writing good though no one can say what changes military need may bring about.[18]

In recognition of the needs of both the military and the congregations of the synod, the seminary commissioned a committee in 1943 to study how the military draft would affect the supply of students;

from this, the seminary adopted a new and accelerated academic calendar in that year, in which the seminary operated year-round so that students could be graduated early. As the *Bulletin* noted in 1945:

> The accelerated schedule compelling us to hold school practically through the entire year also made for much confusion and extra labor. For one thing it overloaded the teaching force, and for another it increased the financial load for the students, who had less time to earn money during the summer.[19]

The article continued by hoping that the seminary would soon be "released" from the accelerated schedule and returned to normal operations.

The jump in enrollments during the 1940s was helpful, because not only were there strong needs for pastors in synodical congregations, there was an equally strong need for military chaplains. In 1943, ten pastors from the Synod of the Northwest (graduates of the seminary) served as military chaplains, and two pastors were called to serve at Lutheran service centers attached to military installations. Recent graduates of the seminary who had gone into the military chaplaincy returned to campus to report on their experiences:

> Maynard Silseth, last year's graduate and now chaplain in the navy told us of his experiences in his new duties. And Army chaplain Marvin R. Moll of the same class visited us for several days while on leave and shared his experiences and new insights with us.[20]

The seminary itself was apparently affiliated with the Navy's V-12 program, whose Theological Units produced candidates for the navy chaplaincy (Luther Seminary was also participating in this program).

THE POSTWAR EXPANSION

As World War II was coming to an end in 1945, the seminary was not only looking forward to resuming normal, prewar operations, but seeking to expand its operations and the number of students it graduated. In a 1945 item in the *Bulletin*, the expectation was noted that this increase would be beneficial for the church and the world:

> The great world need calls for many times the number of men we are sending out. The Seminary is in touch and correspondence with quite a number of men who were looking to the ministry when they were taken up into the war effort and with others who while in the service have felt the call to preach the gospel, and it seems that we shall have increased enrollment as demobilization proceeds.[21]

The seminary also looked toward the government programs to finance education for the returning veterans as an additional bonus. The surge began modestly, as presumably some of the interested candidates had to finish their college education first. But postwar enrollments began to climb; from thirty-five students in 1945 the numbers increased to fifty-two in 1949, and then jumped again as high as ninety-three in 1953 and 1954, settling down to an average of around seventy-five students per year through the 1950s.

This postwar enrollment growth meant that the seminary had to expand both its faculty and its physical facilities in order to deal with a doubling (or more) of its student body. The original Charles S. Pillsbury mansion housed the academic and administrative offices, while the Alfred Pillsbury mansion contained the library. In 1948, the *Bulletin* reported that the synod had authorized the purchase of a house for twenty single students.[22] This building, named after synod founder and seminary faculty member George Gerberding, also housed the boarding club. Another house, along with two apartment buildings (purchased later) housed married students. The postwar surge meant that the old days of the "monkish" single seminary student were over; although there would still be single students attending the seminary, new arrangements would have to be made to accommodate spouses and families. In 1950 the Synod of the Northwest raised $150,000 for the seminary endowment through an appeal across the ULCA named the Christian Higher Education Year Appeal, and another $450,000 was raised in 1959. These funds, which helped to strengthen the seminary endowment and to facilitate the purchase of new buildings, also indicated the pride in ownership that the Synod of the Northwest had in its seminary.

The postwar expansion also necessitated a corresponding expansion of the seminary faculty, the numbers of which had remained fairly steady at four to five during the first twenty-five years (1920–1945). Paul H. Roth, who had been seminary president since 1935, retired in 1950 and was replaced by faculty member Jonas Dresser, who served as president 1950–1956. After Dresser, the seminary brought in Clemens Zeidler, who was president from 1956 to 1976. A number of new faculty were added after World War II, including Axel Ahlén (systematics) in 1945, William Cooper (Old Testament) in 1946, Bryce Schumacher (New Testament) in 1953, and David Belgum (practical theology) in 1955. By the mid-1950s, the size of the faculty increased to seven, and by the end of the decade that number was increased to nine. Faculty added later in the 1950s included Robert Bartels (New Testament) in 1956, George Bass (homiletics) and Dorris Flesner (church history) in 1957, and Robert Paul Roth (systematics) in 1961. Beyond the additional faculty, the seminary relied on quite a number of different occasional faculty, often "borrowed" from Augsburg and Luther seminaries, to deal with the great increase in the student body.

The seminary had shifted to the quarter system in 1941, but the requirement for class hours was retained at 145 for graduation, which left little room for possible electives. In 1952 the total number of hours in required subjects was reduced to 135, and in 1954 to 111 hours. Given that the graduation requirement remained at 145, there was much more room for possible electives, which increasingly show up in the seminary catalog. In 1958 the total number of hours required for graduation was reduced to 135, of which 88 were in required courses. This set of requirements lasted until 1971, after which the seminary adopted the 4-1-4 academic schedule.

The addition of new faculty members meant as well that additional areas of study were offered in the seminary curriculum, especially with the addition of homiletics, practical theology, and church history. Northwestern had not followed the lead of other Lutheran seminaries in adding an internship year until 1955, when this was made available to students on a voluntary basis. The internship year was made mandatory in 1963, following the 1962 church merger that produced the Lutheran Church in America (LCA), which decided that an internship would be required in all of its seminaries.[23] New courses and areas of study appeared in the seminary catalog. Arthur C. P. Hayes, who taught New Testament at the seminary from 1923 to 1953, was a pioneer in the use of the historical-critical method in seminary education, predating the introduction of this material in other Lutheran seminaries by a decade or more. Though the seminary was rooted in the conservative confessional Lutheran theology of the General Council, this development was apparently not controversial among them. As Dorris Flesner observed:

> Since he [Hayes] joined the faculty when Dr. Stump was President of the seminary and they served rather congenially, it does not appear that the strongly confessional Dr. Stump found any difficulty in Hayes' historical-critical approach to the Scriptures.[24]

The historians of Northwestern (Roth and Flesner) emphasize its attachment to traditional Lutheran confessional theology, but it seems clear that this commitment was flexible enough for the seminary faculty to explore new areas of theological inquiry.

THEOLOGICAL CONFLICTS

The confessional nature of the seminary, and of the Synod of the Northwest, was put into some perspective in 1955–1956, when three pastors of the synod, George Crist (NLTS class of 1950), Victor Wrigley (class of 1948), and John Gerberding (class of 1948), were accused of heresy and brought to a trial within the synod. The charges suggested that the three denied the virgin birth and physical resurrection of Christ, the efficacy of intercessory prayer, and the real presence of Christ in the sacrament of the altar. After a synodical examination of these three, Crist and Wrigley were found guilty; Crist left the ministry altogether and eventually went into journalism, while Wrigley wrote a clarifying document and was "unanimously restated" to the synod and his congregation.[25] Gerberding was acquitted of the charges, although the examining committee characterized as "offensive" his testimony, and noted the "obvious confusion, immaturity, and inconsistencies" in his views.[26] Although the incident did not directly involve Northwestern, it indirectly involved the seminary, especially because one of the seminary professors and another synod pastor who would join the faculty were on the trial committee for the three men. Historian of the seminary and former professor Robert Paul Roth also notes the following incident, which appears to be separate from the previous one: "Another accusation of heresy came within the faculty, but after thorough investigation with the writing of papers and reasonable discussion this matter was amicably settled."[27] It has not been possible to determine the facts of this event beyond the information supplied by Roth.

WOMEN AND STUDENTS FROM AROUND THE WORLD

The postwar era at Northwestern brought other changes to the seminary community. Already in 1941, the women associated with the seminary formed the "Women's Auxiliary of Northwestern Lutheran Theological Seminary," signing up over one hundred members at its initial meeting. Their organization was designed not only to support the internal work of the seminary but also to raise awareness about the seminary in the congregation of the synod. The *Bulletin* commented: "With the organized enthusiasm and energy of these women of the Church a powerful new force has been added to the Seminary's support."[28] This group contributed to the support of the seminary in a significant fashion for the forty years of its existence, especially supporting the seminary students. As recounted, the meetings of this group on campus made it possible for synodical women to become acquainted with the seminary and students, "so much that they took a personal interest in individual students, providing them with home-cooked meals and seeing to their other needs."[29]

With the increasing prevalence of married students at the seminary after World War II, the wives of the seminary students brought another dimension to the seminary community. Although women would not be admitted to the seminary for another twenty years, these women were still quite invested in the ministries into which their husbands were being called. In 1959, the *Bulletin* recounted the existence of an organization of seminary wives:

> The "Sem Wives" have started their meetings . . . a variety of edifying topics will be the subject of their interest for the next months, indicating that they are keeping pace with their husbands. . . . A number . . . are meeting informally with Dr. Cooper and Dr. Ahlen every two weeks in the study of Luther's Large Catechism.[30]

The diversity of the campus was also increased by the presence of international students, brought about by the missionary activity of the ULCA. The presence of international students was sometimes an issue for the seminary in segregated south Minneapolis. In 1943 an Indian student and his wife from the ULCA mission in British-occupied Guyana arrived to begin his seminary education, but because of their skin color the seminary could not find an apartment for them in the surrounding area. The solution was to provide them an apartment on the second floor of Passavant Hall, which historian Roth wryly notes "meant ironically that they lived in the luxury of a mansion that they would never have been able to rent outside."[31]

THE LUTHERAN CHURCH IN AMERICA, 1962–1988

After World War II, American Lutherans generally became more serious about further mergers that might reduce the number of major American Lutheran denominations, of which there were about ten to twelve (depending on how you define "major"). With the two largest groups, the ULCA and the Missouri Synod, at somewhat opposite ends of the theological spectrum, the groups in the middle were left to see how they might line up. This process eventually resulted in two major mergers in the early 1960s, with the formation of the American Lutheran Church (ALC) in 1960 and the Lutheran Church in America (LCA) in 1962.[32] The Synod of the Northwest became a part of the newly created LCA when the ULCA merged with the Augustana Lutheran Church (Swedish) and two other small groups, a Danish denomination and a Finnish one. The 1918 merger that created the ULCA had meant no real changes for the Synod of the

Northwest, but the LCA merger in 1962 brought about its end. The congregations of the Synod of the Northwest, together with congregations of the other three merging denominations, were separated into new geographical synods in the upper Midwest.

The new LCA synods in Minnesota and the Dakotas would have the greatest effect on Northwestern, as these would now be the synods that owned the seminary. Although the Synod of the Northwest had a number of prominent congregations in this area, the congregations of the former Augustana church were much more numerous, and they dominated these new synods. This left open the question of the fate of Northwestern Seminary in the new church. But the new LCA synods in the region, and especially the former Augustana congregations, readily embraced Northwestern and brought about another stage of its growth in the 1960s. The reasons for this embrace are complicated but have to do with internal politics and tensions within the former Augustana Lutheran Church. In that denomination, the two rival centers of power were in Illinois and Minnesota; the seminary of the church, and the college that the church supported, were in Rock Island, Illinois.[33] The Minnesota Augustanans thus saw in the new synodical arrangements within the LCA a chance to support their own seminary in the upper Midwest and to no longer have to send their students to Illinois. This is surely part of the reason for the growth of enrollment at Northwestern during the 1960s and 1970s; enrollment jumped to the low 100s beginning in 1962 and climbed again to around 170 students by the early 1970s. The Augustana college in Minnesota—Gustavus Adolphus College, St. Peter—was increasingly a source of students for Northwestern, now rivaling the traditional Synod of the Northwest college, Carthage College in Kenosha, Wisconsin.

The growing allegiance of the Augustana congregations to Northwestern, and the rise in its student body during the early 1960s, came at an opportune moment for the seminary, as there were proposed changes in seminary education in the new LCA that could well have meant major changes, or even its end. As has been seen earlier, the ULCA had quite a few small seminaries, and it had limited power or success in getting these seminaries to merge; with the addition of the other denominations, the new LCA had even more seminaries. Starting in 1963, the new LCA empaneled a new group to study the "seminary situation" and recommend changes. The group's conclusions were outlined in the Bergendoff Report[34] and called for major consolidations of seminaries. Some, such as the combination of Gettysburg and Philadelphia seminaries, were scuttled by vested interests, while the major accomplishment of this report was the formation of the Lutheran School of Theology at Chicago (LSTC) from five smaller Lutheran seminaries, including Augustana Seminary and Chicago Lutheran Theological Seminary in Maywood, Illinois. The future of Northwestern was also debated, with one suggestion being that this seminary, too, be included in the merger that was to form LSTC. Historian Flesner recounts:

> An assistant to LCA President Franklin Clark Fry, thus presumably representing Dr. Fry's wishes, suggested to Northwestern Seminary that it enter discussions looking toward the formation of the new Lutheran School of Theology at Chicago.[35]

A surprise motion to do exactly this was presented at the 1964 convention of the Minnesota Synod of the LCA but soundly defeated; the Augustana contingent "spoke fervently in favor of keeping Northwestern Seminary in the Twin Cities."[36]

A NEW CAMPUS IN SAINT PAUL

The growth of enrollment at Northwestern in the 1950s and 1960s, however, strained the physical resources of the seminary, and leaders began to look around for a possible new location for the institution. Seminary leaders, led by President Zeidler, had already purchased ten acres of property in Bloomington, Minnesota, and developed plans for a campus there. These plans were, however, rejected by the synodical conventions in 1963, when Zeidler and the Northwestern board were "out-maneuvered by people like Cy Rachie, Paul Graf, and Melvin Hammarberg."[37] Increasingly, seminary and synodical leaders were thinking in terms of a possible closer relationship with Luther Seminary in Saint Paul, and this was the direction that was then taken. Discussions ensued between the two seminaries and their respective boards, leading to a proposal from Luther that Northwestern build their new campus on property adjacent to Luther in Saint Paul. After some negotiations between the two seminaries and their respective judicatories, the arrangements were finally approved.

A single new building for Northwestern Seminary, opening in 1967, was located on the southwest corner of Hendon and Fulham streets in St. Paul and sat between the two historic Luther Seminary buildings, Bockman and Gullixson halls, and the old campus of the Breck School that Luther had purchased in 1955. The new Northwestern building, designed by the Northfield, Minnesota, firm of Sovik, Mathre, and Madson, contained all the offices and classrooms needed for the seminary, as well as a chapel and library (the latter was eventually combined with Luther's).[38] Single students lived in the Luther dormitory, while a block of apartments were reserved for married students in the new apartment complex that Luther Seminary was building at the time. The Northwestern building, of which the seminary community was very proud, was designed to operate as an independent or federated seminary, or, if it should come to pass, as a contribution to a fully merged seminary. In 1965 the Minnesota Synod of the LCA started a fund drive that gathered in $500,000 for the new building. Certainly there must have been some nostalgia for the graceful old Pillsbury mansions in south Minneapolis that the seminary had vacated, but as elegant as these buildings were, they had become inadequate for the needs of a growing seminary.

One of the controversial features of the new Northwestern building was the presence of a chapel space, the Chapel of the Cross. As eventual closer relations with Luther Seminary were envisioned even at the time of the construction, some argued that the two communities should begin to worship together in the Luther Seminary chapel in Aasgaard Hall (one of the former Breck School buildings), and that a second chapel was unnecessary and would hinder the integration of the two institutions. But Northwestern had a long tradition of formal worship following the Lutheran hymnals, and they seemed to think that Luther's worship traditions were rather too free for their liking. Historian Roth notes:

> Aasgaard was a converted gymnasium . . . affectionately but aptly called "Calvin's Barn" by the Luther students. . . . [T]his space limited worship

to a meeting house. Northwestern always had a high view of Christ which engendered a high view of Scripture and then a high view of worship.[39]

He notes further that Luther Seminary never had a course on worship in its curriculum. In 1964 one of the new professors, Clarence Lund, had as part of his portfolio teaching classes in worship and liturgics, which was new for both Northwestern and Luther.

It is clear that Northwestern took its daily chapel services and other worship experience seriously, although perhaps not all the students took them equally seriously. The 1955 seminary *Catalog* stated that "the cultivation of spiritual life is one of the goals of the Seminary," to which the 1961 *Catalog* added, "Each student is expected to participate actively in these services unless excused by the Faculty." The idea of requiring attendance was, however, not implemented. In the 1950s and 1960s the sacrament of Holy Communion was offered monthly and on special festivals, while by 1970 it was being offered weekly. Although the intent of the *Catalog* and the faculty was certainly clear, as historian Flesner admitted in 1974, "participation in chapel services leaves much to be desired . . . [and] efforts to control 'competing activities' have long since been abandoned."[40] This is, however, a sentence that could probably be uttered about many other seminaries at many other points in their histories.

GROWTH AND CHANGE IN THE 1960S

The growth of the student body in the 1960s, supported by the new facilities, was matched by a corresponding growth in the size of the permanent teaching faculty. During the 1950s the number of such faculty rose from five to nine, and in the 1960s it rose again from nine to eleven. New faculty included Norman Bakken (biblical interpretation) in 1962, Clarence Lund (Christian education and liturgics) in 1964, Melvin Kimble (pastoral care and internship) in 1965, Martin Lehman (church history) in 1968, and Walter Buschman (systematics) in 1969, along with a number of occasional teaching faculty borrowed from other institutions or from congregations. As was true with many other seminaries of the time, there was also a growth in administrative staff, as functions traditionally handled by faculty members were turned over to other employees. This was a cause for concern among some of the faculty members, who felt that their traditional control over the operation of the seminary was being given over to administrative personnel. But Northwestern was no longer a cozy little operation, and there was need for additional oversight of its operations that the faculty could not provide.

The seminary curriculum was updated in 1970. It retained the overall number of hours (135) needed to earn the basic degree, but the number of hours in required courses was reduced to eighty-eight, which freed up a number of hours for elective subjects. In 1971, Northwestern and five other seminaries (including Luther) formed the Minnesota Consortium of Theological Schools, which was organized to coordinate activities and to allow students to take classes at other local seminaries; Northwestern dean Robert Roth was the second president of the group. In order to allow for more interchange, Northwestern adopted the 4-1-4 schedule in 1972, which meant students took four courses each semester and one intensive four-week course in January (Interim). One problem was that Luther Seminary refused to leave its quarter system, but the two schools worked to find accommodations between the two systems. A concentrated period of chaplaincy training in a clinical setting, Clinical Pastoral Education, was introduced in the early 1970s as an elective and was later required by the LCA as an ordination requirement.

Increasingly students were arguing for a greater say in the composition of their courses and for more flexibility and choice in their electives; the reduction in the number of required courses, along with the January Interim, allowed for some flexibility, although the degree was still rather heavy on required courses. The late 1960s were a time of great controversy and change, and these elements were present at Northwestern, as well. In 1970, with the Vietnam War raging and the Kent State massacre fresh in students' minds, they asked the dean to suspend classes so that some of them could travel to Washington, DC, to participate in protests. When this proved impossible, the students instead sponsored Dean Roth to travel in their stead, so that he could meet with governmental officials to present their concerns. As he would later reflect, "It was the freedom of the Spirit . . .

that provoked [the seminary's] protest against the immorality of the Vietnam War and the oppression of minority people."[41] Around that same time, President Zeidler taught a course on law in theology and society, part of which was focused on the question of conscientious objection to military service; in 1971 a document from this course on this subject was printed in the seminary *Bulletin*.[42] Part of the large increase in students in the seminary, which rose from 95 in 1965 to 173 in 1972, might well have been partly occasioned by avoidance of the military draft.

Another major social change came about in the 1970s and involved the ordination of women as pastors, the first of which occurred in 1970. The Lutheran Council in the USA (LCUSA), a coordinating organization for the LCA, ALC, and Missouri Synod, initiated a study of the question in the late 1960s and carefully laid out the biblical and theological parameters of the question in 1969. The individual denominations were left to act on the report as they saw fit, with the LCA and ALC moving quickly to allow the ordination of women, while the Missouri Synod decided against this move. This meant a small but increasing number of women began enrolling in seminaries like Northwestern beginning in the late 1960s, and a larger movement through the 1970s. Of course this necessitated many changes at the seminary surrounding classes, internships, housing, and many other details. Women pastors, and even clergy couples, were now an increasing phenomenon, signaling a new paradigm of seminary life.

The decade of the 1970s also saw its share of problems for Northwestern Seminary. Like many other schools at this time, Northwestern felt financial pressures through this decade. Up to this point, the seminary had not been forced to charge its students tuition, but this was an option that began to loom larger. In 1960 students paid $35 for room and $120 for board per quarter. By 1969 this had increased to $90 for room and $152.50 for board, and this continued to increase. By 1972 the semester board option was gone altogether, and students paid by the meal at the refectory. Northwestern had to deal with the lingering costs of the new building and its furnishing, an increasing number of faculty and staff, and declining financial support from the synods. But what really brought about the crisis was the rampant monetary inflation of this era, which increased costs much faster than the seminary's financial support. In order to deal with this problem in the early 1970s, the seminary Board of Trustees sought to eliminate two faculty positions in order to save money and balance the budget. However, after studying the situation, Dean Roth felt that all the current faculty were needed and that the budget would have to be balanced in some other fashion.[43] Fortunately for the time, members of the board were able to raise additional funds, but this would only be a stopgap measure, and eventually seminary students would have to start paying tuition, as well.

TOWARD THE MERGER WITH LUTHER SEMINARY

From the late 1950s on, there had been discussions within Northwestern Seminary and in its synods about the possibility of federation, affiliation, or merger with Luther Seminary, discussions accelerated by the 1963 Bergendoff Report and by the 1967 relocation of the seminary to Saint Paul. But though many of those concerned thought that this would be the general direction of Northwestern, the process that led to the final merger of the two institutions was a tortuous path that took over fifteen years to accomplish. There were many questions, reservations, and roadblocks on both sides, and even though the new Northwestern building was a large step in the direction of eventual merger, that step did not necessarily ensure that the merger would ever come. There were many questions concerning the effect of such a move on the respective cultures of the institutions and their differences in size; with Luther at seven hundred students and Northwestern at around two hundred, the partisans of the latter institution were particularly concerned about this.

Alternate futures for Northwestern were offered and rebuffed; merger into LSTC was rejected, as was the new campus in Bloomington, which had its important supporters, including President Zeidler. Already in 1966, ahead of the construction of the new building in Saint Paul, the two seminaries established the Luther-Northwestern Coordinating Committee (LNCC), but progress was slow. Although the two institutions were adjacent to one another and part of the seminary consortium, they did not have a common academic schedule, which limited the amount of interaction that their students could have with each other. Early progress consisted of establishing joint graduate degree programs, publishing common course offerings, and other academic details.

But many barriers needed to be overcome. In terms of structure and governance, the two institutions had very different compositions. Northwestern was owned by its two local LCA synods, Minnesota and Red River, and was an incorporated entity of its own. The seminary and its board were also answerable to the LCA Board of Theological Education, which exercised some control over the institution. In the case of Luther Seminary, however, the seminary itself was owned directly by the national ALC, which exercised control over the school through its Board of Theological Education and Ministry (BTEM). Luther Seminary was not even independently incorporated and legally could not own or control property. Before any kind of merger could possibly occur, Luther Seminary would have to become incorporated in its own right, and there were powerful persons in the national ALC who were strongly resistant to this.[44]

As close as they might seem to outsiders, there were important cultural, structural, and theological differences between the ALC and LCA (which is why the merger negotiations in the 1950s ended up with two denominations rather than one). The issue of ownership had caused the merger discussions to grind to a halt between 1973 and 1974.

The next organizational step came during the 1974/75 academic year, with the formation of a joint Self-Study Committee to examine the histories and cultures of the two institutions and suggest how closer relationships might proceed. The faculty teams worked on two different documents. The first team developed descriptive histories of the institutions (Dorris Flesner for Northwestern and Gerhard Forde for Luther), while the second team (Warren Quanbeck and Robert Roth) wrote a normative plan outlining the pathways toward future work. Driving this effort was the newly installed president of Luther Seminary, Lloyd Svendsbye, who took office in the summer of 1974. The work was made more difficult because the long-time president of Northwestern, Clemens Zeidler, was opposed to a possible merger of the two institutions, and he was joined in this position by a few of the faculty from both schools.⁴⁵ But the momentum was to carry the work forward.

MAXIMAL FUNCTIONAL UNIFICATION

The interim result was a gradual combination of assets and programs, a process that came to be known as "Maximal Functional Unification," or MFU (a perhaps unfortunate acronym). The two schools would move incrementally toward sharing as much of a common program as possible without full organic union. The libraries of the two schools were combined in 1976 in Luther's Gullixson Hall. The two schools also shared a common bookstore in the basement of that building. The Self-Study Committee also ironed out the parameters of common worship and a shared set of regulations for governance, faculty organization, and a single vision for a curriculum.

With the retirement of President Clemens Zeidler in 1976, Luther president Lloyd Svendsbye was elected by the Northwestern board to also become the president of Northwestern. At this point then, "the two schools had one president, one dean, one librarian, one director of graduate studies, one dean of students, one director of continuing education, and one director of contextual education. 'Maximal functional unification' was complete."⁴⁶ Luther being the larger school got most of the positions, but the director of graduate studies and the dean of students were drawn from Northwestern.

There were, however, limits to the amount of unification possible under such interim arrangements. There remained two separate faculties with their own monthly faculty meetings, as well as a monthly joint faculty meeting, after which the two faculties would retire to different rooms to separately ratify the actions they had agreed to jointly. The boards of both seminaries continued to meet independently, and there were separate denominational boards to oversee these seminaries. This meant quite a few meetings and quite a few bosses for Svendsbye. Most of the time things went well, but there was quite a bit of resistance to the new arrangements from the ALC's Board of Theological Education and Ministry and its director, George Schultz, as well as difficulties in balancing and honoring the very different structures and procedures of the ALC and LCA.

Unification efforts are always difficult and fraught with unseen problems along the way. As complicated as it was, the structural elements of moving toward merger, as listed above, were actually the simpler of the processes that needed to happen to make the merger work; the question of campus cultures would also have to be addressed. Seminaries are not just buildings and procedures; they are at the core made up of people—faculty, staff, students, boards, and alumni, with allegiances and opinions. To really make this merger a success, those stakeholders, or at least most of them, would have to be convinced that this merger was in their best interests. The people connected to Northwestern had a particular concern that their traditions and cultures not just be swallowed up in the large whole, dominated by Luther Seminary. As the larger institution, Luther people worried about incorporating the differences of Northwestern into their particular culture.

One particularly sensitive element consisted of the newly merged faculties and the joining together of their common work. Some of this obviously had to do with the practical elements of faculty work—who would teach which courses, who would sit on faculty communities or hold particular leadership positions. But beyond this were the larger theological and personal questions. Surely, they were all dedicated to theological education in the Lutheran tradition, but this is a broad tradition (even within the two seminaries). And faculty being faculty, there were always those perennial disputed questions over which to contend. In the middle of all this was President Svendsbye. Sensing a "negative attitude of a segment of the two faculties toward each other," he had to figure out a way to "soften the relationship and make it positive. The big problem, as [he] saw it, was that the members of the faculties did not really know one another."[47] He organized a series of dinners over the year, bringing together faculty members (and their wives) to meet with each other, which, he thought, gradually helped to overcome the initial reticence.

THE FINALITY OF MERGER

There were two of everything that needed to become one, and unification took time. There were two separate women's auxiliary organizations, and they would need eventually to become one group. Campus organizations, such as housing, dining, bookstores, and other supporting activities, had to be unified, which sometimes required creative solutions. The two groups of students had to become one, something that proved to be more difficult than expected. Svendsbye relates:

> The hostility between the students at the two schools was astonishingly high when I first came to the seminaries. According to the students, the two administrations, without consulting the students, had agreed that Northwestern students would live in Luther housing and that the Luther students would eat at the Northwestern cafeteria.[48]

But many of the Luther students refused to eat in the Northwestern facility and instead resorted to cooking in their own rooms. Eventually a common, seminary-operated food service was implemented, but it took time to overcome these objections. Time, flexibility, and some other accommodations eventually softened the differences, especially as successive new classes of students entered the new institutional situation.

Time, and living together, also overcame other lingering problems, the largest of these were reservations toward the merger on the part of the national ALC Board of Theological Education and Ministry and the daunting legal question of the separate incorporation of Luther Seminary. Without this incorporation, the merger of the two institutions would have been nearly impossible. Eventually, the ALC reticence on the issue was overcome, and Luther formed a new legal entity entitled the Luther Northwestern Theological Seminary, to which the ALC transferred the physical assets of Luther Seminary. It was this new legal entity, then, with which Northwestern merged in June 1982, and the newly merged seminary began operations on July 1, 1982. This marked the end of the separate existence of Northwestern Seminary after sixty-two years of existence. It also predated the merger of the ALC and LCA by six years.

In its seven decades of independent existence, Northwestern Lutheran Theological Seminary created its own distinctive culture and approach to theological education. Coming from the General

Council and the Synod of the Northwest, this seminary demonstrated the strong commitment to the centrality of the Lutheran confessions (in an ecumenical sense) that was the hallmark of these groups. As the Synod of the Northwest was founded as a specifically English-language group, it and the seminary stressed the American nature of their institutions without having any specific ethnic tradition. Northwestern was known for its strong commitment to traditional liturgical worship, to home and world missions, and to a similarly strong emphasis on stewardship, something that allowed a relatively small synod to organize and run its own seminary until the LCA merger in 1962. There was another quality of this institution and its people, however, that was distinctive; they were, in the older sense, churchmen. This term, now out of fashion, meant at its best that they were personally connected with the work of the church at all levels, not just at the congregational level. They had a broad vision of how the work of Christ was incarnated in the organizations of the church and were involved with and supported these efforts; they connected their Christian identities to the work and mission of the broader church. These were qualities that Northwestern contributed to the greater work of Luther Northwestern Theological Seminary as it moved forward.

Notes

1. On the struggle for Lutheran confessional identity in the nineteenth-century United States, see Granquist, *Lutherans in America*, 163–65 and 179–81.

2. The original site of this seminary on the north side of Chicago became the site of Wrigley Field, the home of the Chicago Cubs major-league baseball team. Since the seminary was located in Maywood, it became known informally as the Maywood seminary.

3. See E. Theodore Bachmann, *The United Lutheran Church in America, 1918–1962* (Minneapolis: Fortress Press, 1997), 146–51.

4. Dorris A. Flesner, "Luther-Northwestern Self-Study Affirmations—Descriptive Phase, Northwestern Lutheran Theological Seminary" (manuscript, 1975, Archives of Luther Seminary, Saint Paul, Minnesota). This is a fairly detailed history of Northwestern Lutheran

Theological Seminary written in preparation for its eventual merger with Luther Seminary. On this document, see Lloyd A. Svendsbye, *One in Mission: Luther and Northwestern Seminaries Unite* (Minneapolis: Lutheran University Press, 2012), 25–26.

5. "An Interesting Comparison," *Northwestern Seminary Bulletin* 1, no. 1 (October 1924): 3.
6. Flesner, "Luther-Northwestern Self-Study," 17.
7. The two Nebraska seminaries eventually merged to form Central Lutheran Seminary on the campus of Midland Lutheran College in Fremont, Nebraska.
8. J. K. Jensen, "The Background of the Seminary," *Northwestern Seminary Bulletin* 21, no. 3 (July 1945): 7.
9. "Seminary Notes," *Northwestern Seminary Bulletin* 9, no. 3 (July 1933): 1.
10. *Northwestern Seminary Bulletin* 10, no. 4 (October 1934): 6.
11. Flesner, "Luther-Northwestern Self-Study," 30. Flesner does not name the individual involved, but by looking at the composition of the faculty through the mid-1940s, the only faculty member who departed during this period was Paul Huffman.
12. For a more detailed explanation of the seminary curriculum, see Flesner, "Luther-Northwestern Self-Study," 35–39.
13. "Filled to Capacity," *Northwestern Seminary Bulletin* 3, no. 1 (October 1926): 1.
14. Matthew Haas, "Seminary Life," *Northwestern Seminary Bulletin* 3, no. 4 (July 1927): 9–12.
15. Robert Paul Roth, "Northwestern Lutheran Theological Seminary, 1920–1982," in Gonnerman, *Thanksgiving and Hope*, 62.
16. The Crosby family was a part of Crosby-Washburn Mills, later known as General Mills, so it could be said that the seminary was "in flour." The author of this volume, when a student at Yale Divinity School, lived for a year in quarters attached to a Crosby family home in Woodbridge, Connecticut.
17. Quoted in Roth, "Northwestern Lutheran Theological Seminary," 63.
18. *Northwestern Seminary Bulletin* 18, no. 3 (July 1942): 5–6.
19. *Northwestern Seminary Bulletin* 21, no. 4 (October 1945): 3.
20. *Northwestern Seminary Bulletin* 19, no. 2 (April 1943): 5.
21. *Northwestern Seminary Bulletin* 21, no. 4 (October 1945): 2.

22. *Northwestern Seminary Bulletin* 24, no. 4 (October 1948): 2.
23. Flesner, "Luther-Northwestern Self-Study," 40.
24. Flesner, "Luther-Northwestern Self-Study," 31kkk. In contrast, the historical-critical method was only tentatively introduced at Luther Seminary in the late 1950s.
25. Roth, "Northwestern Lutheran Theological Seminary," 79; and Flesner, "Luther-Northwestern Self-Study," 31(L).
26. Flesner, "Luther-Northwestern Self-Study." This must have been particularly embarrassing to the seminary, given his family connection to the school's faculty.
27. Roth, "Northwestern Lutheran Theological Seminary," 79.
28. *Northwestern Seminary Bulletin* 17, no. 1 (January 1941): 3.
29. Grindal, "Role of Women," 89.
30. *Northwestern Seminary Bulletin* 35, no. 4 (October 1959): 5.
31. Roth, "Northwestern Lutheran Theological Seminary," 78.
32. On these developments, see Granquist, *Lutherans in America*, 271–73.
33. For the details of this history, see Maria Erling and Mark Granquist, *The Augustana Story: Shaping Lutheran Identity in North America* (Minneapolis: Augsburg Fortress, 2008).
34. Named after the panel's leader, Conrad Bergendoff, who was the former president of Augustana College in Rock Island, Illinois.
35. Flesner, "Luther-Northwestern Self-Study," 23–24. The effect of this would have been to reunite Northwestern with the Maywood Seminary from which it split in 1920. Flesner points out that the projection for the size of the new seminary in Chicago was "at least 400 students" but that in 1973 to 1974, the enrollment at LSTC was only 128, in comparison to 171 at Northwestern (22).
36. Roth, "Northwestern Lutheran Theological Seminary," 66.
37. Svendsbye, *One in Mission*, 21.
38. For a long (and sometimes rhapsodic) description of the Northwestern building, especially the chapel, see Roth, "Northwestern Lutheran Theological Seminary," 67–69.
39. Roth, "Northwestern Lutheran Theological Seminary," 67.
40. Flesner, "Luther-Northwestern Self-Study," 34.
41. Roth, "Northwestern Lutheran Theological Seminary," 71.
42. Larry Day, "Conscientious Objection," *Northwestern Seminary Bulletin* 47, no. 4 (1971): 13–16.

43. Roth, "Northwestern Lutheran Theological Seminary," 80.
44. See Svendsbye, *One in Mission*, esp. 8–14.
45. Svendsbye, *One in Mission*, 21–22, 28–29.
46. Svendsbye, *One in Mission*, 76–77.
47. Svendsbye, *One in Mission*, 39.
48. Svendsbye, *One in Mission*, 51.

7

Moving into the Mainstream: Luther Seminary, 1960–1988

The year 1960 has proven to be a watershed year in American history, signaling the coming of age of a new generation, the massive wave of children born to the "greatest generation" of those who had fought in World War II. This new wave of baby boomers would, in the next thirty years, transform American society in ways that would hardly have been thought possible in 1960. The immediate postwar era saw Americans seeking to return home and resume lives that had been interrupted and put on hold. For nearly two decades, Americans' lives had not been "normal," with the dislocations of the Great Depression (1929–1940) and then the all-out national mobilization during World War II, which affected the entire nation, not just those in the military. The postwar mood was marked by a deep longing to get married, buy homes, start careers and families, and in general get on with lives. With these developments, organized religion boomed, and new congregations were established everywhere. Certainly, traumas were yet to come, especially the rise of communism and the Iron Curtain, the Korean War, the outbreaks of polio, and the Cold War, with its justifiable fears of nuclear annihilation. But the country sought safety and continuity, as the two-term presidency of wartime hero Dwight D. Eisenhower indicated.

But "normal" was an illusion of sorts. World War II had changed America in ways that could not have been foreseen. The national wartime mobilization saw large demographic shifts toward the western and southern states, and in all areas the demand for housing pushed the rise of new suburban areas ringing the older urban cores. The postwar GI Bill guaranteed higher education for millions of Americans, who flooded into new and existing educational institutions, straining them to the breaking point. As a country, America had been jolted out of its earlier isolationism, becoming perhaps the major world power of the age. Americans had become personally familiar with countries around the world that had previously only been blotches of color on obscure corners of the globe. The country had shifted socially during the war years, as African Americans began to push for fuller inclusion in American life, and women began to break out of the societal limits placed on them. The return to normal was tempered by the fact that the old normal was gone and could not be restored.

THE OPTIMISM OF THE EARLY 1960S

The election of John F. Kennedy as president in 1960 was widely seen as a sign of a breakthrough, of something new for an expanding and optimistic country. John and Jacqueline Kennedy seemed the very symbol of youth and beauty and grace, and Americans gravitated to their leadership. It was an expansive age, in which anything seemed possible if the national will could be harnessed to create it. Government could develop programs, policies, and procedures to attack long-term social problems, and technology and industry could do their part to ensure that the rising living standards of the postwar period would continue indefinitely, or so it seemed. The Christian denominations were thoroughly imbued with this expansionist spirit and sought to grow everywhere they could.

For many American Lutheran groups, this was a time of maturation and coming of age. Having been built from the massive immigration of the nineteenth century, these denominations had slowly established congregations and institutions and denominations, constructed initially around the primary ethnic and linguistic traditions of the first and second generations. They had done a good job of this, developing the evangelistic tools to gather in at least a portion of the Lutheran immigrants, and growing hundreds of congregations, especially in the expansive period of 1945 to 1965.[1] In this postwar coming of age, American Lutherans felt that they had finally grown out of their hyphenated, ethnically based identities and become equals to other American Protestant groups. Numerically, Lutherans had become the third-largest American Protestant family, behind only the Baptists and the Methodists, and they were eager to join the American Protestant mainline as equal members in their own right (ironically enough, just in time for that mainline to begin to crumble).

THE NEW AMERICAN LUTHERAN CHURCH (1960–1988)

The general ethos of the postwar period was toward larger and more consolidated institutions, whether in business or government or religious denominations. For the churches (especially the mainline Protestants), consolidation and merger were in the air, and the Lutherans responded with the mega-mergers that created out of a host of smaller Lutheran denominations two new, larger bodies, the Lutheran Church in America (LCA) in 1962, and the American Lutheran Church (ALC) in 1960.[2] For Luther Seminary, the latter merger was extremely important. First, no longer would Luther be the sole seminary of a medium-sized Lutheran denomination; now it would be one among several seminaries in the new and large American Lutheran Church. Luther received a very large part of its funding through the ALC but now had to compete for funding from the denomination with three other seminaries: Wartburg (Dubuque, Iowa), Capital (Columbus, Ohio), and Pacific Lutheran (Berkeley, California). In addition, the size of the new denomination, especially the need to fund a large number of new mission congregations in the new suburbs and in the southern and western parts of the country, meant a drain on denomination resources and potentially less funding (by percentage) for all the institutions, including the seminaries. The mergers that would bring in Augsburg Seminary in 1963 and

Northwestern Lutheran Theological Seminary in 1982 would further transform the seminary.

The new ALC was very important to Luther Seminary, because that denomination (like the Evangelical Lutheran Church before it) literally owned the seminary, which was not independently incorporated. Thus many of the important decisions of the seminary, including the ratification of faculty hires and tenure, the physical expansion of the campus, and its general policies were subject to approval by the national church body, especially through its Board for Theological Education and Ministry.

The new denomination was also less homogeneous than the Evangelical Lutheran Church (ELC) had been, presenting further challenges to the seminary. During the years when the Norwegian American–based ELC was in existence, 1917–1960, Luther Seminary was the sole seminary of this denomination. There were therefore tight relationships between those who ran and taught in the seminary and the rest of the ELC. The officials and pastors in the denomination were all graduates of Luther Seminary, and they saw each other constantly, whether on church boards and committees or at the annual convention of the denomination. Certainly those in the ELC did not shy away from internecine conflict; indeed, they seemed sometimes even to relish it. But when there was fighting and conflict, these were "family" fights, with the boundaries that needed to be observed in such fights. There was a strong pattern of interlocking leadership between the ELC headquarters in Minneapolis, Luther Seminary, the four denominational colleges (especially St. Olaf College), and the Lutheran Brotherhood insurance company. After 1960, the ALC contained new, non-Norwegian voices who began to argue for the interests of their seminaries and institutions. The Norwegian Americans' continued domination over the upper Midwestern regions of the new ALC and over much of the ALC headquarters (based in Minneapolis) faded only slowly over the 1960s and 1970s, but it did fade as those denominational, ethnic, and even familial ties grew less intense. Still, the journey was not easy.

One initial challenge to Luther Seminary from the ALC came in 1960, when the denomination proposed a standardization of all its seminaries' curricula in a concept known as the "One Seminary" program. This proposal sought common requirements and number of hours at all the ALC seminaries and made room for some new elective courses. The effect of this proposal at Luther Seminary was to reduce the overall number of hours for required courses from 126 to 119, while retaining the total number of credit hours needed. Eventually this proposal was dropped as being "too cumbersome."[3] Though this overall plan seemed rather modest in both scope and implementation, it was perhaps an early signal that the national ALC intended to have increased control in the lives of its seminaries, something that seemed to concern the Luther Seminary community. After five years in the new denomination, President Alvin Rogness reflected:

> All three schools, in attempting to live and work together as a team or family of seminaries, may have delayed some things that they might have done sooner had they functioned in total independence of one another. But . . . there certainly have been some gains which have enriched the life of the Church.[4]

Despite his diplomatic words, it seems clear that he and many others in the Luther community felt this arrangement was clumsy and confining, and were glad to be free of it.

Another change came in 1963, when the Lutheran Free Church finally passed a denominational vote to enter the new ALC. With this action, the much smaller Augsburg Seminary was decoupled from Augsburg College and merged into Luther Seminary. The overall effect on Luther Seminary was fairly insubstantial; Augsburg Seminary was much smaller and brought into Luther only a few students and two new faculty members, John Stensvaag and Bernhard Christensen—the latter briefly coming over to teach at Luther Seminary in retirement (1963–1967). Paul Sonnack, of the Augsburg faculty, joined the Luther faculty in 1967. The Free Church tradition thus rejoined Luther Seminary after some seventy years, although the Free Church and Haugean traditions tended to get lost in the larger world that was Luther Seminary. But their presence did add to the ongoing diversification of the seminary, if only in a minor way.

EXPANSION AND GROWTH

The postwar growth of the seminary, driven by the returning soldiers and the large expansion of Lutheran congregations, meant that the seminary faculty had to be expanded. In the 1960/61 school year, the seminary faculty expanded to twenty-two full-time positions, with another nine part-time instructors or guest lecturers. In 1965/66 these numbers increased to twenty-four full-time and twenty-eight part-time positions, while by 1970/71 this increased again to thirty-one full-time and thirty part-time positions. This increase in the faculty actually lagged behind the growth in the student body and also signaled an expanded curriculum, especially in the number of new courses and electives. This growth in the faculty also necessitated a new structure in the seminary, as the position of dean of the faculty was established in 1961. Later another position, director of graduate studies, was also created. Although the size of the faculty was increased, its nature remained fairly constant; it was almost uniformly male Lutheran pastors, most of whom had graduated from one of the ALC Lutheran colleges and had degrees from Luther Seminary. But increasingly these new faculty had advanced degrees from leading American and European universities and brought new ideas and perspectives to Luther Seminary.

The size of the student body, which had increased appreciably during the 1950s, actually held fairly steady through the 1960s. In 1960/61 the size of the student body was 573 regular degree students and a total of 721 when summer and special students were counted. By 1965/66 the student numbers actually slipped to 437 regular students, for a total of 681, and by 1970/71 the numbers returned to 588 regular and 735 total students. Until 1964, when the first woman student was admitted, they were all men, and although a few more women would be admitted toward the end of the decade, the student body would remain predominantly male. There was certain uniformity of background to the student body, which came mostly from the five Norwegian American Lutheran colleges: St. Olaf, Concordia (Moorhead), Luther, Augsburg, and Augustana (Sioux Falls). Graduates of these five colleges, usually led by St. Olaf, customarily constituted 70 to 80 percent of the Luther Seminary student body. Not until the

1980s would a public institution, the University of Minnesota, crack the top five of schools providing students to the seminary. The size of the student body also meant that a new administrative position, the dean of students, was established in 1963. The big difference in the student body beginning after World War II was the number of married students, who became a majority of the students by the early 1960s.

The costs of the seminary education were still overwhelmingly subsidized by the ALC, at somewhere in the range of 80 to 90 percent. The denomination also periodically raised money through special appeals to fund capital construction and improvements, but now the funds raised had to be split among the different ALC seminaries. President Rogness, especially, spent much of his time maintaining close relationships with denominational officials and leading pastors and had to be a consummate church politician. Seminary officials were wary of raising money directly from the students themselves; Rogness commented in 1966:

> To levy the charge against the students by increased tuition is hardly wise, in view of the fact that already these men have had to finance four years of college education at high cost.[5]

A nominal student tuition was established in the 1950s at $200 a year, which remained steady until 1970, when it was raised to $500. Room charges were $90–$150 a year in 1960/61 (double or single occupancy), rising to $120–$180 in 1965/66, and $210–$270 in 1970/71. On-campus students participated in a student-run boarding club at the cost of about $50 a month, until that institution was discontinued in the late 1960s. Eventually a seminary-run food service was instituted instead. Seminary-owned apartments, which were introduced in the late 1960s, were available to married students at a rate of $105–$125 per month during the 1970/71 school year. Seminary was still relatively inexpensive, although economic and social forces would change all this in the 1970s.

In 1961, a new addition was made to the Luther Seminary *Catalog*, a statement on the nature and purpose of theological education in the minds of those who ran Luther Seminary. This statement, and especially its timing, represented a significant development in the life of the seminary, especially in view of the fact that the seminary found it necessary to make such a statement at all. That the statement was made on the cusp of a new decade—and in light of both the new denominational situation, not to mention the river of societal changes flowing around it—speaks of an urgency in focusing the mission of the seminary and the challenges it seemed to be feeling from the larger world. Gerhard Forde suggested that this statement, something already anticipated by T. F. Gullixson and others in 1936, was in response to changes in the modern world and in the larger theological climate of the time.[6] This statement, which was extensively revised in the 1973/74 academic year, suggested that theological education was not a means unto itself but something that pointed to the transcendence, truth, and redemption brought by and through Jesus Christ. This theological education, the statement specified, rests on four principles: it is evangelical, it is biblical, it is confessional, and it is comprehensive (or integrative). It seems obvious that this statement was the product of quite a bit of serious reflection and work. Yet Forde continued by suggesting that the statement did not seem to have had much internal effect on curriculum or programs, but:

> Perhaps it is safe to say that the statement is more an attempt to justify to the church at large the way things had as a matter of fact evolved than an attempt to guide or alter the course to be taken.[7]

Given the new realities, perhaps it was time that the seminary did just that, explaining itself and its mission to its larger constituencies.

A NEW CURRICULUM FOR A NEW ERA

The seminary curriculum itself was revised in the 1967/68 academic year, with a substantial reduction in the overall number of total hours needed for graduation, from 144 to 119 hours. Of these hours, 89 (or about three-quarters) were in required subjects, split between Old and New Testament (14 hours each), church history (15 hours), systematic theology (18 hours), and practical theology (28 hours). In 1969/70 the total number of hours was increased to 127, adding one hour each to the biblical disciplines and six more hours to electives. A number of the activities were noncredit courses, including introductory Greek and Hebrew, Clinical Pastoral Education (CPE), and internship. With the growth of the faculty and the room for new electives, the total number of courses offered in an academic year increased steadily over this period of time, nearly doubling in a twenty-year period (1954–1974). In the total course offerings, there were new electives in all the "classical" theological disciplines, especially courses in modern or contemporary theologians, but the bulk of the growth was new courses in practical theology, including new courses in pastoral counseling, worship, homiletics, and Christian education. As Forde states, "Perhaps no department reflects more deeply the changed situation and the demands made on ministry than this one."[8] Much of the growth of these new courses in modern theology and in the arts of ministry was occasioned by student demand. The faculty were hard-pressed to retain the primacy of the older, classical courses in the face of the pressure to show that these core disciplines still had relevance for the modern world and contemporary ministry.

One strong element of the seminary's mission was continuing outreach to its graduates and to other Lutheran pastors. The Midwinter Convocation was one way to bring pastors back to the campus for continuing education, while seminary faculty were often guest speakers at district or regional pastors' conferences. The seminary instigated a new publication in 1961, the *Luther Theological Seminary Review*, with articles on biblical and theological topics and news from the seminary. Summer courses were another form of outreach, especially for those who were considering further education. In 1965 the seminary instituted the Kairos continuing education program, with short-term, focused courses on theological and pastoral topics for pastors and other professionals. In 1969, as a further outreach, the seminary formed a new Luther Seminary Alumni Association. The older, pre-merger activities that had brought all the pastors together each year had shifted, and it was necessary to develop new ways of staying in touch with the pastors of the denomination.

THE CONFLICT OF THE LATE 1960S

The heady optimism of the early 1960s soon shifted into societal conflict over race, government policies, the Vietnam War, and other intractable issues. The assassination of President Kennedy in 1963 and of Martin Luther King Jr. and Robert Kennedy in 1968, the racial conflicts and riots of the decade, the intensification of the Vietnam War, and the rise of student radicalism polarized American society in profound ways, and this polarization was soon apparent in the church and in places like Luther Seminary. As President Rogness later reflected:

> During the 1960s the attack on the seminaries—that they were ivory towers, marooned from the rapid changes in society—was especially strong. . . . The school clung, sometimes with a tenacity born of fear, to the classical forms. . . . The pressures were on, and changes came.[9]

The pressures came from both sides, from those who thought the seminary was not changing fast enough to meet the new realities and also from those who felt that the school was changing too fast, and not maintaining the classical elements of the Christian faith. As Rogness writes, "The mood of the students could hardly be called belligerent, they were a jury putting history on trial. Everything traditional was in the dock. Professors came to the end of the school year emotionally drained."[10] But American Lutherans of this decade, especially in the ALC, were still a rather conservative group, and even the modest changes at the seminary occasioned confusion and hostility from many within the denomination (which, of course, heavily financed the seminary). In the judgment of faculty member Roy Harrisville Jr., "Rogness saved the school. He stood between it and its constituency. He insisted that the tradition had not been forsaken, but had been held to as firmly as in the past, albeit undergoing translation for what he had called 'this turbulent age.'"[11] The ties between Rogness and many of the older faculty, on the one hand, and the pastors and leaders of the ALC, on the other, allowed the seminary to weather these turbulent years.

And turbulent years they were. Students were pushing back against the traditional forms of theological education and against doing things as they had always been done. One requirement that had drawn the ire of the students was that students had to read the entire text of the Bible and the Lutheran Book of Concord and sign a statement to that effect in order to graduate. In the student newspaper, the *Communique*, in 1967 one student expressed a fairly widespread opinion that the requirement was worthless (and much neglected by the students) and suggested that it was pressure from the laypeople that led to the requirement in the first place. "Actually, I think this rule has been made as a result of lay people . . . [now] the seminary can say 'all our students read the Bible and the Book of Concord' and effectively silence anyone who questions seminary education."[12]

In the student newspapers of this time, there were lively discussions about the seminary, its curriculum, the quality of its worship life, and many other controversial issues of the day. One student dramatically opined in 1966, "The seminary is dead. The students, the faculty, the curriculum, the methods, the presuppositions. All are dead. If I have omitted anyone, I will be glad to add them in the reprints."[13] Another student reflected on the new curriculum in 1967 and found it to be a change that went not nearly far enough. He suggested a quite more radical theological experiment: a "free seminary" where the students themselves took an active role in determining what they would study. "We have been given the freedom to work out our own method of study-in-depth; why can we not also begin to determine the subject matter of our study, whether it is 'relevant' or not?"[14] These kinds of opinions, radically questioning the whole established process of seminary education as it then existed, were, if not universally shared among the student population, then at least strongly held in certain quarters.

The seminary took notice of the issues of the 1960s. Students and professors went to various sites in the South to observe the racial conflict there and reported their observations to the seminary community. "More than 100 students" participated in a march to the Minnesota state capitol for equal rights, and various convocation speakers at the seminary spoke on contemporary issues such as these.[15] Students participated in interracial programs, such as the

"Student Interracial Ministry," and brought these insights back to campus.[16] In 1968 elements of the Luther and Northwestern communities combined to offer a program of classes on "Minority Race History," although not as credit-bearing courses. The intensification of the Vietnam War in 1968–1971 drew a strong response from the students; a student-run "Luther Mobilization Committee" was formed in the fall of 1969 and made plans for the seminary community to participate in a moratorium (shared with other educational institutions of the ALC) on October 15 to address their concerns. The results of a student opinion vote at that time were that three-quarters of those responding (admittedly a small sample) supported the mobilization "because I want the war in Vietnam ended now!"[17] The students and faculty seemed to be divided on the issue and the war itself, but any number of antiwar activities occurred on and off campus at the time. In May 1969, President Rogness, reporting in the *Review*, complimented the students:

> And to the credit of our students, I must report that they have for the most part carried on responsibly. They have not had a sit-in, nor destroyed the records. They have pressed to be heard. . . . They do believe (and rightly so) that they have some wisdom and judgement to give us.[18]

The seminary community reflected the turmoil of the larger society, albeit within the context of its theological and societal stances.

CONFLICT SUBSIDES AND A RETURN TO NORMAL?

And then in the early 1970s, it seemed, the turmoil of the late 1960s came to an abrupt end. The Vietnam War was scaled back, American troops were withdrawn, and the military draft was suspended. There was a particularly activist section of the student body that came into the seminary in the late 1960s, some of which were there presumably to avoid the draft. As one historian describes it, "Hundreds of men swarmed to the seminary during the war, then left in droves once peace came. When the draft was cancelled, 50 students from the first year did not return for the second."[19] A contemporary student observer writing in 1971 noted that the "students are quiet this year, even conscientious (to the point of attending class with some regularity!)" and that they hardly seemed to remember the activism of the entering class of 1968/69. He went on to point out that perhaps the school had lost its "activist element," observing that "30% of that class was dropped or dropped out over three years, a record."[20] President Rogness later recalled about this, "Almost overnight, it seemed, calm came. Whether from sheer exhaustion, or from a recovery of historical perspective, students in the 1970s seemed no longer in a panic for change." Rogness concluded that students were not that much less interested in working for justice and serving others, but that they felt they could use the institutional church as a forum for change.[21]

The postwar drop in the number of students was, however, short-term. The regular enrollment in 1970/71 was 588 and with special students totaled 735. In 1975/76 the regular enrollment was 592 and the total 835, and by 1980/81, this had risen to 699 regular and 918 total students (which also included the students from Northwestern). One factor that was perhaps influencing this increase was the demographic wave that was the baby boom generation, the cohort of those born 1946–1962. Starting in the mid-1970s, the peak of this generation were graduating from college, and these students were coming through the seminary. Another factor contributing to this rise was the increasing number of women students (of which more will be said later). Already in 1966, President Rogness was anticipating that the leading edge of the "post-war 'baby boom' should be hitting the seminaries the next few years,"[22] although the effect took longer than perhaps he anticipated, not coming until the late 1970s and early 1980s. This baby-boom effect might also have been a bit delayed by two trends: first, some students were no longer coming to the seminary directly out of college, and second, more second-career students began enrolling in the 1980s.

As the 1970s went on, the background of the student body was becoming increasingly diverse. The number of students who had degrees from the six ALC colleges still constituted a substantial majority of the student body, over 60 percent in 1970, but the number of students with degrees from public universities was on the rise. In 1980, for instance, the institution sending the second-largest number of students to Luther was the University of Minnesota, which was a dramatic rise. With the radicalism of the 1960s and the rise of students from outside the "tradition" came a different type of student. As Harrisville notes, even of students from traditional Lutheran colleges: "Those who managed to survive the pressures of college religion instructors . . . often shared their mentors' assumption that 'provincial,' 'ingrown,' even 'mediocre' were the definition of 'Lutheran.'" Many of these students, he observes, "knew little of life in a Lutheran congregation," and had a faith informed by "extremists left or right." These, he suggests, "knew nothing of a tradition functioning as a norm."[23] Contemporary seminary officials in the 1970s and 1980s decried what they saw as a trend of the best potential Lutheran seminarians being lured away to top North American divinity schools, often by prestige and scholarships, and by pressure from their college advisors. The old "pipeline" between the ALC colleges and Luther Seminary seemed to be drying up, and the collegial relations between the college faculties and the seminary were not as strong as they had been.

Of course, the growth of the student body necessitated a parallel growth in the seminary faculty. From 1962 to 1972, ten older professors retired, and eighteen new persons were added to the faculty, which meant that as of 1972 two-thirds of the faculty were new (from the number in 1962). The total size of the full-time faculty in 1970 was thirty-one, which rose to forty-two by 1975 and fifty-one in 1980 (with the addition of the Northwestern faculty). This rise was occasioned not only by the increasing number of students but also by pressure from academic accrediting agencies, such as the Association of Theological Schools (ATS), which determined that the number of faculty was too small for the enrollment. The new faculty of this time was also much like the earlier postwar faculty, in that they were male Lutheran pastors, mostly graduates of ALC colleges and Luther Seminary, who had earned degrees from top graduate programs in North America and Europe. In subsequent years this would change, especially after 1980.

The growth of the student body and the faculty of course necessitated a corresponding growth in staff and facilities. As the curriculum and academic programs became more complex, there was a need for more professional administrators and staff, including directors of programs such as field or contextual education, graduate education, the library, and other areas supporting instructional efforts. Traditionally, the supervision and assessment of the students had been done by the faculty and president, but now these duties were being handled by professionals in student life. The physical plant of the seminary increased dramatically; though Aasgaard Hall was eventually abandoned (and later torn down), the addition of the Northwestern building compensated for this. All this growth strained the seminary budget in the early 1970s, which was also stressed by declining contributions from the ALC and by the monetary inflation of this decade. Tuition, which had held steady at $200 per year, was raised to $500 by 1975, and this was only the beginning of a shift to tuition as a major source of funding for the seminary. In 1975, newly installed president Lloyd Svendsbye hired Pastor Arvid Bidne to lead a newly created Office of Development, which sought to raise funds directly for the operations and endowment of the seminary. In that this seemed to run counter to the older norm of denominational support for the seminary, this was controversial, but the revenue from the ALC was declining at a noticeable rate, and the balance needed to be filled up.[24] Luther Seminary was by this time one of the largest Lutheran seminaries in the world and increasingly a leading denominationally related seminary in North America.

NEW APPROACHES TO TEACHING AND LEARNING

Although the activism of the 1960s quieted down in the early 1970s, one aspect of the earlier period had permanent effect and that was a change not so much in the curriculum but in the ways the curriculum was being delivered. The early 1970s was a period of great experimentation with the educational process. In a 1970 editorial, a student editor bemoaned the "repetition of the same depressing educational methods and patterns of teaching" and asked, "What can be done to improve the system?"[25] Plenty of new pedagogical elements were introduced in the next few years, and the curriculum was handled differently. Following the emerging pattern of the ATS schools, the old bachelor of divinity degree, long the standard, was replaced by the master of divinity degree in 1970, although this was only a change in nomenclature. Beginning with the 1971/72 academic year, the established letter-grade system was replaced with a system of "Honor, Pass, or No Entry," with the corresponding idea that faculty would give each student a corresponding narrative evaluation. In the 1972/73 academic year, the faculty approved an experimental, alternative system of pedagogy, in which a tutorial system and independent studies would replace the traditional core courses in the curriculum. This system, which seemingly was modeled on educational experiments at the colleges (perhaps most notably the Paracollege at St. Olaf College) was dubbed the "Para-seminary." During this period of time, there was also the addition of a student presence on all the appropriate seminary committees, including student observers at the faculty meetings. Besides the traditional theological degree, now the master of divinity, there were three additional earned degrees at Luther Seminary during the 1970s, the master of arts, the master of theology, and the new doctor of ministry, the latter a professional degree for ministry practitioners.

Many of these new pedagogical and curricular ideas expanded into the larger teaching experience of the seminary. Gerhard Forde noted in 1975 that "styles of teaching have also changed." He noted that the expansion of the faculty and of elective courses made teaching in the seminar-style possible, and beyond that, "there has been an increasing attempt to section courses into smaller groups where more discussion might take place, and to introduce preceptorial discussion groups in core courses."[26] Of course the large size of the student body, even with the growth of the faculty, meant that many classes were still in the large, lecture-style format, but there was a growing realization that the learning life of the seminary had changed and that students expected to be more active in their learning (at least in theory). Surveying all these changes, Forde nevertheless worried, "one can't help but wonder how it is all possible . . . whether the foundation can really bear it and still maintain its integrity?"[27] The changes of this period illuminated the ongoing tensions between the ideal of a normative, core tradition into which students would be initiated, and a new ideal of inquiry free of confining traditional norms. Although perhaps sharp in this period of time, these tensions seemed to have been open questions across the life of Luther Seminary.

THE ORDINATION OF WOMEN

As if these changes in and of themselves were not enough, there was also the decision made by the ALC and LCA in 1970 to allow the ordination of women, which of course meant the regular admission of women to the master of divinity program. As early as 1959, the faculty adopted a resolution in principle allowing for the potential entrance of women students, and in 1960 the faculty approved the admission of a woman as a special student. Still, the path toward ordination was closed to them. In 1964 and 1965, three women were admitted to the bachelor of divinity degree program; as one historian has remarked, "Slowly, the initial prejudices began to wither away."[28] The process toward ordination came slowly. In 1968, in an article in the student newspaper *Communique*, a student noted that two of the senior students, Beverly Allert and Dawn Proux, had fulfilled all the requirements for graduation and ordination, and that "we can admit that they are here . . . and we can, as a community concerned about each of our members, consider the issue and take a stand."[29] A number of Luther faculty participated in the study or the larger discussions that led to women's ordination in 1970, something that happened generally without the kinds of strife one might expect at a contentious time like this and about a potentially contentious issue. As Luther faculty member Gracia Grindal observed:

> The strident debate one associates with any issue that eventually comes to the floor of conventions during these times is simply missing. It feels, at this distance, like a matter whose time had come, even for those who did not like it.[30]

Still, the integration of women into the degree programs and into the ordained ministry was hardly simple and required a major amount of work at Luther Seminary to make it happen. Old patterns of thought and language die hard and would have to be supplanted by new models and new ways of working. Although there were occasional women faculty and staff, they would not become a regularity until the 1980s and beyond. A first step was the appointment of Karen Johnson and then Elizabeth Beissel as assistant dean of students.

The older traditions of women's participation at Luther continued as in the past, although societal changes (especially women working outside the home) brought changes to them. Both Luther and Northwestern seminaries had organizations women participated in, whether as faculty wives, student wives, or other women whose mission it was to support the seminary and seminarians. With the gradual movement toward unification of the two seminaries, the two groups struggled to find common ground. Though women were increasingly students in the 1970s, there was still an active organization of seminary wives at Luther. In 1975 they reported on their activities in the seminary *Review*, acknowledging that the life of a seminary spouse "can be a lonely one." They stated, "The New Sem Wives has added a necessary and stimulating dimension to the lives of women choosing to take part in the wide gamut of activities that foster self-awareness, educational, and community growth."[31] The social changes of the 1970s were, however, greatly increasing the roles that women could occupy at the seminary, although traditional roles also remained important.

THE SVENDSBYE PRESIDENCY AND THE MERGER WITH NORTHWESTERN

A major milestone in the life of Luther Seminary came with the retirement of President Alvin Rogness in 1974. In his twenty-year term, Rogness had greatly expanded not only the size of the seminary but its vision as well and guided it through an immensely difficult period in the late 1960s and early 1970s. The new president, Lloyd Svendsbye, came from outside the seminary. A Luther graduate and pastor, he had a doctorate and was serving as the dean of the faculty at St. Olaf College before coming to Luther. The new challenge that lay before Svendsbye was to consummate the union of Luther and Northwestern seminaries, certainly a daunting task even in the best of times. Although there were many in the larger seminary communities who saw this progression as a natural step, the devil was in the details (at least figuratively), and it took all of Svendsbye's tact and skill to bring the merger about. Rogness was not eager to dive into the merger and retired two years ahead of the normal retirement age. Northwestern president Zeidler was opposed to the merger. Svendsbye was appointed Luther's president in 1975, and when Zeidler retired in 1976, Svendsbye was appointed president of Northwestern, as well.

It is not necessary to rehash the details of the slow and difficult path that led to the merger of the two seminaries in 1982; these details have been covered in chapter 6. Certainly the anxiety on the side of the Northwestern community was probably greater, as they feared the loss of their tradition and identity in being swallowed up by the larger Luther Seminary. But noticeably there were also anxieties on the Luther side; this merger, on top of the merger that had created the ALC in 1960, meant the final and irrevocable conclusion to the Norwegian American immigrant identity of Luther Seminary. Granted, this end had been coming since the language transition to English in the 1920s, but there was still a lingering comfort in that identity. Now that they were completely American Lutherans, what were they supposed to be?

Certainly there were whispered, snide comments about those "high-church, confessionally questionable, liberal" folks at Northwestern (stereotypes that were not particularly true), but the reality of the situation was that there were far more bedrock similarities between the two institutions than the surface differences might have suggested. In the conclusion to his part of the 1974–1975 self-study document, Gerhard Forde notes that the two institutions "bear some subtle differences," and then asks, "How will the theological school which emerges take its place as a Lutheran seminary in America? ... How will it seek to appropriate and perpetuate its own confessional tradition and contribute that understanding to the revitalizing of the Christian church in America?"[32] These questions, among many others, would occupy the Luther Seminary community through the merger period up to 1982 and certainly beyond.

In the merger of 1982, the official name of the seminary was changed to Luther Northwestern Theological Seminary.[33] But the merger itself still left a number of different questions to deal with, including the merger of hearts and minds between the two campus communities. Svendsbye recalled being surprised by the hostility that existed between the two student bodies and the two faculties and worked hard to try and integrate them.[34] On the student level, the situation simply required a couple of years, as new classes came into the community. Faculty turnover was much less rapid, and some problems lingered, although there was a spate of new faculty hiring during the 1980s, which perhaps lessened the tensions. The newly merged seminary did, however, have to deal with two separate and distinct denominations. The ALC and LCA had very different structures and procedures for dealing with seminary education and the approval and placement of theological candidates, which made this entire process more difficult. By 1982 it seemed very probable that the two denominations would be merging with each other (and the smaller Association of Evangelical Lutheran Congregations), but that merger was not completed until the formation in 1988 of the Evangelical Lutheran Church in America (ELCA). Because of these differences, and because of the uncertainty of the denominational merger process, there was much at Luther Northwestern to be negotiated and finessed during the 1980s.

GROWTH OF THE PHYSICAL CAMPUS

One important element of unifying the campus was physical—the building of a new campus center for the merged seminary on land between Bockman Hall and Northwestern Hall, at the northeast corner of Hendon and Fulham streets. Luther Seminary had used Aasgaard Hall for its chapel and public events, but that building was in poor physical condition and was eventually torn down in 1989. Northwestern had an appropriate chapel, but it was not large enough for the entire community to gather. Planning began in the late 1970s with a financial appeal in the ALC for their seminaries, which sought to raise forty million dollars, eleven of which were designated for Luther. From these funds, fifty-one new housing units, the Sandgren Apartments, were built in 1981, and Bockman Hall was also renovated that same year. Money was also designated for the endowment.

The groundbreaking for the new campus center was delayed until 1984.

There were several reasons for the delays in getting the campus center started. The seminary fund appeal in the ALC was largely initially successful, but some of the pledges were slow to arrive. The new apartments and the renovation of Bockman were desperately needed and took priority. The costs of the new building were higher than initial projections and necessitated additional fundraising on the part of the development office. And in some quarters, there was opposition to the new building, especially from the local community. The project needed zoning approval from the Saint Paul Planning Commission and City Council; this complicated process was delayed by the opposition of some neighbors, who felt that the new building would harm the residential quality of the area.[35] Some in the campus community also raised questions about building such a new structure, as one student wrote:

> I find it absurd that we allow ourselves to discuss the "ambience" of our new "worship space," while many other Lutheran brothers and sisters in Africa are struggling just to survive [and] many Americans have been out of work for months.[36]

But eventually the money was found to complete the building, objections were overcome, and the new building was dedicated in the fall of 1985. In 1994, it was named the Olson Campus Center in honor of donors Earl B. and Dorothy A. Olson.

ADMINISTRATION, BOARD, AND FACULTY

The growth of Luther Northwestern was more than just in buildings. It had also grown in the number of students and faculty, to the point that there were by 1985/86 nearly one thousand students and a faculty of over fifty, with an ever-expanding series of programs and degrees. Long gone were the days when the seminary was a simple community of faculty and students; it had grown to be a complex organization with a specialized staff of administrative personnel. The role of seminary president had grown too; the president needed to be the administrator of a complex organization, to relate to the large denominational units, and increasingly to spend significant time overseeing fundraising and development activities. Student life was given over to the dean of students, and the instructional and faculty concerns were the responsibility of the dean of the faculty.

This growth and complexity did, however, lead to some conflict in the 1970s and 1980s between President Svendsbye and the seminary faculty, mainly over the hiring, retention, and tenuring of its members. By this time, these processes were increasingly complex; the faculty would recommend a particular action, the president would either concur or dissent, and the decision would go to the seminary board and then to the appropriate denominational board for ratification. This process was always fraught with possible conflict and often relied on personal relationships and a unified denominational culture to make it work. The new situation was now less clear, and the possibilities for conflict increased. As well, in the new complex organization that was Luther Northwestern, some on the faculty came to feel that their traditional control over the institution was slipping away from them, and they were being marginalized.

Svendsbye and the faculty clashed on a series of faculty personnel decisions and more broadly on the power of the president to shape and control these decisions. In several instances, the faculty voted to hire or approve for tenure certain candidates, decisions that were overturned either by the president, the board, or the ALC Board of Theological Education and Ministry (BTEM).[37] In 1977 Professor Darrell Jodock was approved by faculty and president for reappointment, but this was eventually overturned by the BTEM and the Seminary board. In 1980 Pastor Bruce Westphal was recommended for renewal as associate director of continuing education but was blocked by the president. In 1984 two women candidates were recommended for faculty positions, but Svendsbye would approve only one of them. And in 1985, the faculty recommendation of tenure for Professor Dennis Ormseth was overturned by the president and board. Svendsbye felt strongly that he had "to make independent judgements about each faculty member seeking appointment" but that he "found that making those decisions were [*sic*] wrenching but, however difficult they were, I was obligated to make them."[38] In these processes, the faculty continued to push back against the president's power to control such decisions, perhaps aggravated by all the institutional changes and their perception of their "loss of control" over the seminary.

One of the factors, perhaps, in these conflicts was also the number of new faculty members joining the seminary in the late 1970s and 1980s. Each year it seemed that there were at least three to five new faculty members, especially as the older generation of faculty were retiring.[39] One of the features of this growth was the appointment of the first women as a permanent member of the faculty. Diane Jacobson (Old Testament) was the first, hired in 1982, followed by Gracia Grindal (pastoral care and ministry), who in 1988 was the first woman to receive tenure, and Jane Strohl (church history). Other women faculty members taught for periods of time, including Marcia Bunge, Mary Preus, and Patrice Nordstrand. These faculty were preceded by women serving in the administration, including Karen Johnson, Elizabeth Beissel, and Kathy Sukke as assistant dean of students, Carol Baker as registrar, and Nan Aalborg as associate director of contextual education. This was only the beginning of the presence of women at all levels in the seminary.

A GROWING DIVERSITY

Women also constituted a growing proportion of the student population, although they faced a difficult path through seminary and into the ministry. Their presence on campus caused necessary changes in housing and student life but also sparked new conversations about theology, God-images, inclusive language, and other important aspects. A Women's Center was opened in 1979 to support women students.[40] Now it was possible that there would be seminary husbands alongside the traditional seminary wives. One student recounted in the *Concord* her experience as a pregnant woman going out on her internship year, which she found full of both struggles and joys.[41] Any number of traditional practices would need to be reexamined. By the mid-1980s, nearly half of the students at Luther Northwestern were second-career students; presumably many of them were women who had been dissuaded from entering the ministry in earlier decades and who had finally decided to answer the call to ministry.

The student body in the 1980s at Luther Northwestern was

increasingly diverse. In the fall of 1983, the seminary reported a total enrollment of 841 students across all programs. Of these, 650 were ALC students, 191 were LCA, and 65 were "other," probably including ecumenical students and Lutherans from outside North America. There were in that year 619 men and 222 women in the student body. Programs outside of the traditional master of divinity were growing, with sixty-five students in the master of arts, twenty-six in the master of theology, and seventy-five in the doctor of ministry degree programs.[42] The number of married students was rising at this time, evidenced in the growth of second-career students and increased demand for married-student housing, which usually outpaced the supply. Students from outside North America, primarily from Lutheran churches in Africa, were an increasing presence as well.

One factor that was also changing the seminary was the costs involved in attending. In 1975 the tuition for the year was $800, by 1980 it had risen to $1,200, and by 1985 it had risen further to $1,950. In 1985, a single room ranged from $765 to $1,026 and board was $1,050 to $1,350 for the year; apartments cost $220–$320 a month. In part this reflects the inflation of this period of time, and in part it reflects that the seminary was receiving less direct funding from its two denominations. Direct financial support from the ALC and LCA in 1976 constituted 57 percent of the seminary budget, while by 1995 this had fallen to 27 percent.[43] The establishment of a development office in 1975 had been one reaction to this, but reluctantly the seminary also had to shift a greater part of the burden onto the students themselves. Students had always looked for work to support themselves during seminary, but the pressure was mounting. The seminary recommended that students not work more than twenty hours a week during the school year; in a 1980 survey, one student termed this "ridiculous," while another noted, "It's really frustrating not to be able to take the courses you want because they conflict with work."[44] The old professorial complaint, that students were not doing the reading and not engaging with class, had a basis in these financial realities.

ACTIVISM AND ISSUES

The old campus activism of the 1960s saw a resurgence in the early 1980s, with concerns about nuclear war, the peace movement, abortion, conflicts in El Salvador and Nicaragua, apartheid in South Africa, and racial issues in the United States commonly discussed in the pages of the student newspaper, the *Concord*. Luther Northwestern students protested at Honeywell in 1983 for its production of weapons and were active in other protests and demonstrations.[45] Although it is hard to know the overall position of those in the seminary community on these and other social and political issues, it is clear that there was an activist upsurge in the early 1980s, very possibly in conjunction with the election of Ronald Reagan as president of the United States in 1980. A number of efforts were made to bring cultural awareness to campus, and programs were developed to bring students to places around the country and the world. In 1984 Rev. Steven Charleston was hired as director of cross-cultural studies and proposed programs in Hispanic culture and Native American studies. In 1983 a Racial Minorities Concerns Subcommittee was formed.[46] Although it seems like many of these initiatives were only temporary, they show a growing awareness of these issues on campus.

But this renewed activism and the diversification of the campus and students also caused some strain between the campus and some of its traditional constituencies in the ALC. This denomination was, in the main, moderate to conservative in its social and political leanings, and there was a very conservative element in the denomination deeply suspicious of what was going on at Luther Northwestern. Many held to traditional theology and social ethics and the doctrine of the authority of Scripture, and they worried about losing these positions in the new, merged church.[47] One Twin Cities–based group, the Fellowship of Evangelical Laity and Pastors, was concerned enough to hold a meeting on campus with students, which, if it did not change any minds, was at least a meeting of those minds.[48] But conservative suspicion of the seminary by elements of the ALC did continue and may well have been a factor in the decline in church support for the institution.

NEW PROGRAMS AND NEW INITIATIVES

As a means of trying to connect (or reconnect) with these church constituencies, especially in the new, larger merged churches, the seminaries developed publications aimed at communicating (and explaining) events on campus. Luther Seminary had the *Luther Theological Seminary Review*, and along with this beginning in 1973, the *Semogram*. Northwestern had its publication, *The Bell*. These were merged into the *Semogram-Bell* (1979–1984) and then reformatted into *The Story* magazine in 1985. For more serious readers, the faculty journal *Word & World* was developed in 1981; both *The Story* and *Word & World* continue to be published. After several different iterations in the late 1960s, the student newspaper the *Concord* was begun in 1971.

Two other major institutional developments occurred at Luther Northwestern during the 1980s: the initiation of a PhD graduate program and the formation of the Global Mission Institute. In the midst of the merger of the two institutions in 1981, the chair of the graduate studies committee announced a possible new PhD program for the seminary.[49] There were immediate supporters and doubters of the new initiative, and the proposal wandered through the faculty world for four years, until in the end it was approved in 1985, with a number of caveats, especially that it serve the church and eventually be self-supporting. But faculty approval, tortuous as it was, was only the first step. The new program had to be approved by the boards of the ALC and LCA,[50] the Association of Theological Schools, and other regional accrediting agencies. The first cohort in this new program entered the seminary in the fall of 1987.

Both Luther and Northwestern had traditionally had a deep interest in world missions and the churches in the Global South, and many of their students had served in ministries abroad. There had been, over the years, certain faculty members with special interest and experiences in this area. In 1981, a special endowed chair in missions, funded by the seminary appeal, was founded at Luther, and the chair was filled the next year. In 1985, the chair, Duane Olson, proposed the formation of a Global Mission Institute, owned by Luther Northwestern but with its own board and resources. This program was a link between Luther Northwestern and the global Christian community, as well as an advocate for a world-mission perspective on campus, and looked to bring more global students to campus.

As can be seen in the preceding pages, the term of Lloyd Svendsbye's presidency, beginning in 1975, was a time of great complexity, growth, and sometimes conflict. The merger of the two seminaries and the joining together of the two campuses were immense feats, requiring at times great patience and energy. The seminary community seemed to be moving many directions at once, and there were often disagreements and struggles over the changes, which was only to be expected. But the community seemed to be surprised in January 1986 when President Svendsbye announced his resignation; the faculty then urged him to reconsider this action, which he did.[51] But his reconsideration lasted for only a year, and at the end of 1986 Svendsbye again announced his resignation, effective January 15, 1987. Later that year, he became the president at Augustana College, Sioux Falls, South Dakota, one of the colleges of the ALC.

When Svendsbye left, the seminary board appointed a former ALC bishop, A. G. "Gib" Fjellman, as interim president of Luther Northwestern. But it did not take long for the board to find a permanent president, calling Dr. David Tiede, a Luther Northwestern professor of New Testament, to that position, effective August 15, 1987. There is a sort of biblical quality to this progression, with Svendsbye a type of Moses, leading the seminary to the brink of a new era, in this case the formation of the Evangelical Lutheran Church in America (as of 1988), and Tiede as his Joshua, his successor, to take the seminary into the new situation that lay ahead.

Notes

1. To be sure, this expansion was hardly the automatic gathering in of the immigrants and their children; Lutherans developed an impressive ethos of evangelism to build their congregations. See Mark Granquist, "Exploding the 'Myth of the Boat,'" *Lutheran Forum* 44, no. 4 (Winter 2010): 15–17.

2. But there was a significant downside to this push for a larger American

Lutheran denomination. See Mark Granquist, "The Urge to Merge," *Lutheran Forum* 47, no. 2 (Summer 2013): 20–23.

3. Gerhard O. Forde, "Luther Theological Seminary, 1917–1974," in "Luther-Northwestern Self-Study Affirmations—Descriptive Phase, Northwestern Lutheran Theological Seminary," manuscript, 1975. Archives of Luther Seminary, Saint Paul, MN.

4. Alvin Rogness, "Our President Speaks," *Luther Theological Seminary Review*, November 1965, 5.

5. Alvin Rogness, "A Word from Our President," *Luther Theological Seminary Review*, November 1966, 5.

6. Forde, "Luther Theological Seminary," 30–31. In contemporary terms it might be considered a Mission Statement.

7. Forde, "Luther Theological Seminary," 34.

8. Forde, "Luther Theological Seminary," 37. This whole paragraph is dependent on Forde's analysis of the new curriculum of the 1960s.

9. Rogness, "Reflections on Theological Education," 50.

10. Rogness, "Reflections on Theological Education," 50–51.

11. Harrisville, "Luther Theological Seminary," 52.

12. Earl Hauge, "A Letter to Juniors and Middlers," *Communique*, April 10, 1967, 3.

13. Philip A. Nesset, "A Modest Proposal—Just for Openers," *Communique*, November 7, 1966, 2.

14. Alan Tobey, "Pablum or Steak: The Case for a 'Free Seminary,'" *Communique*, April 18, 1967, 2.

15. Lowell G. Almen, "The Year in Retrospect," *Luther Theological Seminary Review*, May 1965, 9–11.

16. Gary J. Olson, "Student Interracial Ministry: A Challenge," *Communique*, February 23, 1967, 2–3.

17. The student newspaper of the time, *Pax*, ran continuous coverage of the antiwar activities on campus during the period 1969–1971.

18. Alvin Rogness, "From the President's Desk," *Luther Theological Seminary Review* 8, no. 1 (May 1969): 7.

19. Harrisville, "Luther Theological Seminary," 52.

20. "Editorial: Onesimus," *Pax* 1, no. 2 (November 1, 1971): 3.

21. Rogness, "Reflections on Theological Education," 51.

22. Alvin N. Rogness, "A Word from Our President," *Luther Theological*

Moving into the Mainstream: Luther Seminary, 1960–1988

Seminary Review, May 1966, 3.

23. Harrisville, "Luther Theological Seminary," 55. Harrisville was writing from the perspectives of the 1990s and was perhaps anticipating a later trend but one whose beginnings he was seeing in the 1970s.
24. Svendsbye, *One in Mission*, 11–12.
25. "Editorial," *Pax* 2, no. 3 (November 30, 1970): 3.
26. Forde, "Luther Theological Seminary," 38.
27. Forde, "Luther Theological Seminary," 39.
28. Harrisville, "Luther Theological Seminary," 54.
29. Charles W. Bachman, "ALC Ordains Women?" *Communique*, September 23, 1968, 2. A congregation was ready to call Proux but had to wait until the ALC had acted.
30. Gracia Grindal, "How Women Came to Be Ordained," in *Lutheran Women in Ordained Ministry, 1970–1995*, ed. Gloria E. Bengston (Minneapolis: Augsburg, 1995), 52.
31. "The New Sem Wives," *Luther Theological Seminary Review* 14, no. 1 (Spring 1975): 12–13.
32. Forde, "Luther Theological Seminary," 46.
33. This name was short-lived, lasting until 1994, when the name of the institution was changed back to Luther Seminary. Supporters and alumni of Northwestern were obviously displeased by this move, but there was not much they could do to stop the change.
34. Svendsbye, *One in Mission*, 39, 51.
35. "Problems Plague Building Plans," *Concord* 12, no. 17 (March 18, 1983): 1.
36. "My View: New Chapel of New Priorities?" *Concord* 12, no. 3 (November 1, 1982): 7.
37. On the particulars of this, see Kent Johnson, "An Era of Transitions, 1976–1996," in Gonnerman, *Thanksgiving and Hope*, 100–102. On Svendsbye's own view of these conflicts, see Svendsbye, *One in Mission*, 42–46.
38. Svendsbye, *One in Mission*, 43.
39. Until 1991, there was a mandatory retirement age of seventy, and many of these older faculty had come to their respective seminaries after World War II.
40. "Women at LNTS: A Struggle for Place, a Search for Support," *Concord* 12, no. 6 (1982): 1.

41. "What? You Want to Send Us a Pregnant Intern?" *Concord* 13, no. 18 (March 22, 1984): 8.

42. "Enrollment Report," *Semogram-Bell* 4, no. 1 (Fall 1983): 8.

43. Johnson, "An Era of Transitions," 113.

44. "Finances Cause Stress," *Concord* 10, no. 10 (November 14, 1980): 3.

45. See, for example, "Students Protest Honeywell," *Concord* 13, no. 5 (October 27, 1982): 1; or "Faculty Leads Seminary toward Peace Emphasis," *Concord* 12, no. 10 (December 10, 1982): 10.

46. "Seminary Examines Racial Concerns," *Concord* 12, no. 15 (February 11, 1983): 1.

47. In the ALC constitution from 1960, the statement on the authority of Scripture defined it as "divinely inspired, revealed, and inerrant Word of God . . . the only infallible authority in all matters of faith and life" (Article IV, Confession of Faith). The conservatives were very worried (rightly, as it turns out) that this strong language would be abandoned in the new church. A number of conservative congregations did not enter the ELCA because of this.

48. "Prospectus," *Concord* 13, no. 17 (March 15, 1984): 3.

49. Johnson, "An Era of Transitions," 95–96.

50. There was some resistance from the LCA side, perhaps because some wanted to protect the existing PhD program at the LCA's Lutheran School of Theology at Chicago.

51. Johnson, "An Era of Transitions," 102. Johnson believes that the continual struggle with the faculty over appointments and presidential prerogatives played a role in this action.

8

Expansion and Change: Luther Seminary, 1988–2019

In looking at the most recent thirty-year period of the history of Luther Seminary, one thing that is striking is the amount of change that has taken place over this time. Change has always been a significant part of the history of Luther and its predecessors, but the recent developments seem to have been both constant and significant in ways that dwarf those of previous periods.[1] The period of time covered in this final chapter, 1988 to 2019, saw great expansion and development during the first section, followed by painful contraction and retrenchment during the more recent times. The delivery of seminary education has been significantly changed by dramatic social, religious, and technological shifts, things that have only accelerated at the end of the twentieth century. An alum who has not been on the seminary campus for decades might return and wander around the contemporary campus like a modern-day Rip Van Winkle, stunned by the changes wrought in a mere lifetime and wondering if it is really in fact the same institution. And the changes most likely will continue apace, so that an arbitrary date like 2019 is hardly a conclusion to the story.[2] Yet Luther Seminary has continually sought to maintain its focus on educating leaders for the church for the sake of the world, however different these leaders, the church, and the world were becoming.

LUTHER NORTHWESTERN AND THE NEW EVANGELICAL LUTHERAN CHURCH IN AMERICA

This period of change begins in 1988 with the formation of the Evangelical Lutheran Church in America (ELCA). The mergers of the early 1960s that produced the Lutheran Church in America (LCA) and the American Lutheran Church (ALC) seemed to many at the time as merely precursors to a larger development, the eventual unification of all American Lutherans in a single denomination. During the 1960s it seemed for a time that this might be possible, with the LCA, ALC, and Lutheran Church—Missouri Synod (LCMS) cooperating in an increasing range of ministries and activities. But the social and religious turmoil of the late 1960s and 1970s began processes of change that resulted in an ever-widening split between the ALC and LCA on the one hand, and the LCMS on the other, exacerbated by a schism within the LCMS that resulted in 1976 in the formation of a breakoff group, the Association of Evangelical Lutheran Congregations (AELC). Though the dream of a pan-Lutheran merger died hard, it became increasingly clear to many during the 1980s that such a development would be, at best, a distant development (if it ever happened at all). This realization, along with the instability of the AELC, led to the formation of the ELCA in 1988.[3]

This new church (not, it was repeatedly stated, a merger) was formed with a number of initial problems that hung over into the 1990s, many of which directly affected Luther Northwestern Theological Seminary (LNTS).[4] The new church was formed without addressing several difficult issues, which would have to be addressed later and which caused significant conflict. As was seen in chapter 7, the predecessor denominations had very different systems for theological education and the approval of ministerial candidates, and an inability to choose between the two meant that the new system was an unwieldy combination of the two. Unrealistic planning and budgeting for the new ELCA meant that its first decade was rocked by financial crises and organizational retrenchment. Luther Northwestern was spared most of these issues, although the weakness in the ELCA meant that appropriations to the seminaries remained flat and an ever-declining proportion of their overall budgets. For the first time in decades, the seminary ran budget deficits for 1987/88 and 1988/89, which officials attributed primarily to decreasing support from the newly organized regional synods.[5] These new organizations were expensive, and the changes disrupted older patterns of loyalty and support for Luther Northwestern. Each seminary received support from certain synods and was excluded from support by others. In the case of Luther Northwestern, the school was cut off from the support of synods in Wisconsin, Iowa, and the Pacific Northwest, whose support was directed to other ELCA seminaries. Although at the time it was hoped that the budget woes of the national ELCA and its synods would be temporary, the situation only got worse over time.[6]

The new ELCA process for approving students for the ministry was also a difficult change for the seminary and its students. The predecessor church bodies had very different systems, that of the ALC centered around the seminary faculty, while the LCA worked primarily through synodical candidacy committees. Additional differences included psychological evaluations in the LCA and matriculation examinations in the ALC, and different roster options, especially for MA students, between the three merging denominations. Since it proved politically difficult to choose between these systems, they were combined into a single system. Some found the new system—with new requirements, such the mandatory completion of Clinical Pastoral Education (CPE)—cumbersome, lengthy, and difficult. Students and professors criticized the 1989 decision to require CPE as having been made unilaterally and adding another layer of complexity and cost to the seminary process. Professor Bill Hulme, who supported the CPE process in general, nevertheless worried that this mandate was negative and "that requiring it undermines the carefully developed curriculum at LNTS, as well as its relationship to CPE."[7] Officials at Luther Northwestern were concerned but publicly positive about some of the developments. New president David Tiede wrote in 1988, "This is our church, and we are all called to help the ELCA live up to its evangelical commitments."[8]

NEW CURRICULUM AND NEW INITIATIVES

In December 1988, with a new seminary president and a new national church, Luther Northwestern publicly released a planning document entitled "Excellence for Ministry," which enumerated new initiatives and developments for the seminary for the next five-year period. This document called for a revised curriculum, strong admissions and financial initiatives, strengthening the seminary community, and a deeper relation to the ministries of the church. This document set a number of pedagogical and institutional processes in motion. Chief among these was a revision of the seminary curriculum, which required a multiyear process but which was finally implemented in 1993. One feature of this process was a series of conversations with church and congregational leaders to hear their viewpoints on how pastors needed to be educated for the new realities of church and world.[9] A large grant from the Lilly Endowment underwrote the cost of the studies that led to this new curriculum, but it was a struggle to get to faculty agreement on the final plan (these things never come easy). As historian Kent Johnson related:

> On March 11, 1992, the committee presented the third draft of the revised curriculum to the faculty. For more than two hours on that day the faculty debated it.... [T]he meeting ended with general agreement that the outline of the curriculum was in place, following a movement from story to interpreting and confessing to mission.[10]

Given the increasing size and diversity of the faculty, and the institution itself, it is understandable that this process took time and was complex and often conflicted.

The new curriculum, the first since 1977, followed the pattern outlined above, which gave the new plan its shape and purpose. New features included a new push for biblical and cultural literacy on the part of the students. New cross-cultural and contextual experiences were required, as was a course on "Reading the Audiences," all designed to form Christian leaders. There were new requirements for strengthening the biblical literacy, including a Bible Proficiency Exam (BPE) that all students would have to pass.[11] This requirement was controversial with students, as might be expected. Reaction to the overall new curriculum was mixed, with some mourning the loss of older courses, some excited by the new requirements, and some willing to go along with the changes. Some students wanted a curriculum that went even further and allowed the student more freedom. One student wrote in 1993:

> It seems to me, our *new* curriculum is based on some very *old* models for what the goals and objectives of a seminary education ought to be. Moreover, these models . . . actually *undo* the efforts of curriculum reformers to shape a system of pastoral education which is relevant to the world outside academe.[12]

Others criticized the new curriculum as being too unwieldy, having too many noncredit requirements (BPE, biblical languages, CPE, and internship), and having too many required courses, with not enough room for electives. Proponents pointed to the new integrated courses and countered that professional schools (of which a seminary was a type) would naturally have a rigorous and closely defined process for educating their graduates.

Along with these changes to the core master of divinity program came a multiplication of other degree programs and offerings. In the early 1980s the seminary recognized that there was room to grow in the master of arts degree programs; although resistance had previously led to these programs being capped at 5 percent of total enrollment, the student numbers in these areas continued to grow. From 1977 to 1995, the number of individuals in MA programs doubled to nearly one hundred students. New degrees and concentrations were developed, including cross-cultural studies (1983), religious education (1986), and a concentration in Islamic studies (1993). Cooperative degree programs were also begun in aging (1987), in a master of sacred music (1990), and a dual MA-MDiv/MSW with Augsburg College (1999). Master of arts in concentrations such as children, youth, and family (CYF) and congregational mission and leadership (CML) were also added. The doctor of ministry (DMin) cohorts remained strong. The first class of the new PhD program entered in 1987, and this became a growing program, attracting students from around the world, even though the Bible faculty later decided to end their involvement with this degree.

GROWTH AND THE QUESTION OF IDENTITY

The total number of students at Luther Northwestern grew modestly, from 731 in 1988 to 814 in 1994, and then remained at about 800 students into the 2000s. The internal composition of the student body shifted, however. In 1988/89, the entering class (juniors) was 50 percent women, while the graduating class (seniors) was only 27 percent women.[13] By the mid-1990s the total proportion of men and women enrolled was about equal and would remain that way going forward. The number of ecumenical (non-Lutheran) students and international students also increased. Through the 1980s and 1990s, the percentage of second-career students grew, although the percentage of these students at LNTS was considerably less than at the other ELCA seminaries. Increasingly, the percentage of incoming students from ELCA colleges declined, while those from state universities rose.[14] In 1991, a seminary committee urged the increased recruitment of people of color as students, with a goal that they would constitute 10 percent of the student body by 1993/94.[15] An African American pastor, Al Harris, was hired to work in the admissions office, and in 1989 faculty member and director of cross-cultural studies Steve Charleston received tenure, the first nonwhite, non-Lutheran tenured professor in the seminary's history.[16]

This growth, especially the increasing diversity and complexity of the seminary community, naturally raised questions concerning its identity and nature. Certainly the days when the seminary could be considered a Norwegian American institution were gone, although the immigrant background of the seminary continued to be important, if only as a heritage. With an increasing number of ecumenical students and even faculty, the natural questions involved the Lutheran identity of the institution and the role that Lutheranism would play in the seminary's future. In 1991, a group of ecumenical students brought many of these issues to the attention of the seminary community, ranging from their greater integration into the life of the community, the development of alternative curricular requirements, and other accommodations.[17] Although there seemed to be sympathy with this line of thinking, substantive changes were slow in coming, as the percentage of Lutheran students and faculty remained high.

There were several more instances of this search for identity in the 1990s. Although the seminary had taken the name Luther Northwestern as a result of the merger of 1982, the name seemed awkward and clumsy to some in the seminary community. In 1993, the seminary administration and board began to carefully explore a possible change in the name of the seminary, proposing to revert to the name "Luther Seminary." This was, of course, a touchy issue, especially since the unification of the two seminaries was little more than a decade old. But it was believed that the simplification of the title, dropping both the words *Northwestern* and *Theological* would provide for a "simple name that communicates who we are to a broader community."[18] The name change took effect on July 1, 1994, and this has remained the official name of the seminary.

Names, however communicative and important, do not convey the full identity of an institution such as Luther Seminary. As the seminary grew more diverse, it seemed to become necessary to develop a new mission statement, a short paragraph that would encapsulate the core identity and mission of the institution. The statement, as finally agreed to in the spring of 1995, stated:

> Luther Seminary educates leaders for Christian communities called and sent by the Holy Spirit to witness to salvation through Jesus Christ and to serve in God's world.

Even in the most united of communities, the process of hammering out such a statement can be difficult; often each word of the statement is examined in exhaustive detail, and the wrangling can be intense. One participant said of the process: "Coming to that consensus was no easy matter, as those who participated in the discussions will attest."[19] Given the increasing size and complexity of the institution, finding the right words was an arduous task.

INCREASING QUESTIONS ABOUT FINANCING

It was also increasingly difficult to finance such a growing institution.

As was noted above, in its first years the newly formed ELCA experienced a severe financial crisis; in 1989 the church experienced a nearly sixteen-million-dollar deficit (out of a total budget of approximately ninety-five million dollars). Though church support for the seminary began to decline in the late 1950s, financial support from the national church was still an important part of the seminary budget. In 1989 this support made up 38 percent of the seminary budget, and the ELCA was forced to cut this appropriation by 12 percent for 1990. To maintain and grow the seminary, new revenue sources were needed, especially from private gifts and grants, endowment income, and tuition, which supplied about 20 percent each toward the budget. The seminary's development office was expanded to reach additional donors and sources of revenue; that they were successful can be seen in the growth of the seminary endowment, which grew from sixteen million in 1988 to forty-six million by 1998. But the cuts from the ELCA caused short-term pain. As an article in the *Concord* stated in 1990, "The number of faculty and staff has been reduced, and salaries have remained behind inflation for five years."[20]

Increasingly, financial pain fell on the students in the form of increased tuition and fees. Tuition in 1989 was $2,500, but by 1998 it had doubled to $5,950, and by 2008 it had nearly doubled again to $11,000. There was an increase during these years in student financial aid, but this did not fully cover these tuition increases. A news item in *The Story* in 1991 estimated that the total costs that year ranged from $11,000 for a single student up to $19,000 for a married couple.[21] Students living on campus complained about the cost of the board plan and what they saw as the inflexibility of the program. Another significant cost was the ELCA-sponsored (and required) Seminarian Health Plan. This had long been a requirement for students (even going back to Augsburg's "Medical Aid Society"), but up to the early 1980s the costs for this coverage had been modest. Inflation and a dramatic rise in health-care costs began to make this a significant cost. Increasingly seminarians turned to student loans, often on top of loans brought with them from undergraduate education. In 1990, the average student borrower left Luther Northwestern with $12,500 in loan debt (many owed even more), at a time when the income for new pastors (salary and housing) averaged around $26,000.[22] Many students needed to work increasingly longer hours a week while in school just to get by, which cut into their studying.

The life of the campus generally went on as usual in the midst of all of this, sometimes too quietly for some. A 1992 editorial in the *Concord* observed:

> Rumor has it that they used to talk about things on this campus. As a matter of fact, we've heard they used to get into some interesting and occasionally heated arguments. It's hard to imagine that happening here. Who was involved? What did they talk about?[23]

One suspects here a bit of hyperbole and perhaps a grain of truth. Certainly there were lively discussions on campus, in and out of classrooms. Seminary-related issues—tuition, health care, candidacy, the curriculum, and theological issues—were common topics, as has been seen. The campus newspaper regularly carried articles, letters, and opinion pieces on social and political issues, such as race-relations, sexuality, wars in the Middle East, and other political issues. Judging from these items, there was a diversity of opinion among the students (and even faculty) on many of these topics.

CONTROVERSIES IN THE ELCA

There was plenty of controversy occurring in the ELCA during the 1990s that spilled over into the halls of Luther Seminary. As the ELCA was being constructed during the 1980s, a number of thorny issues were put aside for the new church to solve, including ministry and ecumenism, questions that might have delayed or derailed the formation of the new church. These denominational issues, along with the financial crisis of the early 1990s, were regularly discussed at Luther Seminary, and students and faculty were often partisan participants in the larger ELCA discussions.

In the first several years of the ELCA, the irregular ordination of gay pastors by congregations in California led to a crisis in the church, and the congregations that called these pastors, who would not agree to abide by the personal standards then required for ELCA pastors, were removed from the denomination. These incidents led the ELCA to begin to study the issue of human sexuality, with the intention of providing a social statement for the church on these topics. The process led to a great deal of controversy on the Luther campus, as there were passionate supporters on both sides, with the faculty publicly divided on the issue. In the fall of 1993 the study itself was mishandled and leaked to the press ahead of its release to the rest of the ELCA. The subsequent uproar eventually led to the study being suspended, but the questions continued. At the 1994 Winter Convocation, and throughout the spring, members of the faculty presented and debated on the issue, and the wider community and alumni participated. As one observer at the time remarked, "While the faculty probably was never so divided on the issue that it was 'split' . . . the events surrounding the sexuality statement did leave its scars on the community."[24] The issue died down for the time being, but it was not resolved and did not go away.

As it was apparent that there were likely not to be any further mergers involving American Lutherans after the formation of the ELCA in 1988, Lutheran leaders turned their attention to establishing formal ecumenical relations with other Protestant groups. The rubric here was the formation of "full communion" agreements, with the interchangeability of clergy and parishioners as the goal. Such an agreement was reached with Reformed Protestant groups, but the mechanics of full communion with the Episcopal Church were much more difficult to achieve, because of the nature of the ministry in that denomination. Episcopal clergy were ordained by the laying on of hands by bishops in the "historic episcopate," and there were three levels of ordained ministry: deacon, priest, and bishop. Lutherans historically had not maintained the necessity of the historic episcopate (and often avoided it) and had maintained a single ordination to a common ministry. As a means of ensuring full communion and the interchangeability of clergy, in 1997 the two denominations reached an agreement, the *Concordat*, which essentially would have had the ELCA adopting the Episcopal system of ministry; this agreement was narrowly defeated by the ELCA Churchwide Assembly in the same year.

A number of the faculty and alumni of Luther were leaders in the opposition to this adoption of the Episcopal system of ministry and led the charge against the *Concordat*. (Others did support it, however.) With the narrow defeat in 1997, the agreement was reworked as a proposal entitled *Called to Common Mission* (CCM), which was to go to the ELCA Churchwide Assembly in 1999. Opponents of CCM gathered in 1998 to form an organization dedicated to defeating CCM, the "Word Alone Movement," and several Luther faculty were prominent in this organization. Luther Seminary was seen around the ELCA (fairly or not) as the hub of opposition to CCM and the agreement with the Episcopal Church, but in the summer of 1999 CCM was narrowly approved by the ELCA. Word Alone continued as a movement of resistance, with one "wing" remaining in the ELCA, while in 2001 the other wing split from the ELCA to form a new denomination, the Lutheran Congregations in Mission for Christ (LCMC). The new LCMC was heavily populated by congregations in the upper Midwest, and many of these congregations and their pastors had longstanding ties to Luther Seminary. These developments would, over time, have a great effect on Luther Seminary.

The aftermath of the CCM decision lingered on the Luther Seminary campus. Though Luther was a center of resistance to the agreement, opinion on the matter was not uniform. While some faculty and students were in the forefront of opposition to the agreement, other faculty and students welcomed the ecumenical agreement. After the approval of CCM in the summer of 1999, these two sides had to come to some sort of rapprochement, if not agreement. In October 1999 the *Concord* reported: "For almost two months the halls and dining areas at Luther have been buzzing with arguments centering on Called to Common Mission (CCM)." The article reported on a community meeting that had been held to address these lingering issues.[25] One issue was the requirement that candidates for ordination would, in the future, have to be ordained by a bishop. There was a "conscience clause" for students who objected, although some bishops made this arrangement difficult to obtain. The effects of CCM on Luther Seminary were not immediately apparent, but some predicted that the institution would lose pastors and supporters. Faculty member Gracia Grindal wrote an open letter to the ELCA presiding bishop in which she predicted that his ELCA "would lose a 1/3 of your liveliest pastors and growing congregations," many of whom, it would seem, were formerly connected to Luther.[26] It is hard to tell, but the loss of these congregations and alumni probably affected the future strength of Luther Seminary.

THE IMPACT OF TECHNOLOGY

Another major development, and one that would eventually have an immense impact on Luther, was the technological and communications revolution that began in the 1980s with the widespread introduction of personal computing. While the introduction of the IBM Personal Computer in 1981 and the Apple Macintosh in 1984 were the leading edge of this revolution, the cost and usability of these early devices led to a slow adoption of individual computers on campus, which did not begin until the late 1980s. Administrative offices and the library began to move toward computing earlier. By 1985 the library had online connections to over ninety databases, by 1988 the library catalog had been moved to computer, and by 1993 all the books in the library had been barcoded for computerized checkout. In 1990, through a donation by Lutheran Brotherhood, a student computer lab was established in Gullixson Hall, with seven IBM PS/2s, a printer, and word-processing software.[27]

The next major step in this technological revolution was to spread these computers throughout campus and then to link them together. In 1993, all the faculty offices were wired for computing, and computers were distributed to the faculty for their use. Some faculty were eager adapters of this new technology, but historian Johnson observed, "Not all the faculty members were standing in line to take advantage of invitations . . . to develop computer skills." But slowly the computer age permeated the campus, and the seminary moved toward its technological future.

A big step in this direction was the implementation of email capacities on campus, which occurred in 1995. The *Concord* observed:

> Luther Seminary has definitely plunged into the information highway and the reaction from all is very positive. With a completely new computer network fully in place on campus, students, faculty, and staff can enjoy the benefits of Electronic mail (E-mail).[28]

Also in 1995 the seminary developed its first home page for the World Wide Web and began to disseminate news and information by electronic means. In 1996 the seminary announced its intent to begin to wire the entire campus, including dorms and apartments, for electronic communication, in order to replace the older, dial-up modems. All these changes certainly transformed seminary life, though print would still be used for many subsequent years. The downside of all this was the additional costs of this technological revolution, costs that were largely added into already strained seminary budgets.

It was one thing to wire the campus and get people to use computers, but this was only a precursor to the curricular and program revolution that would fundamentally transform Luther Seminary and theological education: the introduction of online and distance education. Email and the internet were developments that would eventually allow theological education to be carried on outside the physical classrooms of the seminary, expanding its reach to students who could not or would not move to the campus in Saint Paul. Satellite campuses and interactive video classes were considered early in this revolution, but these initiatives were not the future of the seminary. Rather, the future lay in the development of online courses, and eventually programs, by which students could receive the bulk of their education. Luther Seminary was a pioneer in developing these programs, which not only transformed the seminary but, some would argue, saved it during the financial crises that lay ahead.

The first attempts at offering online courses came in 1996, when Professor Dick Nysse offered a Pentateuch course electronically, and by 1998 a number of other online classes were being offered. In the beginning, the main students in these courses were traditional commuter students, those within a radius around the Saint Paul campus. In 1998, a group of faculty and staff attended a conference on distance education at the University of Wisconsin, Madison, from which they concluded that distance education should not just encompass isolated classes within the residential learning of the seminary but rather needed to be a whole system of education in which the classes and degree programs needed to be coordinated and integrated into the life of the community. The first attempt at such a coordinated program came in 2000, with the development of a pilot distance-learning (DL) program in the master of arts in children, youth, and family (CYF), which allowed professionals working in these areas to seek the degree while continuing to work in congregations. This pilot program combined online education with intensive on-site courses and independent studies. This program proved to be a popular and successful offering and became a regular part of the seminary degree offerings.

Building on this success, Luther began a similar pilot program for the master of divinity degree in the fall of 2007. This MDiv-DL program began with a cohort of fourteen students who followed the pattern established in the CYF program, with online courses and on-campus intensive courses, usually offered during the January and Summer (June) terms. Since most of these DL students were employed, often in congregations, the program expected that the time to completion of the degree would be lengthened, and students would finish the degree in six or seven years rather than the usual four. The students were organized into cohorts, with the idea that these groups would move through the process together, providing a version of a community for these students. Luther was the first ELCA seminary to offer such a program and one of the first mainline Protestant seminaries to do so.[29] These online programs also required the development of an entire electronic infrastructure that would allow these programs to work efficiently and to integrate them into the existing seminary systems.

Gaining approval for these programs and converting them from pilot programs required the approval of the seminary faculty and of educational regulators such as the Association of Theological Schools (ATS). A number of faculty proponents of these programs were eager to make them work. It seems that while other faculty were not directly opposed to these programs, a number of them were lukewarm to the idea or disinterested in participating in them. To these attitudes, one faculty proponent wrote in 1998:

> Sin, death, and the devil will not be banished by the introduction of computers in the process of education. The *eschaton* did not arrive with the World Wide Web. With that said, I'm finished making concessions

to naysayers. Web-based technology has already facilitated fundamental change; this is not a fad, and the change is not simply a marginal enhancement or costly diversion.[30]

In October of 2004, Luther Seminary formally requested permission from ATS to allow the formation of a DL program in the MDiv degree, with a detailed program outline and a team in place to carry it out. With the ATS approval (with modifications), this program was implemented in 2007.

Beginning these programs was one thing, but integrating them into the life of the seminary was quite another. As long as these initiatives were small pilot programs, they could be ignored or shunted to the margins (by some). But the programs themselves proved to be popular and grew, becoming established elements of seminary itself. Critics worried that these programs lacked the equivalent of residential community formation activities, but the DL students compensated by means of virtual community and gatherings during the intensive on-campus sessions. As one DL student reflected in 2010:

> The DL program truly redefines learning because community is intentionally part of everything we do. No matter if it is living together . . . for two weeks in January or June, or if it is a group of students reflecting on readings and sharing experience in online classes, the DL program embodies the heart of what community is all about.[31]

It seems clear that for some students the online and DL experience did create a new type of community experience, but with the growing popularity of these classes, the question then shifted to concern about their effect on the seminary, especially the full-time residential version of the campus.

Another educational program that was developed was Theological Education for Emerging Ministries (TEEM). This program educated leaders for diverse communities that had a hard time gaining educated leaders, often because their candidates did not have college educations or the time or resources to complete a traditional seminary program. One factor of the new ELCA was the "clustering" of seminaries, which put Luther Seminary together with Pacific Luther Theological Seminary (PLTS) for common work. In 1996, Luther and PLTS agreed to combine their TEEM programs, offering intensive courses October and February on the PLTS campus, and May–June at Luther.[32] This program has been sustained for over twenty years, and a number of Luther faculty have participated in it, but the level of integration of this program into Luther Seminary has been rather low. In some respects, the online and DL offerings at Luther and a successful TEEM program at Wartburg Theological Seminary, Dubuque, Iowa, have siphoned some students away from the PLTS-Luther version of the program.

THE BLIESE PRESIDENCY

New technology and new programs were an important part of the 2000s at Luther Seminary, but certainly other elements of campus life continued as before. A big change for the campus was the retirement of President David Tiede in 2005. Tiede had guided the seminary for thirteen years and was especially important in guiding it through all the transitions and changes that occurred as a result of the formation of the ELCA, the decline in church support, the rise of fundraising activities, and the controversies around ministry, ecumenism, sexuality, and CCM. His successor, Richard Bliese, arrived on campus in 2003, when he served initially as academic dean. Bliese was an outsider to the community, having come from the Lutheran School of Theology at Chicago, and it seemed to some observers that his call to Luther was perhaps in preparation for his eventually being promoted to president. Bliese was an energetic and involved leader with a deep concern for the mission of the church in the world. He sought to grow the seminary even further, with a vision for increasing its role as a leading seminary not only among Lutherans worldwide but also among mainline Protestant seminaries in North America.[33]

This period was an expansive one for Luther Seminary. Besides the two DL programs and the TEEM program with PLTS already discussed, other elements were added to the seminary after 2000. A new doctor of ministry (DMin) degree in biblical preaching was added in 2004 to the existing DMin in congregational mission and leadership. Worried about biblical literacy, the ELCA launched the "Book of Faith" initiative in 2007 to reinvigorate the study of the Bible in congregations. The initiative was launched with Luther professor Diane Jacobson as its director, and other faculty contributing to its resources. In 2008, as a means to improve preaching in the ELCA and other denominations, Luther introduced an online preaching resource entitled Working Preacher. This resource has proven to be very popular and has achieved widespread utilization by preachers and others, garnering good exposure for the seminary, as well. In order to increase biblical literacy in congregations, two Luther professors, Rolf Jacobson and Craig Koester, introduced an alternative lectionary, the Narrative Lectionary, which sought to provide biblical continuity in the Sunday readings. In 2012 a new online resource, "Enter the Bible," was introduced; in the same year Luther bought an established program, the "Festival of Homiletics," again raising the public profile of the seminary. In 2011, in the first major building project at the seminary since 1984, additional space was added to the Olson Campus Center.

Of course, the campus continued to be engaged with events in the church and around the world. Although the possible negative effects of the turn of the millennium in 2000 did not materialize, the controversy over the presidential election that year and the Iraq War beginning in 2003 caused a great deal of discussion, especially regarding military chaplaincy and support for the troops. If the articles and exchanges in the student newspaper, the *Concord*, are any indication, although the campus seemed to lean in a liberal/Democratic direction, there were other voices on campus as well. For example, a campus chapter of the College Republicans formed in 2001, although there is no indication of how long this organization lasted.[34] Students continued to grumble about tuition increases and the board plan, and about an abrupt decision in 2007 to convert the Stub Hall residence to short-term housing for distance learners and guests.

While these issues were important, the major challenge to the ELCA and Luther Seminary during the 2000s was the issue of human sexuality, especially the question of the possible ordination of noncelibate gay clergy. This question had been circulating since the late 1960s, and even though it was temporarily derailed by the failed ELCA study in 1993–1994, advocates continued to push the issue.

The ELCA commissioned a second study of the issue that was delivered and approved in 2009. This social statement recognized that there was a difference of opinion on the matter and did not commit the ELCA to any official position on the issue but for the first time did allow for the ordination and rostering of noncelibate gay clergy in the denomination. The backlash to this proposal was swift; in 2010 and 2011 the ELCA lost 250,000 members a year, which slowed to between 50,000 and 60,000 members in the years following. Many conservatives in the ELCA departed, either for the LCMC or to a newly formed group, the North American Lutheran Church (2010). As with the controversy over CCM, a number of those departing the ELCA had ties to Luther Seminary.

After a long period of expansion, Luther Seminary began to face financial problems. While the endowment grew from forty-five million dollars in 1998 to eighty million in 2007, the seminary budget grew as well, to twenty-three million dollars a year by 2008. Tuition nearly doubled between 1998 and 2008, and average rate of student loan debt for graduating seniors reached fifty thousand dollars by 2009–2010.[35] Financial support from the ELCA and the synods relating to Luther Seminary slowly declined. The size of the seminary faculty and staff continued to increase; by 2009 the faculty had expanded to fifty individuals. Trouble came initially in 2008 and 2009 with a deep financial recession that saw the stock market decline by 50 percent and housing prices crash. The seminary endowment declined in one year by 25 percent. Added to this was the fallout from the 2009 ELCA decision on sexuality and a dramatic financial decline of the denomination.

After 2008, the signs of problems were apparent in many sections of the seminary, with budget cuts affecting staffing and student services, and abrupt decisions not well communicated. In 2010, dean of students Patricia Lull departed in disagreement with the president, and campus pastor John Mann departed after his position was converted to part-time. Faculty teaching loads were increased by half a class per year, and staff positions were scaled back or remained unfilled. In the spring of 2010, the editor of the *Concord* reflected: "What a miserable year. A divided church; fallout from the Churchwide Assembly; increased costs; lousy economy; painful staffing changes and program cuts; communication failures, an antagonistic environment." Though he then listed good elements of the year, he concluded that overall the year was "bizarre."[36] The seminary administration acknowledged the weakness and troubles but remained optimistic in its ability to meet the crises. In a 2010 interview, President Bliese acknowledged the troubles of that year:

> Tuition was down considerably—more students taking less coursework—and so that was a huge gap of $300,000. But secondly, with the Churchwide Assembly and the recession—there are debates on which one has been the largest, but it's a one-two punch. . . . I don't think that we're going to go back to the way we were two years ago.[37]

In an interview earlier that academic year (2009/10), seminary vice president of finance and administration Don Lewis stated: "The seminary is strong. Granted we just came through a horrendous year. We were stronger a year ago. . . . However we have a good endowment, good donor base, and the luxury of being financially healthier than many other seminaries." Suggesting that the previous year was "an anomaly," he continued, "If we take last year out of the mix, we are significantly better off than we were 20 years ago."[38] The feeling seemed to be that these negative developments, as painful as they were, were temporary. The often-heard idea was that the way forward was for Luther to grow to a thousand students and increase its fundraising—in essence, to grow its way out of its temporary troubles.

2012: THE YEAR OF CRISIS

But in the fall of 2012, it became painfully clear just how deep a financial hole Luther Seminary was in. Apparently, most of the community—faculty, staff, students, and board members—had not had a true sense of the depth of the seminary's financial trouble. In a chronology delivered to the accrediting agency the Higher Learning Commission in 2014, the seminary officially reported on the events of the fall of 2012: "October/November Board meetings reveal troubling financial news: $15 M in debt, significant revenue losses for 3 years and pattern of funding shortfalls from loans and tapping endowment funds."[39] In a later interview with Michael Morrow (named vice president for finance and administration in 2014) published in the *Concord* in the fall of 2015, student René Mehlberg summarized what she heard Morrow say were the factors leading up to the 2012 crisis:

> Luther Seminary Administration was using endowment money beyond what was agreed upon by the board, using a process that was not open and transparent. Some money gifted to the Endowment was being spent before deposited in the Endowment fund account. The way Luther Seminary was doing accounting misled people to think there was a balanced budget when there truly wasn't.[40]

As well, depreciation was not being factored into the process, and there was reportedly some imprecision about how grant funding was being handled. The seminary was close to exhausting its lines of credit with its banks.

The result was a campus email sent out on December 10, 2012, that a mandatory community meeting would be held in the chapel at 2:00 p.m. that afternoon. The chair of the seminary board reported a four-million-dollar deficit; a student later recalled hearing from this presentation that "this was a case of mismanaged money. There was nothing criminal about the situation, which was a relief . . . sort of. President Bliese addressed the community with a heartfelt apology . . . ending with the announcement of his resignation, effective immediately."[41] The president's resignation was quickly followed by that of Don Lewis, the vice president for finance and administration. The board of directors set up an oversight committee to manage the situation. The director of contextual education, Rick Foss (a former ELCA bishop), was selected as interim president, and Dr. William Frame (former president of Augsburg College) was brought in as interim vice president for finance and administration. A special "loan" of seven million dollars was arranged from the endowment to begin to put the seminary's finances back on a better footing.

RETRENCHMENT AND REBUILDING

These interim leaders, in close cooperation with the board, began the long and painful process of dealing with this crisis—cutting millions of dollars from the budget and tightening financial controls. Since 2008 there had been a pattern of financial tightening, but the scale of these activities was accelerated starting in early 2013. In his report to the community in spring 2013, President Foss wrote:

> The changes that have come our way recently have not been easy. Last fall, we learned that we had been spending beyond our means over the last few years. In December President Rick Bliese resigned after a decade at the seminary. More tough realities followed. In an effort to lower our annual operating expenses, we made the incredibly difficult decision in March to reduce staff, faculty, and programs. It is an incredibly painful thing to say goodbye to talented and faithful friends and colleagues.[42]

The total budget for the seminary, which had peaked at $23 million in 2008, was reduced to $20 million by 2014, and $16.5 million by 2016. The deficits were reduced, but the budget was not balanced immediately, and the seminary ran deficits for several more years, although they were much less dramatic than in the past. Large-scale layoffs of staff members occurred in March 2013, and further cuts to personnel kept coming as programs were reduced or eliminated. The number of faculty, which had peaked in the 2000s at around fifty, was reduced to the low twenties by 2018, by a combination of buyouts and retirements for the older faculty and departures of younger faculty seeking greener pastures, or reading the writing on the wall. This *ad hoc* process of faculty reduction led at times to imbalances in the disciplines, with some areas having too many faculty and other areas having not enough. Morale on campus was understandably low, as those employees who remained missed their departing colleagues and wondered if they might be next. The students were depressed by the departure of mentors and teachers, which was especially hard on the classes of students who were on campus during the year of trial, 2012/13. Two academic programs were suspended in 2013: the PhD program and the master of sacred music (MSM). The PhD degree program was redesigned and relaunched in 2017, but the MSM was eliminated with the retirement of its main faculty member.

The reduction in staff and faculty was paralleled with reductions in the size of the physical campus. Over the years Luther Seminary had accumulated an expansive campus with many acres and buildings. With decades of deferred maintenance, the financial crises of 2008–2012, and the decline in student numbers, it was clear to many that a campus of this size was unsustainable. Physically, Luther Seminary had to get smaller; the question was, how much smaller? The first sales were the Fulham Street apartments in 2013 and the Sandgren and Burnvedt apartments in 2014. The seminary determined that it could not put into these properties the funding needed to provide them with badly needed renovations. The idea was to sell the apartments to developers who would lease the apartments back to the students, but for a number of reasons this did not generally work out; the new arrangements were more expensive than students could afford, and many students moved off campus. The sale of these apartments gained the seminary $8.5 million, of which $6 million went to repaying the "loan" from the endowment, and the remaining amount to the seminary's cash reserves. In 2016 the seminary sold the large recreational field between the Sandgren apartments and the campus and a portion of the eastern side of the upper campus; these funds were dedicated to future campus renovations.

All areas of seminary life were subject to financial scrutiny, and auxiliary enterprises came under pressure to at least break even. The seminary bookstore, which had been a source of concern for many years, was first downsized and then closed in 2016; it was unable to compete with online book services. The campus food service was outsourced, and its hours and offerings were cut back significantly. While during this period a number of other ELCA seminaries were merging with ELCA colleges and universities, Luther did not take this route. It did, however, enter into a number of cooperative arrangements to share services with Augsburg University in Minneapolis. The seminary's informational technology and communications departments were shared between the two institutions, as were a number of other individual positions, such as the comptroller and seminary pastor. Augsburg leased space in Northwestern Hall and the Olson Campus Center for its physicians' assistant program.

All these changes had a significant impact on student life. The residential nature of campus took a great decline with the sale of the apartments, as many students moved off campus. The dormitory rooms in Bockman Hall were closed in 2012 due to environmental and structural concerns, and the long-term residents were moved to Stub Hall or to various campus-owned houses. These campus houses had traditionally been rented to faculty and staff, who had to vacate them to allow for student living. The reductions in the dining services meant that only breakfast and lunch were offered; students had to find their dinner options elsewhere. Eventually some rooms in Bockman were reopened, but this time for short-term housing, such as for students coming to campus for intensives. These developments all led to fewer students on campus and a sense of dis-ease among the students as to the future of Luther as a residential campus.

There was a national trend during the 2010s of a downturn in seminary enrollment, with a general decline of 20 to 30 percent, across all seminaries, whether Protestant or Roman Catholic, mainline or evangelical. The number of candidates considering candidacy at ELCA seminaries declined even further, from 556 in 2010 to 390 in 2016, sharing in this trend and probably worsened by the steep decline of the ELCA after the 2009 decision.[43] The effect on Luther was substantial, as total student enrollment fell from 830 in 2007 to 490 in 2017, and the "new average" of students is generally reckoned to be about 500 students in any given year. There were internal shifts as well. The number of distance learning (DL) students, which was only 3 percent in 2007, had climbed to 45 percent by 2017, just ten years later. The ratio of male to female students, which was roughly equal over the last decades of the twentieth century, has shifted by 2019 to nearly 60 percent female and 40 percent male. While it is hard to quantify, a number of seminary faculty have commented on their perception that there has been a discernible decline in the number of conservative students enrolled, one that began with CCM in 1999, and was accelerated by the 2009 ELCA sexuality decisions.

All these changes have meant a shift in how students proceed through the seminary. The old model was that students would come to campus for their first two years of education (junior and middler), go off on internship their third year, and return for their fourth (senior) year, finishing the degree in four years. The DL cohorts were built on this same model, although it quickly became apparent that because most DL students were substantially employed, they would normally take six or seven years to complete this program. By the 2010s, these models were in substantial disarray. Residential students were often either accelerating or elongating their programs. Many students pushed for a culminating internship after their course of study, sometimes seeking a part-time internship spread out over two years. Because of work, availability, or even convenience, residential students were taking a number of their courses online. Some DL students, frustrated with the slow pace of their degree progression, decided toward the end of their program to move to campus and go full-time for a year. The number of students Luther had enrolled became a much less precise marker; the only really solid figure was how many "seats" were "sold" in a given year—in other words, how many students took how many classes.

THE STEINKE PRESIDENCY

In 2014, the board of directors voted to call Dr. Robin Steinke as the next president of Luther Seminary, concluding the eighteen-month interim of President Rick Foss. Though she was a native upper-midwesterner, President Steinke came to the seminary from a long tenure as a faculty member and then dean at the Lutheran Theological Seminary at Gettysburg and began her new position on June 1, 2014. The other significant staffing transition that year was the hiring of Michael Morrow as the new vice president of finance and administration later that year. As might be expected, a number of changes in top administrative personnel occurred during the first several years of this new presidential administration, as President Steinke sought to build her own team.

The other major development in 2014 was the introduction of a new curriculum for the master of divinity program, the culmination of several years of working and discussion by the faculty. A number of reasons were suggested for this new curriculum, the first since

1993, most noticeably that the world, the church, and students had changed appreciably over twenty-one years. There was a perceived need to reduce the overall size of the curriculum, especially the non-credit requirements, such as the biblical language, Clinical Pastoral Education, and internship, which in this new curriculum became a credited part of the whole. A four-year master's is a very long degree compared with other professional programs, and the concern over student finances and debt load argued for a shorter list of requirements. The previous seminary curriculum had been rather prescribed, with a high number of required courses, and this new curriculum went quite far in the other direction. To offer greater flexibility and choice, the number of required courses was substantially reduced, giving students great ability to choose elective courses. A set of signature courses to be taken by all MDiv and MA students, and core required courses, constituted about 40 percent of the total required for graduation. The remaining courses were elective.

This curriculum was new in a number of other ways, especially in terms of pedagogy and assessment. It mandated program and learning outcomes for all the courses and for the curriculum as a whole, and for each student to track their own learning and needs, given the large number of electives that they could take. A new initial course entitled "The Learning Leader" sought to have students develop their own path through seminary, guided by portfolio assessment tools that enabled students and faculty to assess their learning. A number of courses were designed to be integrative and team-taught. But almost from the beginning, this new curriculum had problems. In an era of retrenchment and with declining numbers of faculty, this was an ambitious program that could not be sustained with the resources at hand. In 2016 the curriculum was revised. The Learning Leader course and the portfolio program were eliminated, replaced by a new Christian Public Leader course, and there were other tweaks to the curriculum as well.[44] In 2017 there was a substantial reorganization and refocusing of the MA programs to simplify the number of options available for this degree. Also in 2017 a redesigned and somewhat smaller PhD program was introduced that sought to be more collaborative in nature and to move students through the degree more quickly.

The redesign of the campus, which began with the sale of properties in 2013, continued, and plans to redevelop the remaining campus were drawn up. Masterplans for this redevelopment were suggested in 2009, 2012, and 2016, often focusing on an extensive renovation of Bockman Hall for housing, offices, and classrooms; Bockman had not been renovated in decades and needed substantial work. But these plans were stymied by the costs of renovating such an old building and by a curious lack of interest in these plans on the part of major donors, whose contributions were needed to bring these plans to fruition.[45] In 2017–2018, the campus planning shifted to an even more drastic reduction in the campus footprint, as the size of the residential community continued to contract. Proposals were developed to reduce the physical presence of the campus to two buildings, Olson Campus Center and Gullixson Hall, and to sell Bockman Hall and what remained of the lower campus, Northwestern and Stub Halls, to a developer.[46] In 2018–2019, the board voted to accept this two-building approach and signed letters of intent with developers to bring it about. Under this plan, Olson Campus Center and Gullixson would be extensively remodeled, the lower campus would be developed for housing, and Bockman Hall would be turned into residential development, with a section of the building to be leased back for student housing. In the spring of 2019 these plans were postponed for the development of further financing, but the process is seemingly still on track.

There were two major developments in 2018 and 2019 of a much more positive nature. The first was the development of the Jubilee Scholarship program, in which all admitted MDiv and MA students will receive full-tuition scholarship support, essentially eliminating tuition for these students. Driven by increasing concern over student debt loads and to be competitive with other peer seminaries, the Luther program attempted to draw seminary resources and donor support to make this possible. The initial response to this program has been generally positive, as the number of student applicants (and their quality) has gone up substantially. There are drawbacks to this, however; there are unanswered questions as to the sustainability of the program and also about the fact that it, in reality, caps the number of students admitted in any one year and generally precludes the growth of the student population.

The other major development was the announcement of a major grant of twenty-one million dollars to establish a pilot program of pastoral education called the MDivX. This pilot program consists of thirty students a year and compresses the MDiv program into two years. Students in this program will work full-time toward the degree over twenty-four months, and internship and CPE will be done concurrently with the academic program. This all will be made possible for students because they will receive a substantial stipend for the program, on top of the already free tuition. This program obviously depends on cooperation from the ELCA and its synods, as it means a very different candidacy process for the students. The first cohort of the MDivX program began at Luther Seminary in June 2019.[47]

In 2019, it is rather stunning to think back on the amount of change that Luther Seminary has undergone in the past dozen years. Certainly the crises of 2008–2012 have remolded this institution in profound and probably permanent ways, and the seminary community itself is still searching for the "new normal," if such a thing exists. It seems, if the pronouncements of the seminary administration are to be believed, the institution is financially stable and is moving with confidence into its new future. There is no current reason not to believe this, although the radical changes of the recent past have made the community somewhat skittish of such pronouncements. But Luther Seminary continues to try, as best it can, to educate Christian leaders for Christian communities in the midst of an ever changing world.

Notes

1. A historian's disclaimer is in order here. This writer has been directly involved with the developments at Luther Seminary since being first employed there in 2007 and has similarly been involved in developments and controversies in the ELCA since its inception in 1988. While every effort will be made to be as fair and balanced in these historical accounts, the reader will have to adjust for these factors.

2. Given the obvious limitations of doing contemporary history, the discussions and conclusions of this final chapter will be, understandably, hardly the last word. The writer begs the indulgence of the reader to understand that this chapter is the first draft of the historical record and that time and space may well adjust these conclusions in the future.

3. On the formation of the ELCA and its early issues, see Edgar Trexler, *High Expectations: Understanding the ELCA's Early Years, 1988–2002* (Minneapolis: Augsburg Fortress, 2003).

4. This chapter will continue to use the name Luther Northwestern for the seminary as long as this was its official name (1982–1994). After 1994, the name of the institution was changed back to Luther Seminary, and the narrative will revert to that for events beginning in 1994.

5. "Student Council Views Student Financial Burdens," *Concord* 18, no. 15 (May 4, 1989): 1.

6. On the continuing financial and membership decline in the ELCA, see Mark Granquist, "The ELCA by the Numbers," *Lutheran Forum* 50, no. 3 (Fall 2016): 17–21.

7. Hans Wiersma, "ELCA to Require CPE," *Concord* 18, no. 16 (May 18, 1989): 3.

8. "Seminarium," *The Story* 4, no. 3 (Fall/Winter 1988/89): 2.

9. Roland Martinson, "Seminary Aims at Education for Faithful, Effective Leadership into 21st Century," *The Story*, Spring–Summer, 1993, 13.

10. Johnson, "An Era of Transitions," 109.

11. Steve Anderson, "Bible Literacy Exam Proposal Approved," *Concord* 23, no. 10 (February 24, 1994): 1.

12. Paul Skistad-Kimmel, "The New Curriculum: Geared for Obsolescence?" *Concord* 23, no. 3 (October 21, 1993): 7.

13. Rolf Jacobson, "Enrollment Is Up, More Women Attending LNTS," *Concord* 18, no. 8 (January 18, 1989): 1.

14. Rolf Jacobson, "Flesner Reflects on Admissions Trends," *Concord* 18, no. 14 (April 20, 1989): 2.

15. Johnson, "An Era of Transitions," 105. The goal of 10 percent mirrored that of the quotas for participation in the ELCA, but it was a goal that has never been met. Hiring multicultural staff and professors has also been a goal, but these results have not been much better.

16. Brett Carter, "Charleston Receives Historic Tenure Friday," *Concord* 19, no. 5 (October 11, 1989): 1. Charleston did not remain long at LNTS, as he was elected the Episcopal bishop for Alaska.

17. Tor Kristian Berg, "Non-Lutheran Students Seek More Integration at LNTS," *Concord* 20, no. 7 (February 20, 1991): 1.
18. "Luther Seminary Approved by Directors as New Name," *The Story*, Fall–Winter 1993, 15. The same article quoted former Northwestern dean and professor Robert Roth as endorsing the change, although there was, as might be expected, unhappiness with the move by some supporters of the former seminary.
19. Johnson, "An Era of Transitions," 93.
20. Greg Peterson, "Expected 12% Cut in Churchwide Financial Support Could Mean More Cuts Here and Possible Tuition Hike," *Concord* 19, no. 10 (January 17, 1990): 1. Through the 1980s inflation was a big problem, and the seminary had a tough time raising enough revenue to keep up with it.
21. "What Does Education at Luther Northwestern Really Cost," *The Story*, Fall 1991, 13.
22. John Paulson, "Commitment Doesn't Buy Groceries," *The Story*, Spring 1991, 5–7.
23. "Thunder of Silence at LNTS," *Concord* 22, no. 4 (October 14, 1992): 6.
24. Johnson, "An Era of Transitions," 113.
25. "Luther Community Gathers to Discuss CCM," *Concord* 29, no. 3 (October 18, 1999): 1.
26. Gracia Grindal, "Open letter to Presiding Bishop H. George Anderson," *Concord* 29, no. 2 (October 4, 1999): 3. The actual loss of pastors and congregations from the ELCA was slow, but fifteen years later the new LCMC had 750 congregations and 375,000 members. See Mark Granquist, "A Slow Disaster and a Proposal for Reform," *Lutheran Forum* 46, no. 2 (Summer 2012): 23–26.
27. Jeff Mach, "Student Computers Go 'Online' Sept. 4," *Concord* 20, no. 1 (August 29, 1990): 2.
28. S. K. Hannan, "Luther Successfully on E-Mail," *Concord* 24, no. 8 (January 26, 1995): 1.
29. Laura Kaslow, "Distributed Learning M.Div. Pilot Program Launches This Fall," *The Story*, Summer 2007, 7.
30. Richard W. Nysse, "Online Education: An Asset in a Period of Educational Change," in *Practical Wisdom: Theological Teaching and Learning*, ed. Malcolm L. Warford (New York: Peter Lang, 2004), 197. Nysse made this statement in a communication in 1998 and was quoting himself in an article six years later.

31. Jodie Becker, "Redefining Learning," *Concord* 40, no. 3 (December 8, 2010): 3.

32. Andy Behrendt, "Luther and PLTS 'TEEM' Up to Provide Innovative Theological Education," *The Story*, Fall Supplement 2006, 2.

33. Sheri Booms Holm, "A Heart for Mission," *The Story*, Summer 2005, 6–7; and Andrew Plocher, "Infallible: President Richard Bliese Entertains a Few Questions," *Concord* 35, no. 1 (September 28, 2005): 8–9.

34. "Survey Says . . ." *Concord* 40, no. 5 (February 16, 2011): 13; about 60 percent of faculty and 50 percent of the students polled identified themselves as Democrats. On the college Republicans, see "College Republicans Chapter Formed at Luther Seminary," *Concord* 30, no. 9 (May 10, 2001): 2.

35. "Facts and Figures," *Concord*, April 11, 2012, 11. Of course, a significant portion of this debt made been incurred by students as a part of their undergraduate educations.

36. Nicholas Weber, "Letter from the Editor," *Concord* 39, no. 6 (April 29, 2010): 2.

37. Where We Stand: A Q & A with President Bliese," *Concord* 39, no. 4 (February 24, 2010): 3.

38. "Facing Financial Realities at Luther Seminary," *Concord* 39, no. 2 (November 4, 2009): 5.

39. Luther Seminary, "Self-Study Report for Continued Accreditation with the Higher Learning Commission," March 2015, 14.

40. Rene Mehlberg, "Interview with Michael Morrow," *Concord* 45, no. 3 (December 2015): 5.

41. Jenn Herron, "The Fall of 2012," *Concord* 45, no. 3 (December 2015): 3. Herron reported her personal evaluation of the situation, "In the outpouring of a standing ovation filled with love and reverence, Dr. Bliese walked away from the pulpit and right out of the chapel with tears running down his face. No longer was this an ordinary day. This was a defining moment. Luther Seminary would never be the same again." If truth be told, not all in attendance that day shared this assessment.

42. Rick Foss, "Changing Lives," *The Story*, Spring 2013, 4.

43. Kenneth Inskeep, "A Review of Candidacy Applications Submitted from January 1, 2010 through May 23, 2017," ELCA Office of Research and Evaluation, unpublished paper, July 2017. The figure for 2017 was 202, but presumably this was lower because it was a partial year.

44. On the new 2014 curriculum, see John Klawiter, "A New Curriculum for a Changing Church in a Changing World," *The Story*, Spring 2014,

17–19. There was, and still is, a division among the faculty on the 2016 revisions of the curriculum. Some saw the 2014 program as too ambitious for the new reality of Luther Seminary, while others think that the innovative features of the new curriculum were not given a full chance to succeed.

45. Curious, because the Development Office tried to push this program and was not successful. Their conclusion, after conversations with donors, was that the Luther Seminary donor base was more interested in supporting scholarships than it was in brick-and-mortar projects.

46. There were even suggestions of more radical possible shifts—one that the entire campus be fit into a single building, or even more radically, that the entire campus be sold and relocated to another location.

47. Certainly the Jubilee Scholarships and the MDivX program are exciting new initiatives, even as it remains to be seen as to whether they are the models for future seminary education. But in some respects, they do harken back to older models, as well, back to the time when the seminary was tuition free, or, in the case of the MDivX, the compressed programs of theological education during World War II.

Epilogue

At the conclusion of their works, historians are often tempted (or urged) to be either moralists or prophets. "Tell us," historians are often implored, "what conclusions the reader should draw and what this narrative implies for the future." If they are wise, historians should resist these temptations, because, if anything, the history of such attempts often shows only two things: historians are lousy moralists, and their prophecies far too often go laughably astray. Some very fine historians, people who have done marvelous historical work, have found their reputations rather sullied by the conclusions they attempted to spin from their works, conclusions that say more about what they wish would happen than what the historical evidence might suggest.

On the other hand, after having worked within their subject matter for as long as they have, historians often come to see recurring and important patterns, trends, and developments. These elements can be extrapolated into the future, not as suggestions of what will happen, but as frameworks that focus the questions asked in the future and that suggest responses to such questions. These responses quite often fall within generally predictable parameters, although occasionally new or unexpected developments arise. It is often said that history repeats itself, but this adage seems too mechanistic. Rather, history more likely rhymes, and future developments might be seen as echoes of the past, shaped and directed by the previously established patterns. History is, above all, about people and groups of people, and the human response, while often predictable, is not universally so.

So if it is understood that what follows is neither moral nor prophecy, but personal, authorial reflections on the patterns and tendencies observed in this historical narrative, this author takes it as somewhat of a duty (and perhaps privilege) to reflect on the past, present, and future of Luther Seminary. Certainly, to some extent the entire narrative presented so far contains elements of this, and a completely objective history is rather impossible ("*wie es eigentlich gewesen*"[1]). Yet, at this point, the reader is invited into an active engagement with the materials and with the author's reflections on them, and to begin a dialogue over the past and its implications. If such an engagement does occur, it would be a great compliment to this author.

There are twin approaches to history that tend to distort the historical record and that do damage to it. The first is the curt dismissal of the past as having no relevance to the present and future. This sort of ahistoricism finds the past to be hopelessly compromised, and the only thing that is useful is as a reminder that we have "evolved" beyond such things. But simply living with the persons narrated in this volume is to discover that many of them were wise, dedicated, and faithful individuals. They may not have thought the same way as present-day individuals, but they had great courage and determination, things that might be a model and correction to such ahistoricism. The other approach, equally dangerous, is the popular attempt to repristinate a "golden age" as a model from the past. If history teaches anything, it is that there never was such a golden age, except perhaps in the imagination of the reader. This second approach is equally problematic, for there is no way to recapture the past, and even if it were possible, it would not be advisable. History shows us people, otherwise commendable, who were also flawed, petty, and limited, and reminds us to be on the lookout for such human frailties and foibles among ourselves. The Lutheran theological tradition speaks of human beings who are *simul justus et peccator* (at the same time saint and sinner), and this limitation applies equally to the past, present, and future. In fundamental ways, human beings have not and will not progress morally.

The history of Luther Seminary, then, belies both ahistoricism and the "golden age." What it does seem to show is a state of both constant challenge and faithful innovation. At no time in its history did Luther Seminary (and by this is meant the living, breathing group of people who constituted and sustained it, and all its constituent parts) "have it made," nor was it in a position such that the present and future seemed to be settled. Bluntly, the position of a stand-alone denomination seminary has always been precarious, although at some times more so than others. This difficulty is more than just financial, although the ongoing financial pressures have been a major part of this history. A major theme of this history is the ways in which the people of Luther Seminary have responded to these pressures, often in a heroically self-sacrificing manner. They did so because they believed in the mission of the place itself and that behind Luther Seminary stood not only a group of supporters and denominations, but also the Spirit of God moving in and among them. Their attitude was similar to that of Rabbi Gamaliel, who said "if . . . this undertaking is of human origin, it will fail; but if it is of God, you will not be able to overthrow them" (Acts 5:38–39). This sense of God at work through (and sometimes in spite of) their efforts seemed to keep them going in the midst of turmoil and stress. For them, their current situations were often indeed dire, but they still had hope.

Another major positive element of this history is the general sense of vision and community among many of those associated with Luther Seminary. These terms are often romanticized as meaning a harmony and unanimity of purpose, something that is generally not found in actual human communities. Rather, what is evident throughout the history of Luther Seminary is a gut-level commitment to the mission of the seminary and the people involved. Fights? There were major conflicts, often of a fundamental nature. But they fought within the boundaries of a common commitment to their students, their congregations and denominations, and their Lord. Human nature being what it is, there were also petty jealousies and power-plays—of course there were. But there were also at times restraint, and confession and forgiveness for these all-too-human actions. Luther Seminary has often enough been a community of people who sought to meet the future head-on and to improve the school as an institution for educating pastors and others to be leaders for Christ's mission on earth. There were instances when individuals and the institution as a whole sacrificed mightily for the furtherance of this mission. Whether this stance holds true for the future is yet to be seen.[2]

One significant element of change for Luther Seminary has involved the larger community to which it reports and for whom it is operated. One constant in the first one hundred years of this history was that Luther Seminary had a very close and singular relationship with the denominations that, in fact, owned the seminary itself. This was a one-to-one relationship; Luther was the one and only source for new pastors for these denominations, and the denominations were the major source of income for the seminary. There was between the two a significant relationship, not always harmonious, but the lines of accountability were clear. To be sure, some of those in Luther Seminary chafed at the amount of control the denomination had over the institution, but this closeness also had its advantages, as the denomination regularly raised significant capital funding for the seminary.

With the ALC merger in 1960, this pattern was disrupted somewhat, although the proximity of the seminary to the ALC's headquarters in Minneapolis was still very important. But the financial contributions from the ALC were not enough to sustain an expansive seminary; a growing reliance on tuition and development funding took up the slack but also meant that denominational control was loosened. The separate incorporation of the seminary as its own legal entity was also another step in that direction. With the formation of the ELCA in 1988 and that denomination's dramatic numerical and financial decline across its history, the relations between the national church headquarters and Luther Seminary were loosened even further, especially when elements of the seminary faculty were leaders in the fight against the first sexuality study and CCM in the 1990s. The recent dramatic fade of the ELCA since 2000 has also meant a vacuum in power and leadership, which in some ways has devolved on the regional synods. From the seminary's perspective there are advantages and disadvantages to this shift. It has meant more freedom of movement, but also the complication of dealing with a number of different individual synods and entities. It also makes the question of the seminary's identity all the more complicated; to whom, ultimately, is it accountable? Can Luther Seminary develop and cultivate a community of stakeholders that are as invested in its survival as were the denominations to which it was previously related?

One final set of observations has to do with a more nebulous aspect, something that might have to do with the "ethos" of the seminary—its vision and its sense of the future. One common thread to the history of Luther Seminary was that, even in times of great challenge and difficulty, its leaders generally had an expansive vision of the seminary and its future. Things may have been difficult at the time (and often were), but these faculty and leaders seemed to have had an assurance that these difficulties were temporary and that in the future Luther Seminary would grow and expand to meet the growing needs of Christ's mission in the United States and around the world. They expected and planned for this growth, assuming it would happen and that they would need to be ready for it. Indeed, through much of the history of the seminary, they were generally playing "catch-up" to this growth. The most recent period of difficulty, since 2008 and especially since 2012, seems different in this respect. Perhaps we are simply too close to this period of difficulty, but to an inside observer it seems that this optimism is lacking. The current prevailing attitude seems to be one in which the contraction of the seminary is accepted as permanent and that its future is to be a smaller institution. Perhaps this attitude has a basis in reality, but it also seems to be a buy-in to the prevailing defeatist attitude prevalent in mainline Protestant circles in which decline is often simply accepted and at times even celebrated as the cost of faithfulness.[3]

A question that has often been asked by anxious friends over the last decade is, "Will Luther Seminary survive?" The answer is that yes, Luther Seminary will survive. It is very tough to kill an institution that has the amount of capital and resources that Luther Seminary currently has. Institutions, congregations, and denominations have a way of surviving, even in decline, and Luther Seminary will tough it out, most assuredly. But survival is not the important question. The central question is this: Will Luther Seminary flourish? Will it regain its equilibrium and its expansive vision of Christ's mission on earth? Will it find its confidence in the leadership of the Spirit of God and link its mission to this? If so, then Luther Seminary will be an important factor in the Christian community, both in the United States and around the world. It has the resources, but does it have the vision?

Historian Martin Marty, the doctoral advisor of this author, is famous for saying of such challenging situations that while he is not optimistic, he does have hope. Optimism and hope are two very different things, and perhaps hope is much better than optimism. So let's say for the last word on the future of Luther Seminary that we rest its future in hope in the power of God to maintain and expand its God-given mission on earth.

Notes

1. Leopold von Ranke's famous formulation of a completely objective history, things "as they actually were," which is generally doubted by historians these days. I like to think of it as the "Sergeant Joe Friday" school of historiography—"Just the facts, Ma'am."
2. One disturbing trend across American academia in general is a change in the ways faculty relate to their institution and how their institution relates to them. In previous generations, the faculty saw that their primary identity and allegiance was to the institution that employed them; in recent decades there has been a shift, whereby the faculty are now often more loyal to the circles of their academic discipline than to their institution. On the other hand, many institutions are now more willing to see their faculty less as the core of the institution and more as interchangeable parts that can be replaced. There is no knowing which came first; probably they developed simultaneously.
3. For an exploration of this attitude in the ELCA see Mark Granquist, "The ELCA by the Numbers," *Lutheran Forum* 50, no. 3 (Fall 2016): 17–21.

Appendix: Professors and Numbers of Graduates to 1936

This listing,[1] compiled for the seminary's sixtieth anniversary, is perhaps helpful in two ways, first, to give a visual record of the relative dates of the predecessor seminaries and their personnel, and also to provide a relative gauge of their sizes by means of the total number of graduates they produced. This list, of course, is incomplete, in that it does not go past 1936, nor does it include the elements of Northwestern Lutheran Theological Seminary.

AUGSBURG SEMINARY

August Weenaas	1869–1876
Sven Oftedal	1873–1904
Georg Sverdrup	1874–1907
Sven Gunnersen	1874–1883
Marcus Olaus Bøckman	1890–1893
Friedrich Augustus	1890–1893
Emil Gunerius Lund	1891–1893

AUGUSTANA SEMINARY

August Weenaas	1868–1869
David Lysnes	1874–1890
K. O. Lomen	1888–1890

APPENDIX

LUTHER SEMINARY

Ole B. Asperheim	1876–1878
Friedrich Augustus Schmidt	1876–1886
Hans G. Stub	1878–1917
Johannes Ylvisaker	1879–1917
Johannes Bjerk Frich	1888–1902
W. Petersen	1894–1899
Olaf E. Brandt	1896–1917
Elling Hove	1901–1917

RED WING SEMINARY

Ingvald Eisteinsen	1879–1881
August Weenaas	1882–1885
Sven Gunnersen	1883–1884
O. S. Meland	1884–1887; 1889–1892
Hans H. Bergsland	1887–1907
Martin G. Hanson	1886–1887; 1898–1910
Erik Kristian Johnsen	1892–1897
E. W. Schmidt	1908–1917
Mons O. Wee	1908–1917
Gustav M. Bruce	1911–1917

NORTHFIELD SEMINARY

Marcus Olaus Bøckman	1886–1890
Friedrich AugustusSchmidt	1886–1890

THE UNITED CHURCH SEMINARY

Marcus Olaus Bøckman	1890–1917
Friedrich Augustus Schmidt	1890–1917
Emil Gunerius Lund	1891–1904

Appendix

Erik Kristian Johnsen	1900–1917
Carl M. Weswig	1906–1917
Michael J. Stolee	1911–1917
J. N. Kildahl	1914–1917

LUTHER THEOLOGICAL SEMINARY, 1917–1936

Marcus Olaus Bøckman	1917–1936
Johannes Ylvisaker	1917
J. N. Kildahl	1917–1920
Olaf E. Brandt	1917–1936
Gustav M. Bruce	1917–1936
Erik Kristian Johnsen	1917–1923
Carl M. Weswig	1917–1936
Elling Hove	1917–1927
Michael J. Stolee	1917–1936
Jacob Tanner	1925–1936
Thaddeus Franke Gullixson	1930–1936
Mons O. Wee	1917–1936

THEOLOGICAL GRADUATES TO 1917

Augustana Seminary	32
Luther Seminary	475
Northfield Seminary	33
Red Wing Seminary	183
United Church Seminary	559
Total	1,282

LUTHER THEOLOGICAL SEMINARY, 1917–1936

Candidatus Theologiae	646
Certificates of Graduation	4

APPENDIX

Baccalaureus Theologiae	185
Magister Theologiae	5
Doctor Divinitatis (Honoris Causa)	11
Total Number *Candidatus Theologiae* (1876–1936)	1,928

Notes

1. *Luther Theological Seminary St. Paul, Minnesota, 1876–1936*, Sixtieth Anniversary Service at the Twelfth General Convention of the Norwegian Lutheran Church of America, June 6, 1936, 45–47. Note that this is the sixtieth anniversary of Luther Seminary from 1876 and does not count back to 1869, as the current history does.

Bibliography

Aaberg, Theodore A. *A City Set on a Hill*. Mankato, MN: Board of Publication of the Evangelical Lutheran Synod, 1968.

Aasgaard, Johan Arnd. "Unpublished Autobiographical Interview." In the Region 3 Archives of the Evangelical Lutheran Church in America, 1957.

Arden, G. Everett. *School of the Prophets: The Background and History of Augustana Theological Seminary, 1860–1960*. Rock Island, IL: Augustana Theological Seminary, 1960.

Bachmann, E. Theodore. *The United Lutheran Church in America, 1918–1962*. Minneapolis: Fortress Press, 1997.

Belgum, Gerhard Lee. "The Old Norwegian Synod in America, 1853–1890." PhD diss., Yale University, 1957.

Bergmann, Leola Nelson. *Music Master of the Middle West: The Story of F. Melius Christiansen and the St. Olaf Choir*. Minneapolis: University of Minnesota Press, 1944.

Bodensieck, Julius, ed. *The Encyclopedia of the Lutheran Church*. 3 vols. Minneapolis: Augsburg, 1965.

Bruce, G. M. "The Theological Department of Red Wing Seminary." In *Red Wing Seminary, Fifty Years of Service*, edited by Arthur Rholl, 34–42. Red Wing, MN: Red Wing Seminary, 1930.

Burkee, James C. *Power, Politics, and the Missouri Synod: A Conflict That Changed American Christianity*. Minneapolis: Fortress Press, 2011.

Burtness, James. "Reaching Out in World Missions." In *Striving for Ministry: Centennial Essays Interpreting the Heritage of Luther Theological Seminary,* edited by Warren A. Quanbeck, Eugene L. Fevold, and Gerhard E. Frost, 173–85. Minneapolis: Augsburg, 1977.

Carlsen, Clarence J. *The Years of Our Church*. Minneapolis: Lutheran Free Church, 1942.

Cherry, Conrad. *Hurrying toward Zion: Universities, Divinity Schools, and American Protestantism*. Bloomington: Indiana University Press, 1995.

Chrislock, Carl H. *From Fjord to Freeway: 100 Years, Augsburg College*. Minneapolis: Augsburg College, 1969.

Erling, Maria, and Mark Granquist. *The Augustana Story: Shaping Lutheran Identity in North America*. Minneapolis: Augsburg Fortress, 2008.

Fevold, Eugene L. "Laying Foundations in a New Land." In *Striving for Ministry: Centennial Essays Interpreting the Heritage of Luther Theological Seminary*, edited by Warren A. Quanbeck, Eugene L. Fevold, and Gerhard E. Frost, 11–44. Minneapolis: Augsburg, 1977.

———. *The Lutheran Free Church: A Fellowship of American Lutheran Congregations, 1897–1963*. Minneapolis: Augsburg, 1969.

Finke, Roger, and Rodney Stark. *The Churching of America, 1776–2005: Winners and Losers in Our Religious Economy*. New Brunswick, NJ: Rutgers University Press, 2005.

Flesner, Dorris A. "Luther-Northwestern Self-Study Affirmations—Descriptive Phase, Northwestern Lutheran Theological Seminary." Manuscript. 1975. Archives of Luther Seminary, Saint Paul, MN.

Foelsch, Charles B. "Ministerial Education." In *The Encyclopedia of the Lutheran Church*, edited by Julius Bodensieck, vol. 2, 1564–74. Minneapolis: Augsburg, 1965.

Forde, Gerhard O. "Luther Theological Seminary, 1917–1974." In "Luther-Northwestern Self-Study Affirmations—Descriptive Phase, Northwestern Lutheran Theological Seminary." Manuscript. 1975. Archives of Luther Seminary, Saint Paul, MN.

———. "The 'Old Synod': A Search for Objectivity." In *Striving for Ministry: Centennial Essays Interpreting the Heritage of Luther Theological Seminary*, edited by Warren A. Quanbeck, Eugene L. Fevold, and Gerhard E. Frost, 67–80. Minneapolis: Augsburg, 1977.

Frost, Gerhard. "Maintaining the Pastoral Stance." In *Striving for Ministry: Centennial Essays Interpreting the Heritage of Luther Theological Seminary*, edited by Warren A. Quanbeck, Eugene L. Fevold, and Gerhard E. Frost, 162–72. Minneapolis: Augsburg, 1977.

Gonzales, Justo L. *The History of Theological Education*. Nashville: Abingdon, 2015.

Granquist, Mark. "A Comparison of Swedish- and Norwegian-American Religious Traditions, 1860–1920." *Lutheran Quarterly* 8, no. 3 (Autumn 1994): 299–320.

———. "The ELCA by the Numbers." *Lutheran Forum* 50, no. 3 (Fall 2016): 17–21.

———. "Exploding the 'Myth of the Boat.'" *Lutheran Forum* 44, no. 4 (Winter 2010): 15–17.

———. *Lutherans in America: A New History*. Minneapolis: Fortress Press, 2015.

———. "The Scripture Controversy in American Lutheranism: Infallibility, Inerrancy, Inspiration." In *Rightly Handling the Word of Truth: Scripture, Canon, and Creed*, edited by Carl E. Braaten, 71–88. Delhi, NY: ALPB Books, 2015.

———. "A Slow Disaster and a Proposal for Reform." *Lutheran Forum* 46, no. 2 (Summer 2012): 23–26.

———. "The Urge to Merge." *Lutheran Forum* 47, no. 2 (Summer 2013): 20–23.

Grindal, Gracia. "How Women Came to Be Ordained." In *Lutheran Women in Ordained Ministry, 1970–1995*, edited by Gloria E. Bengtson, 33–44. Minneapolis: Augsburg, 1995.

———. "The Role of Women in Seminary Life." In *Thanksgiving and Hope: A Collection of Essays Chronicling 125 Years of ... Luther Seminary*, edited by Frederick H. Gonnerman, 83–92. Saint Paul: Luther Seminary, 1998.

Hamre, James S. "Augsburg Theological Seminary, 1869–1963." In *Thanksgiving and Hope: A Collection of Essays Chronicling 125 Years of ... Luther Seminary*, edited by Frederick H. Gonnerman, 9–34. Saint Paul: Luther Seminary, 1998.

Harrisville, Roy, Jr. "Interpreting the Scriptures." In *Striving for Ministry: Centennial Essays Interpreting the Heritage of Luther Theological Seminary*, edited by Warren A. Quanbeck, Eugene L. Fevold, and Gerhard E. Frost, 123–46. Minneapolis: Augsburg, 1977.

———. "Luther Theological Seminary, 1876–1976." In *Thanksgiving and*

Hope: A Collection of Essays Chronicling 125 Years of... Luther Seminary, edited by Frederick H. Gonnerman, 35–58. Saint Paul: Luther Seminary, 1998.

Huber, Donald L. *Educating Lutheran Pastors in Ohio, 1830–1930: A History of Trinity Lutheran Seminary and Its Predecessors*. Lewiston, NY: Edwin Mellen, 1989.

Inskeep, Kenneth. "A Review of Candidacy Applications Submitted from January 1, 2010 through May 23, 2017." ELCA Office of Research and Evaluation, July 2017. Archives of the Evangelical Lutheran Church in America, Elk Grove Village, IL.

Jacobson, Thomas E. "Hauge's Norwegian Evangelical Lutheran Synod in America and the Continuation of the Haugean Spirit in Twentieth-Century American Lutheranism." PhD diss., Luther Seminary, 2018.

Johnson, Kent. "An Era of Transitions, 1976–1996." In *Thanksgiving and Hope: A Collection of Essays Chronicling 125 Years of... Luther Seminary*, edited by Frederick H. Gonnerman, 93–115. Saint Paul: Luther Seminary, 1998.

Lagerquist, L. DeAne. *The Lutherans*. Denominations in America 9. Westport, CT: Greenwood, 1999.

Luther Seminary. "Self-Study Report for Continued Accreditation with the Higher Learning Commission." March 2015. Archives of Luther Seminary.

McArver, Susan Wilds, and Scott H. Hendrix. *A Goodly Heritage: The Story of Lutheran Theological Southern Seminary, 1830–2005*. Columbia, SC: Lutheran Theological Southern Seminary, 2006.

Meyer, Carl S. *Log Cabin to Luther Tower: Concordia Seminary during 125 Years toward a More Excellent Ministry, 1839–1965*. St. Louis: Concordia Publishing House, 1965.

Miller, Glenn T. *Piety and Intellect: The Aims and Purposes of Ante-Bellum Theological Education*. Atlanta: Scholars Press, 1990.

———. *Piety and Plurality: Theological Education since 1960*. Eugene, OR: Cascade, 2014.

———. *Piety and Profession: American Protestant Theological Education, 1870–1970*. Grand Rapids: Eerdmans, 2007.

Nelson, David T. *Luther College, 1861–1961*. Decorah, IA: Luther College Press, 1961.

Nelson, E. Clifford. *Lutheranism in North America, 1914–1970.* Minneapolis: Augsburg, 1972.

———, ed. *The Lutherans in North America.* Philadelphia: Fortress Press, 1975.

Nelson, E. Clifford, and Eugene Fevold. *The Lutheran Church among the Norwegian-Americans.* 2 vols. Minneapolis: Augsburg, 1960.

Nysse, Richard W. "Online Education: An Asset in a Period of Educational Change." In *Practical Wisdom: Theological Teaching and Learning*, edited by Malcolm L. Warford, 197–214. New York: Peter Lang, 2004.

Placher, William C., and Derek R. Nelson. *A History of Christian Theology: An Introduction.* Philadelphia: Westminster, 1983.

Preus, Herman Amberg. *Vivacious Daughter: Seven Lectures on the Religious Situation among the Norwegians in America.* Edited and translated by Todd W. Nichol. Northfield, MN: Norwegian-American Historical Association, 1990.

Quanbeck, Warren A. "Keeping Faith with the Reformation Heritage." In *Striving for Ministry: Centennial Essays Interpreting the Heritage of Luther Theological Seminary*, edited by Warren A. Quanbeck, Eugene L. Fevold, and Gerhard E. Frost, 147–61. Minneapolis: Augsburg, 1977.

Ringenberg, W. C. "Education, Protestant Theological." In *Dictionary of Christianity in America*, edited by Daniel C. Reid, 378–80. Downers Grove, IL: InterVarsity, 1990.

Rogness, Alvin N. "Reflections on Theological Education in a Turbulent Time." In *Striving for Ministry: Centennial Essays Interpreting the Heritage of Luther Theological Seminary*, edited by Warren A. Quanbeck, Eugene L. Fevold, and Gerhard E. Frost, 45–66. Minneapolis: Augsburg, 1977.

Rohne, J. Magnus. *Norwegian American Lutheranism up to 1872.* New York: Macmillan, 1926.

Rønning, N. N. *Festskrift udgivet I Anledning af Red Wing Seminariums Femogtyve Aars Jubiläum.* Red Wing, MN: n.p., 1904.

Roth, Robert Paul. "Northwestern Lutheran Theological Seminary, 1920–1982." In *Thanksgiving and Hope: A Collection of Essays Chronicling 125 Years of . . . Luther Seminary*, edited by Frederick H. Gonnerman, 59–82. Saint Paul: Luther Seminary, 1998.

Satre, Lowell J. "The Hauge Synod." In *Striving for Ministry: Centennial Essays Interpreting the Heritage of Luther Theological Seminary*, edited by Warren A. Quanbeck, Eugene L. Fevold, and Gerhard E. Frost, 81–96. Minneapolis: Augsburg, 1977.

Shall Red Wing Seminary Be Closed? Red Wing, MN: Red Wing Printing Company, [1932?].

Shaw, Joseph M. *A History of St. Olaf College, 1874–1974.* Northfield, MN: St. Olaf College Press, 1974.

———. *John Nathan Kildahl.* Northfield, MN: Highland Books, 2014.

Skillrud, Harold. *LSTC: Decade of Decision.* Chicago: Lutheran School of Theology at Chicago, 1969.

Solberg, Richard W. *Lutheran Higher Education in North America.* Minneapolis: Augsburg, 1985.

Sonnack, Paul. "The 'United Church': A Comprehensive Sense of Mission." In *Striving for Ministry: Centennial Essays Interpreting the Heritage of Luther Theological Seminary*, edited by Warren A. Quanbeck, Eugene L. Fevold, and Gerhard E. Frost, 97–110. Minneapolis: Augsburg, 1977.

Stensvaag, John M. "The Lutheran Free Church: For the Upbuilding of the Congregation." In *Striving for Ministry: Centennial Essays Interpreting the Heritage of Luther Theological Seminary*, edited by Warren A. Quanbeck, Eugene L. Fevold, and Gerhard E. Frost, 111–22. Minneapolis: Augsburg, 1977.

Svendsbye, Lloyd A. *One in Mission: Luther and Northwestern Seminaries Unite.* Minneapolis: Lutheran University Press, 2012.

Sverdrup, Georg. *The Heritage of Faith: Selections from the Writings of Georg Sverdrup.* Translated by Melvin A. Helland. Minneapolis: Augsburg, 1969.

Tappert, Theodore G. *A History of the Lutheran Theological Seminary at Philadelphia, 1864–1964.* Philadelphia: Lutheran Theological Seminary, 1964.

Trexler, Edgar. *High Expectations: Understanding the ELCA's Early Years, 1988–2002.* Minneapolis: Augsburg Fortress, 2003.

Wee, M. O. "Along the Years Together." In *Luther Theological Seminary St. Paul, Minnesota, 1876–1936.* Sixtieth Anniversary Service at the Twelfth General Convention of the Norwegian Lutheran Church of America, June 6, 1936.

———. *Haugeanism: A Brief Sketch of the Movement and Some of Its Chief Exponents.* Saint Paul: n.p., 1919.

Wentz, Abdel Ross. *A Basic History of Lutheranism in America*. Rev. ed. Philadelphia: Fortress Press, 1964.

———. *Gettysburg Lutheran Theological Seminary*. Vol. 1, *History 1826–1965*. Harrisburg, PA: Evangelical Press, 1965.

Wisoff, Carl F. "Theological Schools, IV: In Europe." In *The Encyclopedia of the Lutheran Church*, edited by Julius Bodensieck, vol. 3, 2353–71. Minneapolis: Augsburg, 1965.

Index

1960s, 214–16

Aalborg, Nan, 227
Aasgaard Hall, 138, 191, 219
Aasgaard, Johan A., 98, 119
Ahlen, Axel, 185
American Lutheran Church (1930–60), 23
American Lutheran Church (1960–88), 46, 123, 167–69, 207–9
American Lutheranism, 27
Andersen, Paul, 68
Anti-Missouri Brotherhood, 44, 80–81
apprenticeship model, 8, 18–19
Asperheim, Ole B., 53, 79
Association of Evangelical Lutheran Congregations, 236
Association of Free Lutheran Congregations, 169
Association of Theological Schools, 218
Augsburg Medical Aid Society, 149
Augsburg Seminary, 72–77, 86–89

Augsburg University, 256–57
Augustana Seminary (1860–1962), 69
Augustana Synod, 43, 188–90
Aus, George, 109–10

baby boom, 205
Baker, Carol, 227
Bakken, Norman, 192
Bartels, Robert, 185
Bass, George, 185
Beissel, Elizabeth, 227
Belgum, David, 185
Bell, The, 230
Bergsland, Hans, 62
Bible schools, 21
Bidne, Arvid, 219
Bliese, Richard, 250, 253–54
Board of Theological Education (LCA), 196
Board of Theological Education and Ministry (ALC), 196, 199
boarding club, 149
Bøckman, Marcus Olaus, 80, 93, 100–101, 128
Bockman Hall, 106, 225

285

INDEX

Boehlke, Terry, 137
Book of Faith initiative, 250–51
Brandt, Olaf E., 55
Breck School, 119
Brohaugh, G. O., 60
Bruce, Gustav, 62
Bunge, Marcia, 227
Burgess, Andrew, 117
Burntvedt, T. O., 119
Buschman, Walter, 192

Called to Common Mission, 244–45
campus redevelopment, 260
candidacy process, 237
catechetical schools, 7
catechumenate, 7
Charleston, Steven, 229
Chicago Lutheran Theological Seminary (Maywood), 176–77
Christensen, Bernhard, 161–68, 209
Church of the Lutheran Brethren, 44
Clausen, Claus Lauritz, 46, 75
Clinical Pastoral Education (CPE), 193, 213, 237
college controversy, 81–83
Communique, 215
Concord, 230
Concordia Seminary, St. Louis, 49–52
Conference, The. *See* Conference for the Norwegian Danish Evangelical Lutheran Church in America

Conference for the Norwegian Danish Evangelical Lutheran Church in America, 43, 72–77
Cooper, William, 185
crisis of 2012, 253–54
Crist, George, 186
curriculum, 103, 185–86, 193, 212–13, 219–20, 238–39, 259

Dahle, John, 56, 107
Deerfield, Wisconsin, 60
degree programs, new (1980s–1990s), 239
Depression, Great, 108–9, 113–15, 157–59
Dietrichson, J. W. C., 43
distance learning cohorts, 248–49, 257
doctor of ministry program, 239
Dresser, Jonas, 185

ecumenical students, 240
Eilesen, Elling, 43, 57
Eilesen Synod (Evangelical Lutheran Church in America), 43
Eisteinsen, Ingvald, 60
Enlightenment, 13
Enter the Bible, 251
Erlangen school, 14
Ermisch, Karl, 156
Evangelical Lutheran Church, 95n32, 117–19, 208
Evangelical Lutheran Church in America, 32–33, 224, 236–37
Evjen, John, 148, 154–55, 170n13

286

Index

Fargo, North Dakota, 177
Fellowship of Evangelical Laity and Pastors, 229
Festival of Homiletics, 251
Field, Laurence, 117
financial crisis, 242–43
first form and second form, 98, 109–10
Fjellman, A. G. "Gib", 231
Flesner, Dorris, 185, 196
Forde, Gerhard, 196, 211–13, 220, 223
Formula of Concord, Article IX, 78
Foss, Rick, 254–55, 258
Frame, William, 254
Free Seminary, 215
Friends of Augsburg, 44, 86–89
Friends of Luther Seminary, 122
Frost, Gerhard, 120
fundamentalism, 111, 161–62

General Council, 175–76
General Synod, 175
Gerberding, George, 175, 177
Gerberding, John, 186
Gjertsen, M. Falk, 74, 148
Global Mission Institute, 230–31
Grindal, Gracia, 221, 227
Gullixson, Thaddeus Franke, 107–9, 136
Gullixson Hall, 106
Gunnersen, Sven, 74, 128

Halvorson, John Victor, 117
Hamline area, St. Paul, 55
Hanson, Martin, 62

Harbo, Elias, 148
Harris, Al, 240
Hauge, Hans Nielsen, 38–39
Haugeanism, 59, 61
Hauge's Norwegian Evangelical Lutheran Synod, 44, 56, 62–64
Helland, Andreas, 148
Hove, Elling, 55
humanism, 145–46
human sexuality, 251–52

immigration, Lutherans to North America, 24–25
international students, 121, 142, 188, 240
internship, 113–14, 213
irregular ordination of gay pastors, 243–44

Jacobson, Diane, 227, 251
Jacobson, Rolf, 251
Jodock, Darrell, 226
Johnsen, Erik Kristian, 85
Johnson, Gisle, 40–41, 67
Johnson, Karen, 227
Jubilee Scholarships, 260
Juel, Don, 138

Kairos, 213
Kildahl, J. N., 85
Koester, Craig, 251

language transition, 85, 103–5, 174
Larsen, Peter Laurentius (Laur), 48
Lehman, Martin, 192

INDEX

Lewis, Don, 253–54
Lillehei, Lars, 155–56
living Christianity, 76–77
Lull, Patricia, 252
Lund, Clarence, 192
Lund, Emil Gunerius, 81
Luther, Martin, 9
Luther College, 52–53, 63
Luther Mobilization Committee, 216
Luther Northwestern Theological Seminary, 224
Luther Seminary (1876–1917), 52–56
Luther Seminary Alumni Association, 213
Luther Seminary Bookstore, 137
Luther Theological Seminary Review, 213, 230
Lutheran Church–Missouri Synod, 28, 49–52, 122–23
Lutheran Church in America, 123, 188–90
Lutheran Congregations in Mission for Christ, 245
Lutheran Daughters of the Reformation, 114
Lutheran Free Church, 44, 86–89, 143–44
Lutherans, Scandinavian American, 29–30
Luther-Northwestern Coordinating Committee, 195
Lysnes, David, 72

Madison, Wisconsin, 53–54, 127

Madison Agreement (Opjør), 45, 92–93
mainline Protestantism, 21, 207
Mann, John, 252
married students, 165, 184
Marshall, Wisconsin, 71–72
Martinson, Rollie, 138
Maximal Functional Unification, 197
MDivX pilot program, 261
Melanchthon, Philip, 10
Mergenthal, Jennings, 137
Midwinter Convocation, 213
Milton, John, 109, 112
Minnesota Consortium of Theological Schools, 193
missions: foreign/world, 114–15, 120–21, 150–51; home, 149–51
mission societies, 14–15
mission statement, 241
modern (higher) biblical criticism, 166
Morrow, Michael, 254, 258
Muhlenberg, Henry Melchior, 25
Muus, Berndt Julius, 79

Narrative Lectionary, 251
National Lutheran Council, 122
Nelson, E. Clifford, 117–18
neoconfessionalism, 14
neoorthodoxy, 22
Nielsen, Peter, 87
Norborg, Sverre, 162–63
Nordstrand, Patrice, 227
North American Lutheran Church, 252

Index

Northfield Seminary, 80–81
Northwestern Lutheran Theological Seminary, 132–33
Norway, Lutheranism in, 38–41
Norwegian American Lutheran colleges, 210–11
Norwegian American Lutheranism, 41–46
Norwegian Danish Augustana Synod, 43, 68–72
Norwegian Evangelical Lutheran Church in America, 43, 46–56
Norwegian Lutheran Church in America, 45, 91–93, 97–102
Norwegian Synod. *See* Norwegian Evangelical Lutheran Church in America

Oftedal, Asmund, 161–62
Oftedal, Sven, 74–77, 86–89, 128, 147–48
Olson Campus Center, 224–25
Olson, Duane, 231
Olson, Iver, 164
One Seminary program, 208–9
online education, 247–48
ordination of women, 194, 221–22
Ormseth, Dennis, 226
orthodoxy, 11

Para-seminary, 220
Passavant, William, 175
PhD program, 230, 259
Pietism, 13
Pillsbury mansion, 182

Pontoppidan, Eric, 38, 79
preachers seminaries, 15
predestination controversy (election), 77–80
Predigarseminar, 13
Preus, Herman Amberg (1825–94), 46–48
Preus, Herman Amberg (1896–1995), 100, 109–10
Preus, Mary, 139, 227

Qualben, Lars, 155
Quanbeck, Philip A., 164, 169
Quanbeck, Warren, 117, 196

Racial Minorities Concerns Subcommittee, 229
Rasmussen, Peter Andreas, 57–59
Red Wing, Minnesota, 58–64
Red Wing Seminary (1878–1917), 60–64
Robbinsdale, Minnesota, 55, 130
Rogness, Alvin N., 118, 136, 211, 214–17
Rosenius, Carl Olof, 41
Roth, Paul, 177, 180, 196
Roth, Robert Paul, 185
Rozentals, Janis, 117

sale of apartments, 256
Sandgren Apartments, 225
Schiotz, Frederick A., 136
Schmidt, Friedrich Augustus, 51–52, 78–80
Schmucker, Samuel Simon, 26, 175
Schumacher, Bryce, 185

289

INDEX

Scripture, authority of, 110–12, 161–62
Second Great Awakening, 20
Self-Study Committee (joint), 196–97
seminaries: Lutheran, 25–33; Protestant, 19–23
Seminary choir, 107
Seminary Wives Organization, 121–22
Seminettes, 165
Semogram, 230
Semogram-Bell, 230
Skrefsrud, Lars O., 90
slavery, controversy among Norwegians, 50–51
Small Catechism, 10
Smits, Edmund, 117
Sonnack, Paul, 164, 169, 209
Spener, Philipp Jakob, 12
Sponheim, Paul, 138
St. Anthony Park, St. Paul, 84
Steinke, Robin, 258
Stensvaag, John, 164, 169, 209
St. Olaf College, 63, 80–81
Stolee, Michael J., 85, 106
Story, The, 230
Strohl, Jane, 227
Stub, Hans Andreas, 46, 79
Stub, Hans G., 98, 111
Stub, Valborg Hovind, 55–56
Stump, Joseph, 177, 180
Sukke, Kathy, 227
Svendsbye, Lloyd, 196–97, 222–24, 226–27
Sverdrup, Georg, 74–77, 86–89, 128, 144–48

Sverdrup, George, 148, 151–62
Synod of Northern Illinois, 68–69
Synod of the Northwest, 176–77
Synodical Conference, 52

Tanner, Jacob, 100
technology, 246–47
tenure controversies, 226–27
Theological Education for Emerging Ministries (TEEM), 249–50
Tiede, David, 231
Trabert, Georg, 175
tuition, 211, 228

United Church, The. *See* United Norwegian Lutheran Church
United Church Seminary (1893–1917), 81–86, 129
United Lutheran Church in America, 122–23, 176–80
United Norwegian Lutheran Church, 44, 81–86

Vietnam War, 194
Voltz, Carl A., 138

Walther, C. F. W., 49, 78
Wee, Mons O., 62, 101–2
Weenaas, August, 69–71
Westphal, Bruce, 226
Weswig, Carl M., 85, 106
women, 187–88
Women's Center, 227
Word & World, 230
Word Alone Movement, 245
Working Preacher, 251

World War I, 105–6
World War II, 115–16, 164–65, 182–83
Wrigley, Victor, 186

Ylvisaker, Johannes, 53, 93

Zeidler, Clemens, 185, 190–91, 196–97

www.ingramcontent.com/pod-product-compliance
Lightning Source LLC
Chambersburg PA
CBHW020357080526
44584CB00014B/1053